OMAHA
BEACH
and
BEYOND

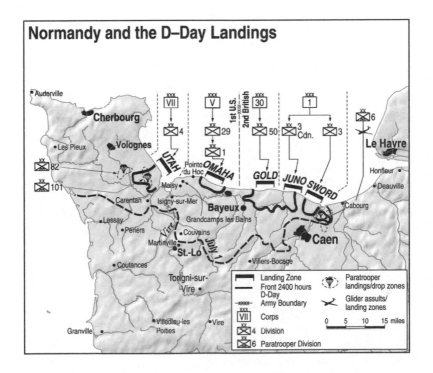

Normandy and the D–Day Landings

Landing Zone	Paratrooper landings/drop zones
Front 2400 hours D-Day	Glider assults/landing zones
Army Boundary	
VII Corps	
4 Division	
6 Paratrooper Division	

0   5   10   15 miles

OMAHA
BEACH
and
BEYOND

THE LONG MARCH OF
SERGEANT BOB SLAUGHTER

JOHN ROBERT SLAUGHTER

ZENITH PRESS

First published in 2007 by Zenith Press, an imprint of
MBI Publishing Company LLC, Galtier Plaza, Suite 200,
380 Jackson Street, St. Paul, MN 55101 USA

Zenith Press titles are also available at discounts in bulk quantity for industrial or sales-
promotional use. For details write to Special Sales
Manager at MBI Publishing Company, Galtier Plaza, Suite 200,
380 Jackson Street, St. Paul, MN 55101 USA.

To find out more about our books, join us online at www.zenithpress.com.
Library of Congress Cataloging-in-Publication Data

Slaughter, John Robert, 1925-
  Omaha Beach and beyond : the long march of Sergeant Bob Slaughter / By John
Robert Slaughter.
    p. cm.
  ISBN-13: 978-0-7603-3141-5 (hardbound w/ jacket)
  ISBN-10: 0-7603-3141-3 (hardbound w/ jacket) 1. Slaughter, John Robert, 1925- 2.
United States. Army. Infantry Regiment, 116th. 3. World War, 1939-1945—
Campaigns—Western Front. 4. World War, 1939-1945—Campaigns—France—
Normandy. 5. World War, 1939-1945—Personal narratives, American. 6. Normandy
(France)—History, Military—20th century. 7. United States. Army—Biography. 8.
Soldiers—United States—Biography. 9. Veterans—Virginia—Biography. I. Title.
D769.31116th .S52 2007
940.54'21421092—dc22
[B]
                                        2007009185

Layout: Jennifer Maass
Cover: Tom Heffron

Printed in the United States of America

All photographs from the author's collection. Maps on pages 284 and 285 from *29 Let's
Go! A History of the 29th Infantry Division in World War II* by Joseph H. Ewing. All
other maps by Phil Schwartzberg, Meridian Mapping.

On the front cover: Staff Sergeant Bob Slaughter. Germany, 1945.

On the spine: The 29th Infantry Division patch. The "Blue and Gray" Division was
composed of regiments which traced their lineage to
Colonial times; during the Civil War, some had served the Union, some
the Confederacy.

On the back cover: Bill Hurd, John Stinnett, Pat Sibold, and Rufus Carr (standing); Vic
Crimone, Bev "Razz" Jones, and Ed Walton (kneeling). England, 1943.

CONTENTS

FOREWORD

It was a beautiful fall afternoon when I pulled up in my rental car in the driveway of Bob Slaughter's home in the gentle, rolling hills outside Roanoke, Virginia. I was emotionally drained. I had just spent several days talking to the relatives of nineteen young men—the so-called Bedford Boys—who had died in a matter of minutes on Omaha Beach.

That very morning, I had managed with great difficulty to coax a few painful memories from the only officer still living from Company A, 116th Infantry Regiment, 29th Division—the first unit of Americans to hit the most lethal beach on D-Day and to which the Bedford Boys had belonged. Perhaps Mr. Slaughter, a fellow survivor of "Bloody Omaha" would be just as reluctant to talk, just as cautious as others in casting his mind back to days that Virginia communities such as Lynchburg, Bedford, and Roanoke struggled for many years to try to forget.

I had heard so many overwhelming stories of grief and loss, from widows who still cry when they remember, from brothers and sisters, from a daughter who never did get to meet her father. Frankly, I was depressed. But then Bob greeted me at his front door with a firm handshake and a warm welcome, and a smile finally returned to my face. For a couple of hours I sat transfixed in his study as he told me the amazing tale of how he also landed on Omaha Beach on June 6, 1944, and managed not only to get off that killing ground without injury but also, by some miracle, to fight on across Normandy and then France until the fall of the Third Reich.

Bob Slaughter told his story with clarity, humor, and sometimes brutal honesty. I knew from the first few minutes of our conversation that I had found a very important source, a man with a keen and accurate memory who had experienced the same upbringing, induction to the army, and buildup to D-Day as the young men from Bedford whose story I was trying to tell. I discovered that he was just fifteen when he joined the National Guard. "I was tall for my age—six foot two," he told me. "We got a dollar every drill and went to Virginia Beach in the summer." He grew another three inches by D-Day.

I will not spoil Bob's riveting narrative by revealing what happened to him on D-Day. Suffice it to say that when he told me I was shocked to the core by the random nature of the slaughter—life and death were separated by a bullet going a fraction of an inch one way or the other. Many of Bob's friends from Roanoke were killed before his eyes. It was almost impossible to stomach, and it was even harder to then find the strength, the guts, to get the job done and get off that beach. But all six foot five inches of Bob Slaughter managed it.

By the end of June 1944, Bob Slaughter had fought through hedgerows and ruined villages toward St.-Lô. Very few of the men he had landed with on D-Day were still alive. All knew that they would either be killed or wounded. There was no other fate. "Your best hope was for a million-dollar wound, nice clean sheets, and a pretty nurse," Bob told me. "You didn't want to lie out there and bleed for a long time. I'd see guys on a stretcher, and they'd been shot through the leg and they would be smiling. 'I'll see ya buddy!' they shouted. You didn't want to get it in the groin or stomach but the legs, arms, shoulders, hands. That would have been wonderful. Fingers didn't count."

Thankfully, every day Bob Slaughter spent in combat counted. Indeed, every yard he advanced counted a great deal. He and his ilk—liberators, not conquerors—earned America an inestimable prestige in the eyes of an eternally grateful continent. Visit hamlets where Slaughter and his brothers fought, as I did on the sixtieth anniversary of D-Day, and you will find that today people still remember the heart-wrenching sacrifice of young American lives. Some of the locals saw the cost of freedom with their own eyes: the twisted corpses dotted along hedgerows, the lines of young Virginians, limbless, disfigured, waiting in some shell-holed church to be evacuated.

I don't care if this sounds shamelessly sentimental. It is the truth: Bob Slaughter and his kind walk like giants among us today. They are not long for this world. So while they are still here to shake our hands, we should read what they write and listen to what they say. They were there. They can tell us what it was like to fight during America's finest hour—June 6, 1944. They can tell us that only for the greatest of causes should any young American lay down his life.

I owe a two-fold debt to Bob Slaughter. As a Brit, I grew up in a Europe that he helped liberate. I have enjoyed what so many of his childhood friends never lived to see—over sixty years of peace and prosperity on a continent that had been scarred by war since the beginning of history. I am also indebted to Bob because I benefited enormously in my research from a carefully typed manuscript that he loaned to me—the origins of the book you are reading now. The manuscript has changed a great deal since then. But the story is essentially the same: Bob Slaughter's memoir *Omaha Beach and Beyond* is a powerful and moving tale of a teenage warrior who came of age on D-Day. It is the story of a man who could not forget, who walked the sands on Omaha with President Clinton at his side in 1994, on the fiftieth anniversary of the invasion, and who more than any other is responsible for the building of America's finest war memorial—the National D-Day Memorial in Bedford, Virginia.

If you ever happen to be in Bob Slaughter's neighborhood, take a detour and visit the memorial. It lies in the lee of the Blue Ridge Mountains. It is a beautiful place, a fitting tribute to the men who fought and died alongside Bob Slaughter. And if you ever happen to find yourself in Normandy, the setting for so much of this cracking good story, you must pay a visit to the American cemetery at Colleville sur Mer. Bob knows the place well. Several of his good friends are buried there in graves overlooking the beach, beside 9,386 other American dead from the battle for Normandy. In the near future, I will take my young son to the graveyard to make him proud to be an American. I will talk to him about men like Bob. I will tell him it was my honor to spend time with them. I will also take him to a chapel at the heart of the rows of dead, a chapel Mr. Slaughter also knows only too well. On a wall of that chapel the following words are inscribed for all to see: "Think not only upon their passing. Remember the glory of their spirit."

—*Alex Kershaw*

INTRODUCTION

Historians, scribes, and screenwriters have long featured World War II as the global event of the twentieth century, and D-Day at Normandy on June 6, 1944, was indisputably one of the greatest battles of the war. Yet by 1944, the German army was severely crippled and stretched to the limit. Through 1944 and 1945, the once-potent Luftwaffe was almost nonexistent.

Why then, did the twelve-nation Allies have so much trouble bringing the war-weary Nazi empire under control? The cost of the war had reached into the billions and billions of dollars, and had caused the loss of many millions of human lives. Why then, was this war so difficult for so long?

This book fails to answer any of that.

My purpose instead is to tell the untold story of a few young citizen soldiers, including myself, who were caught up in a world war that turned out to be so utterly brutal that it still remains difficult to write about it even now, over sixty years later. Much of this account tells the story of the melding of national guardsmen and drafted soldiers into a fighting unit that defeated a well-disciplined, well-equipped, and well-led professional Axis army.

Before D-Day, the regular army called 29th Division soldiers "home nannies" and "weekend warriors." Some volunteer or drafted soldiers actually regarded former national guardsmen as inferior. Major General Leslie McNair—later killed by friendly fire in Normandy —wrote to Washington that in his opinion, National Guard officers were unfit for combat.

A few guardsmen and reservists were indeed deficient, and were quickly separated out. A relatively few other guard officers were too old or otherwise unfit, but the vast majority became the nucleus of the wartime army. Many former Virginia National Guard officers and noncoms led the 116th Infantry Regiment, which stormed Omaha, the most viciously defended of the Allied landing beaches.

Most of these men became outstanding wartime leaders. Technical Sergeant Frank Peregory of K Company, 116th, for example, first won the Soldiers Medal by plunging into a frozen North Carolina canal to save a fellow soldier's life. Later, he posthumously won the nation's highest award, the Medal of Honor, for extreme valor in combat. He hailed from Charlottesville, Virginia, and was a former national guardsman. In the name of fairness, I hasten to add that the 29th Division was blessed with many great drafted and volunteer soldiers as well.

This book portrays the months and months of man-killing assault training and physical conditioning that we soldiers willingly accepted. Despite enduring those many, many months of unbelievable hardships and harsh military discipline, many of my comrades were killed within minutes on the bloody sands of Omaha Beach, or mere days later in the entangling Normandy hedgerows. Others survived only to be killed within a few months, on the wintertime battlefields of Nazi Germany.

INTRODUCTION

Recalling events of long ago and in the proper chronological order is, at best, an educated guess. However, many of my long-dormant memories, fuzzy at first, crystallized into focus with the help of reliable evidence from other credible eyewitnesses. We are not talking about information from best-selling books about World War II, but unique, untold stories set down in the words of ordinary former officers and men of the 116th Infantry and the 29th Division. Many of these contributors have now answered the last roll call. Thankfully, their memories are not buried with them and will live for all eternity!

During early D Company reunions, a pseudo committee of "intellectuals" engaged in many serious roundtable discussions. These stories often conflicted at first, but usually after recourse, evolved into almost unanimously accepted facts. For some, recurring flashbacks would not evaporate easily into oblivion. Many vivid episodes often resurfaced while lying in bed, only to return in sweaty nightmares after sleep arrived.

All of us vividly remembered the history-changing event that occurred on December 7, 1941, when an audacious Japanese sneak attack destroyed the American Pacific Fleet at Pearl Harbor. This single event drew the United States and much of the world into the second great war of the twentieth century.

The men of the 116th Regiment also recalled the danger of the transatlantic crossing as we sailed for war in October 1942. As we watched from the deck of one of the largest ocean liners afloat, 332 Englishmen perished. In an incredible midocean shipwreck, the RMS *Queen Mary* sliced through one of our light cruiser escorts, the HMS *Curacoa*. This tragedy occurred on a calm and sunny afternoon in the North Atlantic Ocean.

Nor did those of us who volunteered for the 29th Rangers ever forget the harsh, wintertime physical training we endured at the Commando Training Depot in the rugged highlands of Scotland. The British commando instructors were given the task of preparing one thousand American volunteers for a tough special assignment. Half of us washed out, and the five hundred that were left wondered why we had accepted the hardships in order to become 29th Rangers.

There were greater and lesser adventures, but all are worth retelling. The amphibious assault training at southern England's beaches; living and hiking on the water-soaked and utterly bleak English wintertime moors; D-Day briefings at the marshaling area; and, of course, the terrible disaster suffered by the 116th RCT (Regimental Combat Team) at Omaha Beach on June 6, 1944. That fatal day, the Allied navies and air forces undoubtedly saved the lodgment at Omaha by keeping Jerry's vaunted panzers at bay until our depleted and vulnerable V Corps was adequately replenished and reinforced. In my opinion, the Omaha Beach sector would have failed had it not been for the supporting warships and airplanes.

It was comforting to have nearby the elite 2nd and 5th Ranger Battalions, the veteran Big Red One 1st Division, the 4th Ivy Division, and two airborne divisions—the combat-tested 82nd All Americans, and the 101st Screaming Eagles. They were just as scared and shaken as we were, but we knew that if we could just hold on for a few days, reinforcements were on the way. Who could ever forget D-Day, even if it were one hundred years ago!

I remember buddies with whom I spent passes to London, men I played cards with a couple of days before the landing, who signed their autographs on my Eisenhower D-Day missive, who shook hands with me on the *Javelin's* deck—young men, as I was, all killed during the largest air, land, and sea battle ever fought. Many more were maimed and never seen again. How could I forget this epic event, even if I fail to recall all the proper names and faces?

Memoirs are not history. But history is someone's recorded memory.

Most of us remember noble and heroic deeds, but conveniently forget or fail to record the less than noble. I am no different. Many times I did and saw things that are best forgotten or left unwritten.

Introduction

War brings out the best and worst in most of us. The Nazis were accused of killing, raping, pillaging, and burning. A few on our side were also guilty of all these crimes. Soldiers on both sides looted for souvenirs, as did I. Many men lost their lives in their quest for booty. And yet cruel treatment of the enemy was an unusual occurrence. I, myself, am proud to say that I once saved an enemy soldier's life.

This book will attempt to show that ordinary men and women can do extraordinary feats if they believe the cause is great. Many GIs have said that they were merely "fighting for each other." True, but I maintain another factor played a more important role, and it can be summed up with one word: pride. Regardless of their motives, I saw very few cowards in the 116th Infantry Regiment. May God bless the many, many, more heroes.

CHAPTER ONE

HOW IT ALL BEGAN

WAR AND REMEMBRANCE

In September 1988, on a cloudy, windy afternoon, I was among a group of 29th Division veterans who were making a pilgrimage to Normandy. Many of us had participated in the initial 1944 amphibious assault on Normandy's Omaha Beach on D-Day, one of the bloodiest and most epic battles of World War II.

We were there to dedicate the 29th Division Memorial-Monument that had just been erected on hallowed ground at the maw of the D-1 exit draw at Vierville, on the *Dog Green* Sector of Omaha Beach. The draw, referred to on military maps as D-1, is an eroded ravine that leads off the beach to the village of Vierville-sur-Mer. Near here, well-entrenched German defenders mauled hundreds of our proud 1st Battalion in the early morning of June 6, 1944. The memorial erected and paid for by 29th Division Association members, honors the legions of comrades who lost their lives on D-Day and in the eleven months of bitter fighting that followed.

It was my first visit to the Normandy beaches since the end of World War II. My initial reaction was pride in being one of the men who had participated in the pivotal battle of the war in Europe. But I was also saddened for all those brave young men who fought and died that day. Now 9,387 of them are forever interred under crosses and stars on the scenic 172-acre bluff at the Colleville-sur-Mer American Cemetery.

Now, forty-five years later, my wife Margaret and I were standing about two hundred yards to the east of the Vierville Draw. I looked westward toward Pointe du Hoc where the 2nd Rangers did the impossible, then eastward up the beach where the 1st Infantry Division, the Big Red One, stormed ashore. I then scanned the foreboding bluffs, and finally looked out to sea.

Memories of that fateful day long ago overwhelmed me. Tears welled up and began to run down my face. I knew most of the forty brave young men of my D Company who died that day on the sand and in the water. Diehard German machine gunners supplemented by untold numbers of riflemen sent streams of 8mm bullets at anything and everything that moved. Slightly wounded men, who under ordinary circumstances could have been saved, were left to bleed, suffer, and die, because it was impossible for the understaffed medics to attend to all of them. Remembering it all left me speechless.

Margaret tried to make sense of the battle scene by asking me probing questions. I simply didn't know how to answer, or my brain just couldn't handle her queries.

I could only wonder, shaking my head, how in the world had we ever managed to cross that long, slightly graded expanse of beach, moving upward into the teeth of a determined enemy? To cross those four hundred yards of mushy sand and gain a modicum of precious cover, my squad and I had to run through a gauntlet of chattering machine guns that sent strings of fiery tracer bullets crisscrossing our front. Many bullets popped and cracked over and about our flattened bodies as we tried to escape the fusillade coming from the bluffs. What scared me the most was the screeching and booming of the German artillery and mortars zeroing in at the shoreline.

And then there were the screams from men being hit, and dire pleadings for help from the drowning.

There were decisions to be made: when to abandon the armpit-deep water at the shoreline, knowing the flooding tide would soon swallow us. If we stayed where we were, the tide would soon force us closer to the gun sights of the well-entrenched and well-camouflaged enemy.

It was much different on this gray and breezy afternoon forty-five years later. I tried to recall the low tide, 200 yards lower, and the nearly five thousand ships of all kinds and descriptions out in the English Channel, forming the largest armada in history. I also recalled other images: a burning landing ship, tank (LST) with its ramp down, an amphibious tank on fire, men and equipment floating in the water and nobody moving on the beach. And then there were the ugly antilanding obstacles, made of timber posts with mines tied to them, that hindered our landings during the flooding tide. The obstacles themselves were bad enough, but the early waves were forced to land at extreme low tide to avoid the potent twenty-pound teller mines tied at their apex. This meant the battalion was forced to run across a much deeper stretch of flat sand, advancing 400 to 450 yards under withering fire.

Forty-five years had done nothing to erase the vividness of these memories.

Preparing for D-Day, the largest air, land, and sea battle ever fought, began for me on my sixteenth birthday, February 3, 1941. Ironically, this was also the date the Virginia National Guard, of which I was a member, was inducted into federal service. Following twenty months of training in the United States and the Japanese bombing of Pearl Harbor, my unit, Company D, 116th Infantry

Regiment, 29th Division, was sent to the war zone in the British Isles. We didn't know it then, but our ultimate goal would be to spearhead the invasion of Normandy, France, in less than two years.

The world was at war. Adolf Hitler and Benito Mussolini were hell-bent on conquering the world by using devious diplomacy and the iron fist. The United States was struggling to get back on its feet after the devastating economic depression of the 1930s. Unemployment was strangling the country—and its feeble military defenses invited these ambitious despots and the Japanese to take bold military gambles.

My decision to join the National Guard was not entirely patriotic. My family was financially pinched. I believed that I could help and, too, I was impatient to become a mature man. Hollywood movies had already become the favorite propaganda medium, and the silver screen's biggest stars played larger-than-life war heroes. The War Department and the film industry collaborated to make the handsome and brave American soldier, sailor, marine, or pilot always the winner. He might suffer a heroic wound, but it was seldom fatal. The military hero always ended up with the most beautiful girl, too, which attracted the attention of many naïve schoolboys. *For Whom the Bell Tolls, Sergeant York, A Yank in the RAF,* and *Dawn Patrol* were a few of my favorites.

Rousing John Philip Sousa martial band music saturated the airwaves. Thousands of posters and billboards promoting jingoistic patriotism enticed youngsters to *"Join the Navy and See the World!"* On zillions of posters, a stern Uncle Sam pointed directly at me and declared: *"I Want YOU!"* All these gimmicks had an effect on the subconscious thinking of eager young men and boys, and long lines began to form at recruiting offices. Many of my fuzzy-chinned school chums were joining the navy or the marines and some made a point of showing off their splendid uniforms. These branches of service didn't interest me, though, because the regular enlistment for a marine was four years and for a sailor it was six.

One evening, a neighborhood schoolmate came by our house on his way to National Guard drill, wearing an olive drab (OD) woolen dress uniform. His name was Medron R. Patterson, but everyone called him Nudy. Nudy's brass buttons glistened, and the military insignias revealed the colorful history of his regiment in the last war. He had already made corporal, and explained that with each promotion came extra pay.

Corporal Patterson was a well-built lad and, I thought, looked very impressive in his olive drab woolens. He proudly told me he was allowed to keep a uniform at home to wear to the weekly drills. I could picture myself wearing a uniform like that, a uniform that would help me to gain respect. Patterson assured me that his company commander, Captain William Stinnett, might consider my application.

Captain Stinnett was looking for a few good men, but not necessarily a naïve, smooth-faced schoolboy. He questioned my decision, but said that if my parents signed, he would consider the request. It was well known that the Virginia National Guard was to be activated into federal service for a year of intense military training. But I doubt that one person in D Company believed at the time that the United States was gearing up for a world war. I know I didn't.

My family prior to 1937 lived in Bristol, Tennessee. My father had joined the army in 1918 during World War I and was assigned to the coast artillery at Fort Story, Virginia. During his military service he contracted the dangerous pandemic Asian flu virus, and almost died. This illness so weakened his system he never fully recovered.

After the war, John W. Slaughter settled in Bristol, Virginia, where he found work as a lumber salesman and billing estimator at the Bristol Builders Supply Company. Although he had only a tenth-grade education, my father was considered a gifted mathematician. He met and married my mother, Vera Hunter, who was then working in Bristol as a medical secretary for the Massengill Pharmaceutical Company. I was born nine months later on February 3, 1925; then came William Hunter fifteen months later, and James Walker about four years after that. After an interval, Mary Louise entered the picture.

The stock market crash that led to the great worldwide depression of the 1930s caused the nation to hunker down and try to weather the very serious financial crisis. The Slaughter family, although struggling a bit financially, was no worse off than its neighbors. We lived moderately on my father's salary until the building trade hit a slump that forced Bristol Builders to drastically downsize its work force. My father was one of the employees the company cut loose. This move caused the Slaughter family much physical and mental stress.

After weeks of searching for work, my father finally found it in Roanoke, Virginia. We lived for a few weeks at a public boarding house on Patterson Avenue until we were able to rent a house within walking distance of my father's new job at the Skyline Lumber Company. This lumber supply company was similar to the one he left in Bristol, but he was forced to accept much less responsibility and less pay. Due to circumstances, he considered himself lucky to find this job as the warehouse superintendent. His weekly paycheck was thirty-five dollars.

There were four children to feed, and increasingly frequent doctor bills. My father's health was deteriorating, and it became hard to make ends meet. I was almost fifteen years old and wanted to do my part with the household expenses.

In 1940, Roanoke was a midsized southwest Virginia town with a population of about fifty thousand. The Norfolk & Western Railway was headquartered in Roanoke and was the chief employer. The coal-burning N&W steam engines were infamous for depositing black coal dust on front porches, white linen suits, and straw hats. Tree-climbing children like us caused our mamas to work extra hard washing the black coal dust out of our play clothes.

The smaller Virginian Railway was electrified and much cleaner. N&W employees were comparatively well paid and most of them lived comfortably on a fifty-dollar paycheck a week. And then there were the trolley cars that ran on tracks to almost every section of the city. The clanging trolleys rambled noisily over paved streets through neighborhoods on up to, and past bedtime. But the electric streetcars offered cheap and dependable fare—a one-way token cost seven cents, allowing many Roanokers to leave their expensive automobiles at home.

The morning *Roanoke Times* newspaper, and the evening *Roanoke World-News* were the news-gathering print media of that day and time. *WDBJ* and *WSLS* were the major radio broadcast stations. Several movie houses downtown furnished popular entertainment for all ages.

My brothers and I had a newspaper route in a distressed section of Roanoke, where many of the customers were either late paying or simply couldn't keep up the payments at all. Paper carriers, being contractors, are required to pay the company up front for the product they carry and sell. After many months of losing money, we were forced to give up the paper route.

We also mowed our neighbors' lawns and did other odd jobs to earn money. Mrs. Poindexter, who lived up the street, hired Billy and me to pick all the cherries off a large tree in her front yard. We were paid fifty cents a day and all the cherries we could eat. Our clothing was hopelessly stained with red cherry juice and the black N&W coal dust.

During the summer of 1939, I heard about a sawmill job that paid fifty cents a day, with a brown bag lunch thrown in. Brother Billy and I signed on to work as lumber stackers. Billy was then about twelve years old, and I was fourteen. Mr. Carroll, the owner of the mill, rounded up the work crew at 7 a.m. sharp, Monday through Friday. His pickup truck arrived at the work site in Bedford County about 8 a.m. We were supposed to work eight-hour shifts, but we never returned home until after 5:30 or 6 p.m.

My job was to catch and stack the sawn yellow pine boards as they came off the circular saw blade. The sappy lumber was sticky, and the boards were much too heavy for young boys to handle. As the saw log was drawn into the whirling saw blade, a piercing scream ensued, causing our eardrums to ring and ache. Worse than that, large and small wood chips went flying in all directions. I was lucky my face and eyes were spared; the rest of me wasn't so lucky.

Working close to that saw blade was very dangerous, and the noise of the whining blade was ear shattering. There were no goggles or gloves to protect the worker. Billy and I gave Mr. Carroll notice after the first week that we were quitting. He offered a nickel a day raise, but we had to refuse the offer.

That was how it was in the 1930s. Almost every neighborhood chum I knew was desperate for a decent paying summertime job.

I began asking Nudy Patterson questions about how I might join the National Guard. Patterson liked to show off his army uniform, and he always had green folding money in his wallet for movies and cigarettes. I was lucky to have a dime or a quarter for the weekly Saturday morning shows at the downtown Rialto Movie Theater. Our favorite Saturday morning ritual was to buy a nickel bag of chewy caramel kisses at Woolworth's Five & Dime Store, and pay fifteen cents to watch a cowboy movie at the Rialto. The clincher that lured most of the rowdy juveniles each Saturday was a Mickey Mouse or Bugs Bunny cartoon, a Three Stooges comedy, and a hair-raising serial that always left us hanging until the next week's show.

I reasoned that one year of army life would do me good, and afterward I could finish my education. I would have spending money for myself and still send at least half of what was left home to the family. The National Guard was paying one dollar per drill. It seemed too good to be true. But first, I had to get my parents' approval for the one-year enlistment.

I remember the evening I tried to get my parents' attention at the supper table. After a few attempts, I blurted out, "Daddy, I want to join the National Guard like Nudy Patterson." He could tell I was serious. "*BOBBY, WHAT ARE YOU THINKING ABOUT?*" he cried, as he slammed his fist to the table.

Both parents explained that first I had to complete high school. Then it might be all right to enlist. They reasoned that maturity and education would help my military career. I knew they were giving good advice, but I had no intention of making the military a career. I promised I would send at least half my thirty-dollar-a-month private's pay to help with household expenses and besides, I reasoned, there would be one less mouth to feed.

When they saw my determination, they signed.

I enlisted with Roanoke's Company D, a heavy weapons company that supported rifle companies in combat. The company was made up of eight Browning .30-caliber, water-cooled, heavy machine guns and four 81mm mortars. I had heard that the life span of a machine gunner was about three minutes in the last world war—a grim statistic that was grounds for bragging, and it added prestige and honor to being a machine gunner. There was no hint, however, that any of us would ever see combat in any form.

Before our departure to Fort Meade, we received a military sendoff by the City of Roanoke and Roanoke Post 64, 29th Division Association. The parade began at Elmwood Park, passed through downtown Roanoke, and ended in front of the City Court House on Campbell Avenue. After the ceremony, we marched back to the Roanoke Auditorium encampment and to the crowded gymnasium floor.

A newspaper article that appeared in *The Roanoke Times* on February 8, 1941, quoted Roanoke's mayor, Walter W. Wood, as he addressed the young men about to leave home:

> "I do not know what tasks will be assigned you. . . .
> I do know that whatever the tasks are, or whatever
> the sacrifice required of you, that not one single
> member of the 1st Battalion, 116th Infantry, 29th
> Division will be found wanting. Your Battalion has
> a splendid and noble record. Many of its members
> in the World War I are standing here beside me.
> They are not handing the baton to you, but merely
> back standing you here, for their services may be
> needed before the insane dictators of Europe are
> crushed. . . . Good luck and God bless you."

CHAPTER TWO

STATESIDE TRAINING

1941 CAROLINA MANEUVERS

There we were, eight hundred troops clad in woolen olive drab or cotton blue denim uniforms, sitting or lying on canvas cots in a basketball arena, many of us smoking cig arettes or shooting the breeze with friends. The setting was the multipurpose auditorium and arena that the city of Roanoke used for recreational sports, concerts, and dances. But on this occasion, the arena was the temporary quarters for the newly inducted Roanoke, Virginia, National Guard companies.

The facility, near the Norfolk & Western railway passenger station, was across the way from the elegant Hotel Roanoke. Once a week, before the National Guard had been federalized, local units of the 116th Infantry had drilled at the arena on weeknights, using the basketball court for close-order drill and other exercises, and the classrooms for instruction in soldiering. Now we were federalized, and we were allowed to leave the crowded confines of the auditorium only to go out for meals.

The local units of the 116th Infantry that shared the armory included Regimental Headquarters Company, 1st Battalion Headquarters Company, D Company, Service Company, Antitank Company, Band Company, and a Medical Detachment of the 104th Medical Company. D Company's first sergeant, George W. Boyd, was the epitome of an army "top kick." He was older than most of us, for one thing. Plus, he was blessed with a special military presence and a booming, commanding voice. He immediately took charge of the company as we formed for the short march to breakfast at the Manhattan Restaurant on North Jefferson Street.

In early 1941, all of us in D Company knew we were a comical sight as we attempted to march in step to chow. I prayed that no one I knew would recognize me. Many of us wore ill-fitting, hand-me-down uniforms, could not stay in step, and looked like a proverbial "sad sack." At night, loud snoring and whispers kept many of us from getting our eight hours of sleep. To break the boredom, some of the older men played tricks on gullible privates by sending them on supposedly important errands, and by short-sheeting their beds and other asinine pranks.

For most of the men, it was very frustrating to stand in a long line for a warm shower or a basin for shaving. I was not old enough to shave, but I still had to wait for a shower. We frittered away many hours reading dime novels and comic books, and playing checkers or nickel knock-rummy. The confinement gave me a chance to become acquainted with many of my peers. These friendships, which began so easily, would be cemented later as we shared the extreme hardships of training and fighting a desperate and bloody war.

After spending ten days bivouacked on the crowded hardwood floor of the auditorium, we were finally told to pack our gear. Without fanfare this time, we formed a column of twos to the train station. We descended a few steps to the depot platform, and waited to board the Norfolk & Western passenger train. I found a seat next to Jack Ingram, whom I knew from having played basketball and baseball against each other in junior high school. Several schoolyard acquaintances from my neighborhood made it a little easier to leave home. Fort George G. Meade, Maryland, situated between Washington, D.C. and Baltimore, was our destination. Every click of the rail took us farther from our parents, siblings, girlfriends, and, for a few of the men, wives, and children.

The noisy steam engine idled and puffed at the siding, waiting for all hands to climb aboard and be seated. Then a uniformed conductor cupped his hands to his mouth and yelled, "All aboard!" The engine bellowed white steam, and the train began to move, slowly at first, then faster and faster. We could not imagine it then, but many of the men on that train would never return home.

About five hours later, we pulled into the train station at Odenton, Maryland. As we piled out and marched the short distance to our new homes, some of them still under construction, it suddenly dawned on me that I was a soldier in the United States Army. I was barely sixteen years old, and had never spent a night away from my mother and father. I became queasy with a bad case of homesickness. Wearing the uniform of a U.S. soldier had not in the least turned me into a man. Wondering what I had done to myself, I nevertheless consoled myself into thinking that we would return home in twelve months.

What a strange-looking place this newly built army base was! I was amazed at all the coarse brown sand. The streets were unpaved and there was not a blade or branch of anything green. I remember the uniformity of all the plain, unpainted new buildings, which my regiment was the first to occupy. Behind our barracks was the battalion drill field. There we assembled for daily reveille and retreat formations, and spent many hours of close-order and other sorts of drill. Old World War I army tanks lined up on the upper end of the drill field like dormant war-horses served as subjects for many GI photo opportunities. On the outskirts of the encampment, a boomtown grew out of the coarse brown sand. Slick entrepreneurs were anxious to take advantage of our gullibility, pushing cheap souvenirs, mostly made in Japan. Rowdy beer joints sprouted and prospered. A carnival also came to town in order to fleece us of our paychecks.

The first sergeant called the roll, and then ordered: "Right face, *forward* march!" A mile away from our destination, a cacophony of carpenters hammered and sawed more pine barracks for the next batch of new recruits who followed. Could it be the country was gearing up for another world war?

Across the way were more permanent brick buildings that housed the regular army contingent at Fort Meade, peacetime regular soldiers whom nobody could mistake for new arrivals. These were career professionals, whose tailor-made military uniforms fit like gloves. Their leather shoes and belts were spit-polished, and their brass buttons glistened. Many old-timers had hash marks running up their arms to their elbows, despite the fact that they were still privates or corporals. Many were thirty-five or forty years old, and looked like the real thing to us. Off post, many of them often changed to civilian clothes.

Our barracks were long, unpainted, yellow pine clapboard, two-and-a-half stories high. Each company also had an orderly room, supply room, and mess hall. Company D had three two-and-a-half-story buildings that housed noncommissioned officers (noncoms) and privates. There were two floors of sleeping dormitories that had twenty steel cots on each floor. The foot of each cot faced the middle aisle. Each had two white sheets, a pillow with a white pillowcase, and two woolen OD blankets. At the foot of each cot was an OD-painted wooden footlocker. At each end of the dormitory were two small private rooms with two sergeants to each room. If you entered the barracks from the back door and turned to the right, you went down about four steps to the washroom. Straight ahead were about eight or ten washbasins with mirrors above each one. At the left were shower stalls with an alum-water footbath. Around the room were toilets and urinals.

Outside were the mess hall, kitchen, and a smaller building that housed the orderly room, where the captain, first sergeant, and company clerk worked. Corporal Joseph M. Young, a large, amiable redhead, was selected to be company clerk. He worked under the supervision of the first sergeant, keeping records of payrolls, sicknesses, AWOLs (absent without leaves), promotions, and the like. He was required to type and communicate with other companies, and battalion and regimental headquarters. (After Young left the company, he was replaced by Tech 5 William Rauch, a drafted soldier from Pennsylvania.) Adjoining the orderly room was the supply room, where Supply Sergeant Arthur Joseph (Joe) Lancaster issued clothing and equipment. The sergeant kept an inventory of what was issued to each man. If someone's equipment was lost or stolen, the unlucky fellow could expect the cost to be deducted from his next paycheck.

One morning in formation, Lancaster had us scratching our heads. He tried to explain that three bed sheets would be issued to each man and that the top sheet would be turned in for washing each morning. His instruction was to "put the top sheet over the bottom sheet, the bottom sheet goes under the top sheet, and the third sheet on the . . . uh, uh, oh hell, you know what I mean!"

We were given ill-fitting woolen uniforms that reeked of mothballs, undoubtedly recycled from the World War. There were also .30-caliber machine guns and 81mm mortars that had been packed away with Cosmoline and crated. Our job was to uncrate and clean these weapons with gasoline-soaked rags. Afterward they were inspected to make sure they were properly cleaned and in good working order. Each of us was given a physical examination, immunization shots, and very short haircuts.

A different way of life soon became apparent to the bewildered newcomers. Discipline and organization were foreign to most of us, and our first task was to learn that infractions were not to be tolerated. Basic instructions included: march in step, perform manual of arms drill, make beds the military way, police company area, clean and press uniforms, shine shoes, tend to personal hygiene, cut hair short, perform weapons drill, memorize the general orders of guard duty and recite them upon command, and salute and say "sir" to officers.

For all of this, in 1941 the army soldier's pay per month was: private, $30; private first class, $36; corporal, $54; sergeant, $60; staff sergeant, $72; technical sergeant, $84; and first sergeant, $96. A newly drafted private was paid $21 the first four months and then his pay was raised to $30. Some of the older men had spent years in the National Guard or Civilian Conservation Corps (CCC) and seemed comfortable in the military. But those of us new to this routine often forgot or made mistakes, and were constantly being embarrassed.

Our commanding officer, Captain Walter O. Schilling, demanded unyielding compliance to all military rules and regulations, and he threw in a few of his own for good measure. Under his command, the military book of rules had to be read and learned. Punishment was meted out to the slow learners, and rewards of weekend passes and promotions to the willing achievers. The captain was not a large man, but he was wiry and tough. He threatened to take his bars off and step behind the barracks with any noncompliant malcontent. No one doubted his sincerity.

Once, a noncom was caught stealing from another soldier, and he soon felt the captain's iron fist. This was a severe breach of army conduct. It was rumored that Schilling met the lawbreaker behind the barracks. Although we could only speculate about what actually happened, the crook disappeared and we never heard of him again. Another time, one of the squad leaders, was not getting compliance from one of his men. The corporal, Hartman, marched the troublemaker to the captain's office. In his squeaky, high-pitched voice, he whined, "Captain, Sir, Private Stevenson won't do a damned thing I asked him to do."

Captain Schilling rose from his chair, eyes squinting over his round wire-rimmed glasses, and said, "God damn it, Corporal, how much do you weigh?"

Hartman, feeling sheepish, quietly answered, "About two hundred, Sir!"

The captain then said in a rising voice, "Now Corporal, how much does Private Stevenson weigh?"

Hartman mumbled, "Uh, er, I'd say about one-fifty, Sir!"

Schilling then screamed, *"Get the hell out of here!"*

Other unforgettable people included Staff Sergeant John B. Sink, our mess sergeant. He was in charge of the kitchen and supervised the full-time cooks and part-time kitchen police. Nothing seemed to bother the sergeant. The men frequently complained about the quality or the quantity of the food, and Sergeant Sink always had a ready answer:

"I take boys and make men out of you," he would say. When one of the men accused the sergeant of starving him to death, Sink grinned and said, "We haven't lost a single man, as far as I know, from malnutrition!" Another time, someone complained that he found rocks in the beans. Sink put his index finger to his lips and whispered, "Shh, don't let anyone hear you. They'll all want them in theirs."

The first draftees assigned to the company arrived in the early spring of 1941. These men were from southwest Virginia, eastern Tennessee, and eastern Kentucky. They had been students, farmers, coal miners, lumbermen, and factory workers.

Curtis C. Moore had previously worked at his grandfather's Moore Milling Company in Salem, Virginia. He recently recalled his first impression of army life: "I marched into the area with a formation of fresh recruits. As we entered D Company, there was Private Johnny Steeleton digging a four-by-four-by-four-foot hole, using a pick and shovel. Standing over him, armed with a baseball bat, was this tough-looking sergeant." Steeleton, perspiring profusely, was armpit-deep in the cavity, throwing dirt onto a huge pile. The sergeant measured the dimensions of the hole, making sure the walls were straight. After the hole was completed to his satisfaction, the sergeant ordered the private to shovel the dirt back into the hole. It was stressed to the newcomers that the same fate or worse, awaited them if they stepped out of line. They never forgot that scene.

Another unpardonable sin was to "fall out" during a hike. Many of us suffered from blisters, heat exhaustion, leg cramps, and even the flu, but we never considered falling out. Captain Schilling almost always suffered, too, during our biweekly fifteen- to twenty-five-mile hikes. Usually after about five or six miles, the captain's shoulders began to droop and he began to limp, sometimes badly.

On the night before one of the dreaded summertime fifteen-mile hikes, new arrival Private Curtis Moore and Sergeant Harry Ferris went to town and drank most of a fifth of bourbon. They paid the price for it beginning when the reveille bugle blew very early the next morning. In June, the weather at sandy Fort Meade was always hot and very humid. We were told that one canteen of water had to do until we returned to camp late that evening. After about six or seven miles, Moore had emptied his canteen. As the hot, dusty miles rolled on, the private developed a splitting hangover headache, and his throat was parched. His platoon brought up the rear of the column.

Sergeant Ferris, who liked to play jokes, told his drinking buddy that Captain Schilling might let him ride in his jeep. The jeep, used for emergencies, led at the head of the column. Private Moore ran about thirty yards from the rear of the column to near the front. Huffing and puffing, he said, "Captain, Sir, I'm sicker 'n hell! Would it be okay, Sir, if I ride back to camp in the Jeep?" The captain, limping badly himself and toughing it out, screamed: *"Not no! But hell, no! Get your fat ass back in that line, right now!"*

After we completed the ordeal and were back at camp, the four platoons assembled in formation. The captain screamed, "*Attention!* Now, whose damned platoon is Private Moore in?" First Platoon Sergeant Willard R. Norfleet sheepishly replied, "Sir, Private Moore is in my platoon, Sir!" "I'd be damned ashamed, Sergeant Norfleet, to admit it!" the captain admonished.

A few weeks later, a second group of draftees was integrated into the company. These men came from north of the Mason-Dixon line (Pennsylvania; Washington, D.C.; and Maryland), which explained the division's nickname, *"Blue and Gray."* Many of the new arrivals were Irish, Polish, German, Greek, and Italian, and were mostly Catholic.

Those damned Yankees brought with them strange customs and a funny way of speaking. They, in turn, laughed at the slow, thick-tongued drawl of the Appalachian mountaineers: *"Y'all come ovah, ya heah."* And the southern "rednecks" had to strain their ears to understand *"Geez, goiz, I'm from Sout' Philly."* It wasn't long before the Yankees had adopted *"y'all come"* and the Southerners were imitating their northern buddies with, *"Croist kid, deal the ciads!"*

Over time, some of the older men left the company and were discharged; others qualified for OCS (officer candidate school). The recently drafted men not only filled the void but swelled the ranks to near capacity. First Sergeant George Boyd left the company as a second lieutenant and eventually became Company H's commanding officer. James H. Obenshain was promoted to first sergeant after First Sergeant James Mabes left D Company for Antitank Company. All of these are remembered as fine soldiers.

During the time I was a corporal, most of the noncoms were selected to teach basic training to a third group of recruits from New England. I was assigned to the 5th Provisional Training Company. Upon completion of thirteen weeks of basic infantry training, the cadre and the graduates joined the regiment at Camp

A. P. Hill Military Reservation near Bowling Green in Caroline County, Virginia.

Hiking 125 miles in ninety-degree heat while carrying our weapons with full field packs was a fitting infantry graduation exercise. Few of us will forget the last mile up a steady grade into the 116th Regiment's bivouac area. It was drilled into the cadre that all the companies were to finish the hike on their feet.

This class produced many great combat soldiers who would prove themselves in 1944–1945, but as new graduates of basic training they were not, as yet, in top physical shape. The heat and humidity, plus the steep mile-long grade caused many of the recruits to become nauseated, and the cadre had to help them to the finish line in order to keep them on their feet. I ended up carrying three extra rifles and two field packs. An impromptu welcoming committee of spectators clapped and cheered as every member of the 5th Training Company staggered to the finish line. The former soldier candidates were now proclaimed proud members of the Stonewall Brigade's 116th Infantry Regiment.

Camp A. P. Hill Military Reservation was a hellhole. The United States military has a knack for finding god-forsaken wastelands for army campsites. In 1941, Caroline County was miles of scrubby briar thickets, sappy bull pine trees, wood ticks, and chiggers. We all called the reservation A. P. "Hell," and its thousands of acres covered most of Caroline County.

The new arrivals marched up the dusty company streets before separating into individual company areas. I was filthy, sweaty, and very thirsty. The camp was dotted with scores of eight-man pyramidal squad tents. Wood smoke from the various company kitchens filled our nostrils. And something else caught my eye, too. There were three or four large water-filled rubberized canvas bags hanging from tripods, called "lister bags." A fellow had to be extremely thirsty to drink that tea-warm, foul tasting, chlorine-laced water. We were warned to hold our noses before drinking the foul stuff.

Another unpleasant element was the twice-weekly cold shower. Smart army engineers had invented a makeshift field shower, which pumped unheated water into ten-gallon bags that hung from overhead poles. Drinking water was warm and shower water was cold! Long lines of bare-ass GIs waited for their turns to bathe. After soaping up, you pulled a lever to pour a gallon or so of breathtakingly cold water over yourself. And so we learned to live with misery.

We also hiked all day on one canteen—about a quart—of that foul-tasting A. P. Hill water and two sandwiches for lunch, one bologna and one jelly. There were no recreational outlets or acceptable towns to visit during our stay. This, however, did not much matter, because after two months of chiggers and ticks, the division motor-marched south in July to the more unfriendly North and South Carolina war games.

Carolina newspapers followed the division into the field, bragging that these war games were as close to actual combat as possible. One team was *Red* and the other *Blue*. If the officers knew what was going on, the news didn't trickle down to the bewildered enlisted soldiers. All we knew was we began the day early, received two sandwiches—one bologna, the other jelly—and an apple in a brown paper bag. We were either loading into trucks or hiking out of camp to where the action was.

On rare occasions, a formation of military single-engine biplanes flew over the column of troops. We had no clue where we were going or what we were supposed to do. The maneuver arena was similar to Caroline County, Virginia: a backwash hellhole of a deeper hot and humid South.

I was born and raised a southerner, but I had never seen hundreds of blacks—men, women, and children—bent over cotton plants in ninety-degree heat for ten hours a day. I had always believed that slavery ended with the Civil War. Another shock for me was witnessing Carolina chain gangs working on state infrastructure. Muscular black men were dressed in black-and-white striped uniforms, with ball-and-chain leg irons. Dripping sweat, these Carolina road gangs were swinging heavy sixteen-pound sledgehammers, singing as they swung. Many of these convicts spent most of their lives making little rocks out of big rocks. Mounted guards with shotguns kept the crews working and sweating. For once, I saw people I wouldn't trade places with.

On our return trip to Fort Meade we motor convoyed through the outskirts of Savannah and bivouacked in woods ten miles north of the city. As usual, Captain Schilling ordered that no one was to leave the bivouac area.

Corporal Aaron Bowling and I had already made plans to scout the restaurants in the Georgia city. We were aware the captain didn't want to have to send a search party into town to round up soldiers who had lost track of time. Even so, Bowling and I changed into our starched khakis and caught a ride with the battalion water truck going to town.

On the outskirts of Savannah we spotted a roadside diner and asked the driver to let us out. This was late afternoon and we knew it would be difficult to hitch a ride after dark. Our plan was to eat and get back to camp before sundown.

We chose a booth in back of the restaurant, hung our caps on the hat rack at our booth, sat down, and ordered two steaks. I was facing the front door. We both were anxiously awaited the arrival of our meal twenty minutes later, when Captain Schilling and his driver, Private First Class June McDevitt, walked in the door and took a booth near the front. I couldn't believe my eyes.

I slid down behind the booth and whispered to Bowling, "It's Captain Schilling and Mack." Our hearts were pounding in our chests. I knew those caps hanging on the wall with the 116th insignias showing were dead giveaways.

McDevitt excused himself to go to the washroom and saw us hiding. He grimaced at us as he walked by, but he knew and we knew our goose was cooked. Captain Schilling soon followed, and immediately pounced on our table. "Do you two assholes think you can get by with something like this? If you aren't back in camp by the time I'm there, you both can kiss your stripes goodbye!" Both of us had just been promoted to corporal, and his threat meant a lot.

We canceled the order, caught a ride, and were back in camp before the Captain arrived. For months we both were at the top of his "s—" list.

It was a chilly late evening on Sunday, December 7. The 1st Battalion and D Company were bivouacked in woods near South Hill, Virginia. The division was returning to Fort Meade and would soon be saying goodbye to Uncle Sam. The 1st Platoon was huddled around a blazing campfire. Some of the men played cards on a blanket while others watched the game or the fire. I was lying on a blanket on the ground, almost asleep. We had almost completed our year of obligatory training, which would be over come February 1942.

Suddenly, Motor Sergeant William R. Hurd burst into the area screaming, *The Japs have bombed Pearl Harbor! The Japs have bombed Pearl Harbor!*"

Hurd was known for his practical jokes. "Shut up, Bill!" I replied. "We're trying to sleep!"

"I'll swear it's the truth!" he shouted.

The attack had occurred earlier that morning, Pacific time, but we were so isolated and communications were so rudimentary, that it was late afternoon before we heard what had happened. Radios scattered throughout the area verified the terrible news. The Japanese had made a sneak attack on the Pacific outpost and had almost destroyed the American fleet anchored in the harbor. At first, we felt anger and frustration at such a cowardly act—and then we realized that we would not be going home.

The next day, Japan, Germany, and Italy declared war on the United States. Discharges were suspended, and many of us who sang the song "I'll Be Back in a Year, Little Darling," changed the words to "in for the duration." Many civilians and merchants who had previously scorned the military suddenly began to treat us with respect.

Soon afterward, D Company and the 116th were selected for an important wartime mission. The regiment was assigned motorized patrol duty guarding the Maryland eastern shore coastline to the Virginia border. Bridges, tunnels, and other coastal infrastructure were vulnerable to enemy naval attack, or enemy saboteurs slipping ashore.

D Company's eight heavy machine guns were ordered mounted on swivels fixed to weapons carriers. The guns were fully loaded with live ammunition. While performing this duty we stayed in vacant CCC barracks at Westover, Maryland. After a few weeks of patrolling the eastern shore, we were relieved and headed for another assignment in Virginia.

On one of the coldest nights of the year, the regiment loaded onto transport trucks and headed for Camp Pendleton near Virginia Beach. The temperature hovered at thirty degrees, but it felt even colder. A loose, flapping canvas fanned us as we rode, causing my teeth to chatter uncontrollably. My dream as we high-balled down the highway was getting under a hot shower in one of those steam-heated barracks at Camp Pendleton. I had never been so cold for so long. I believe that dream was all that kept me from dying of hypothermia.

It was impossible to sleep. In the darkness of early morning, the trucks pulled into a pine forest and shut off the motors. There were about three inches of ice and snow on the ground. Because we were near water, the windchill made the cold even worse. Where were those steam-heated barracks?

Someone up front yelled, "De-truck! Pitch tents!" I couldn't believe my ears. In the icy darkness we pitched pup tents on the frozen tundra. Three hours later, we were awakened; we broke camp and headed east. This time, our job was to protect the coast from the "enemy"—the invading Bataan-bound 1st Division Marines. They waded ashore from landing craft and simulated assaulting the beach.

Digging gun emplacements in the frozen ground wasn't easy, but wading ashore from landing craft through the icy surf was much worse. Many leathernecks were paralyzed when they hit the cold water. But it was good training. After this landing, those same 1st Division Marines sailed for the tropical Japanese-occupied Philippine Islands.

We spent the spring and summer of 1942 in the heat and red clay dust of North and South Carolina, fine-tuning our skills and slowly being reequipped with more modern weapons. Eventually, we worked our way down to Camp Blanding, Florida, a beautiful setting with white sand beaches around clear, seven-mile-wide Kingsley Lake. Our training was momentarily suspended, and many of us acquired golden Florida suntans.

Nearby Jacksonville was the home of Sergeant Jimmie L. Hamlin. One night he invited a few of us for an evening on the town. We ordered a fine dinner at the elegant Roosevelt Hotel. I wasn't used to crystal chandeliers, oriental carpets, and excellent food and drink. I hoped it would never end. I prayed that we would spend the war at Blanding, training other infantry troops for oversea duty.

But that prayer was not answered. Before long, we heard once more, "Pack up, we're heading out!" Again, the regiment loaded onto passenger trains headed we knew not where. All we knew was that the tracks pointed north. As the train departed, there were many teary-eyed wives and girlfriends waving goodbye to their husbands and boyfriends. My last memory of Camp Blanding was that of a sobbing wife running beside the slow-moving train, waving a damp handkerchief at her sad-faced husband. Hours later, the train pulled into the passenger depot at New Brunswick, New Jersey. At the platform we were surprised to see many of those same wives and girlfriends who had watched us depart Blanding.

Camp Kilmer was an East Coast processing center for troops being shipped overseas. The camp had a ten-foot fence with barbed wire reenforcing the top. No one was allowed passes to town. We were told German intelligence officers were eager to learn the sailing schedules of departing troopships. Also, when orders were given to board ship they didn't want to have to send military policemen (MPs) into town rounding up soldiers. By now, this was a familiar tune.

But "orders from headquarters" was never much of an obstacle for Corporal Dick Owensby. He had previously spent time in New Brunswick selling war bonds for the government. On this occasion, Owensby told me he had gotten the phone numbers of some local girls. We knew that if we were caught going over that fence, Captain Schilling would skin both of us alive. We also knew we were going overseas to goodness knows where—or what. Okay, we decided, *let's go!*

We dressed into our starched khakis and rolled the fence. That was the easy part. We couldn't find the girls, and neither of us had much money after paying the taxi fare. As the clock ticked, I began to worry.

We decided that we had better get back before the 6 a.m. reveille roll call. We caught a taxi back to camp and as we paid the driver and departed the cab, we could see D Company already in early morning formation. We were AWOL and in trouble. Quickly, we concocted a tale about playing poker with Service Company men and that both of us had fallen asleep.

We climbed the barrier and tiptoed into the barracks. First Sergeant Obenshain was waiting. With hands on his hips, he sarcastically asked, "Where in the hell have you two been?"

We replied in unison, "Playing cards at Service Company."

He then said, "You have just lost your ass!"

Obenshain grabbed Owensby as he told me to stay put. He then led Owensby into Captain Schilling's small office and closed the door. I could hear angry shouting, and looked for a hole to crawl into. Shortly, I, too, was ordered into the captain's office. I could imagine it being an execution chamber. It had only been a few weeks ago that Bowling and I had been caught sneaking off to Savannah.

Schilling squinted over his glasses and growled, "Damn it, Slaughter, don't you lie to me!" He bellowed as he pointed to a pale-faced Owensby. "That excuse for a soldier lied through his god-damned teeth! I want to hear what *you* have to say! Just where have you two assholes been?"

I knew my corporal stripes and the monthly $54 were as good as gone. I told him the truth. I don't believe that the captain ever forgave me, and I know that the distraction of going overseas saved us from very severe consequences. He sentenced us both to a month's confinement at Tidworth. We knew we were lucky to get off so easily.

CHAPTER THREE

GOING ABROAD

THE SINKING OF THE *CURACOA*

I n September 1942, Camp Kilmer was a beehive of activity. Thousands of men at this huge overseas supply depot were all preparing to ship out to the European Theater of Operation (ETO), and I was one of them. The 116th Infantry and the 111th Field Artillery, plus attachments—about twelve thousand of us in all—were measured and outfitted for the upcoming ocean journey, and for what lay ahead. We stood in long lines before table after table piled with equipment and clothing. Much of the new-issue equipment had been improved, while some of it was merely new.

Most importantly, we exchanged the bolt action Springfield '03 rifle for the semiautomatic M1 Garand. We also exchanged our flat, dishpan-shaped helmets for new ones that looked like coal buckets, and traded in our blue denim fatigues for better-looking green herringbone twill. Photograph mug shots and fingerprints were taken and made into neat, wallet-sized identification folders that we carried until we were discharged or buried.

We received vaccination shots for every disease known to man, and we took them in both arms and where the sun doesn't shine. With both sleeves rolled, we walked single-file through a gauntlet of needle-pricking medics. The first two fellows painted iodine circles, many of them off-target, for the picadors to stab with long, dull needles. Then we dropped our pants and bent over to get more shots. For days after, it was hard to either salute the flag or sit down.

Our last few hours on American soil were an unforgettable nightmare. The army has "standard operating procedures" or SOPs, thought up by smart officers, and passed down to mean NCOs to implement. We now became the victim of the SOP concerning the two barracks bags that we were using as carry-on luggage, and for storing excess uniforms and equipment.

Our barracks bags were large, bulky, and heavy, made of olive drab canvas duck with a rope tie on one end to keep things from falling out. First Sergeant Obenshain labeled one of the bags the "A" bag and the other the "B" bag. Simple enough. Essential gear that would stay with us went in the "A" bag, and anything not needed for the journey went in the "B" bag, which would be stored in the hold of the ship.

Obenshain read a long list of items that were to be packed in each bag. No sooner had we packed everything up according to his explicit instructions, than we got a countermanding order to take certain items from the "B" bag and put them in the "A" bag, and vice versa. This went on and on. Eventually we dumped the contents of both bags in one huge pile and started the entire process over again. Looking back, the incident seems amusing now, but at the time, it greatly added to the deteriorating mood. Our sagging morale just plummeted!

On the afternoon of September 26, the 116th Infantry, along with others, left Kilmer by passenger train and headed for Jersey City, New Jersey. From there, we hiked over to a small boat that ferried us across the North River and to the troopship loading dock. Heavily loaded down, our two barracks bags filled to the brim, our M1 constantly sliding off our shoulders, we marched double-file to dockside in a late summer rain. Anchored alongside the pier was one of the largest ocean liners in the world. We fussed and cussed in the soaking September downpour, burdened by the ever-shifting load we carried.

On this trip the British Crown provided us with free transportation aboard the famous luxury liner, the RMS *Queen Mary*. The 115th and 175th, the other two regiments of the 29th, sailed a week later on her sister ship, the RMS *Queen Elizabeth*. These twins were the largest and fastest ships afloat. Each was capable of doing at least thirty knots, which enabled them to cross the Atlantic Ocean unescorted in about five days.

We were scheduled to maintain 28–29 knots. To foil the German torpedoes, the ship changed course every seven or eight minutes in a maneuver the British navy dubbed "zigzag 8."

The *Queen Mary* and *Queen Elizabeth* were outfitted like most other luxury passenger liners, which early in the war had been pressed into troop-carrying service. Stripped of extravagance and retrofitted with troopship austerity, the *Queen Mary* was repainted a dull camouflage gray inside and out. Backbreaking, double-decker hammocks replaced the ocean liner's comfortable beds. There was room for less than half of us to eat or sleep at any one time, so we ate and slept in shifts.

Upon arrival at the ship, the American Red Cross issued each of us a handy ditty bag. Special guides escorted individual companies to their assigned areas of the ship. It was after midnight when we finally climbed aboard. Single lines of khaki-clad men strained up the steep gangplank like pack animals. As each of us boarded, our last name was called, and we answered with our first name and middle initial.

The next morning, after breakfast—Sunday, September 27— New York tugboats pushed the giant transport and her valuable cargo into the channel, and she steamed out into the Atlantic Ocean. We were leaving our homeland for a strange and hostile land. No rousing band music, no throngs of waving spectators sent us off to our destination and fate. Out on the deck, I watched the Statue of Liberty fade into the distance. Our harbor escort vessels waved goodbye and peeled off. This was the last time many of the men would ever see the American shore. The lucky ones returned home about three years later, some of them forever maimed.

The wet autumn weather cleared and the moderating gulf currents made the voyage warm and enjoyable. The ride was relatively smooth, even though I felt a little woozy at times and never quite up to par. Many avid landlubbers spent time in the head, but most of us enjoyed the ride. A school of playful porpoises followed the ship, and a few misguided flying fish landed on deck. One day, we even sighted a whale off the starboard side, spewing water and rolling in the ripple-smooth water.

The British food was, in a word, terrible. This was my introduction to wartime British rations, and I never did get used to them. To make matters worse, eating the awful stuff was a physical challenge. If you didn't anchor your dinner plate, it slid across the table. Spots of bitter tea sloshed out of lip-burning tin cups. Although we longed for better food, the rolling sea and the meager rations did keep our normal hunger pangs in check.

Then, in the middle of this uneventful trip, a terrible tragedy occurred—a calamity caused not by the German Luftwaffe or U-boats, but by the British Royal Navy. On Friday, October 2, we were about two hundred miles from our destination when the *Queen Mary*, our troop transport, collided with another British ship, slicing it in two. In minutes, 332 British sailors died before our horrified eyes.

When the catastrophe occurred, we felt a distinct bump. Many of us ran to the rail just in time to see the bow of the *Curacoa*, nose up, scraping the starboard side of the *Queen Mary*. I was horrified to see a frightened sailor performing semaphore signals from the ship's horizontal-to-the-water crow's nest. I couldn't imagine what he was thinking, or whom he was signaling.

There was little we could do except throw life preservers to the stricken sailors. The larger ship, unable to stop, kept going, but at a reduced speed. Sadly enough, it would have been imprudent to endanger twelve thousand men to save a few hundred.

The stern of the cruiser bumped the port side, and quickly sank in the *Queen Mary's* wake. The much larger bow—black smoke pouring from its funnel—stayed afloat for about six minutes before it too was swept into our wake. The broken *Curacoa* slowly raised its nose until it was almost vertical, and then slid backward into a sea of bubbling foam.

Following is an excerpt of a British Admiralty special hearing:

> . . . HMS *Curacoa*, a twin-screw, antiaircraft light cruiser of 4,290 tons displacement, 450 feet in length, assigned, with a six-destroyer antisubmarine screen, to guard the [*Queen Mary*], sighted her at a given position in about longitude twelve degrees west. The [*Queen Mary*] was relying on her speed and a planned zigzag, known as a "zigzag 8" for her chief defense.
>
> The zigzag took about 40 minutes to complete, steering to port and starboard, and her speed was taken as about 28 1/2 knots. Her main course was 106 degrees, and it was calculated the ship would advance on it 93 per cent of the total distance run. The *Curacoa's* best speed was 25 knots and so the [*Queen Mary*], despite the zigzag, would ultimately overtake her escort.
>
> At about 1220, Captain Boutwood of the *Curacoa* sent a hand signal to his convoy, which

was still well astern, 'When you are ahead I will edge in astern of you.' His duty, of course, was to guard the transport against air attack. They were now in a zone where the danger was increasing, and although the sea was rough with a heavy westerly swell running, the weather was fine and clear, with visibility extending for miles.

By 1330, the [*Queen Mary*] was close astern of the cruiser. The *Curacoa* had a complement of 430 officers and men, and in broad daylight under a shining sky, just 42 minutes later, the [*Queen Mary*] had killed 332 of them. Her bow struck the *Curacoa* on her port side aft at a fine angle and divided the warship into two parts, which sank in minutes. By the hard practice of the war, the [*Queen Mary*] went straight on, over and through the wreck, the still living, the dying and the dead.

All of us aboard the *Queen Mary* were aghast at the great loss of human life. This was war—but the enemy was blameless for this careless mistake. Very luckily for us, the ship was partitioned with separate compartments, which saved thousands of 29ers from the same fate.

All Browning automatic riflemen (BAR) were ordered to assemble on deck. Private First Class Curtis Moore and other BAR men were ordered to retrieve their crated weapons, and go to the upper deck to stand watch against possible Luftwaffe or U-boat attacks. Although I was not aware of it at the time, it was also reported that Captain Schilling ordered Company D's eight .30-caliber heavy machine guns to be uncrated and manned.

As we exited the ocean liner at Greenock, Scotland, we discovered a puncture so large we could hardly believe that the ship had remained afloat. The hole in her bow could easily have swallowed a truck.

After that horror at sea, it was doubly good to be on *terra firma* again. It took a while to calm our unsteady sea legs and our nerves. As we left the ship and the balmy weather of the Gulf Stream behind, it was clear that early winter had arrived in Scotland. Friendly British NAAFI (Navy, Army, Air Force Institutes) girls, much like the American Red Cross, greeted us with small cake-like doughnuts and hot coffee. A British army band played a snappy tune that helped to ease the sharp pangs of homesickness.

Late that afternoon, we boarded the London, Midland, and Scottish Railway train that headed south toward the English midlands. Wartime English trains were smaller but more agile than those back in the United States. After dark, blackout curtains covered the windows and the coach lights were dimmed. High-stake poker games kept some of the men occupied, while others of us just rode in idle bewilderment. The speeding little train shook us from side to side as the shrill, eerie whistle screamed throughout the dark night.

Early the next morning we arrived at the Andover, England, train station. I hadn't slept ten minutes the entire trip and it was already daylight. The sky was overcast and the forecast was cloudy and cool. I was tired, hungry, and severely sleep deprived. British troop-carrying trucks, called lorries, were lined up along the road waiting for us. We now convoyed to our temporary homes at Tidworth Barracks, a regular army cavalry base about halfway between Salisbury and Andover on the Salisbury Plains.

The square, two-story, Elizabethan-era exterior was constructed of antique red brick and wrought iron. The interior living quarters looked more like a penitentiary than an army barracks, and the English winter made it even worse. Gone were the heated barracks we had enjoyed at Hotel Fort Meade; gone were white sheets and soft bedding. Each floor had two small, coal-burning, pot-bellied stoves that died soon after the lights went out.

The double-deck bunks in these frigid quarters were much too small for my six-foot five-inch frame. Less than six feet long and about three feet wide, they had straw mattresses, two GI wool blankets, and no pillow—all of which made sleeping very uncomfortable.

There was simply no way I could fit into the bed. If I curled into the fetal position, my rear end and knees hung over the sides; if I straightened, my feet were exposed. I had the upper bunk so there was nothing I could do to improve the situation, but I was so tired that I managed to sleep anyway. I supplemented my bed covers with the contents of my barracks bag, which always spilled onto the floor by morning. We slept in our uniforms and socks, and when the 5:30 a.m. wake-up bugle blew, we were almost dressed.

Within days, we were sightseeing in the English countryside via biweekly twenty-five-mile hikes. The training was seven days a week, and once a month we were given forty-eight-hour passes to Salisbury or Andover if we kept our noses clean. We saw such landmarks as Stonehenge and Salisbury Cathedral, but I'm not sure we adequately appreciated them under the circumstances.

Britain had been at war for three years and food was in short supply. During this period we received food rations directly from the British army. Typical army fare consisted of Australian mutton (we called it goat meat), salt fish, Spam, cabbage, Brussels sprouts, potatoes, powdered eggs, powdered milk, brown bread, unsweetened (and bitter) orange marmalade, and tea or coffee. Portions were small and we were not allowed to waste food. Garbage was strictly forbidden.

As the odor of goat meat permeated the chow lines, the hungry GIs bleated, "baa, baa!" Lying in bed hungry brought me dreams of thick steak, mashed potatoes, hot biscuits, butter, and sweet, ice-cold milk, and when I woke up I was hungrier still.

We made nightly visits to the NAAFI canteen, which kept us from starving. English wartime sweets were not actually sweet, and the warm soft drinks were merely colored, semisweet carbonated water. We preferred Coca-Colas, but they, too, had gone to war. Their popular green bottles were now clear, as the color green in the glass was in demand for the war, and the lack of carbonation and reduced sugar changed the familiar taste. Ice for drinks was just a fond memory.

The cool, cloudy weather in Britain turned worse. Now it seemed that the sun was also rationed. A thick fog, biting wind, and cold drizzle were typical during November and December. Our condition improved a bit as the navy and merchant marine grew more successful at avoiding the dreaded torpedoes of the U-boats, and thus were able to provide us with a few more supplies. Meanwhile, we had to accept it all: the bland, scanty food, the lack of sleep, the dearth of warm clothing. The English kept reminding us, *"Yank, don't you know there's a bloody war on?"*

The highlight of any day was the much-anticipated mail call. "Mail call! Mail call!" The company clerk was the most popular man on base after we heard that yell. All of us dropped whatever we were doing and ran to the caller. The officers and first sergeant were the first to go through the mail, so whatever was left was intended for the rest of us. "Journell!" "Here!" "Phillips!" "Over here!" "Sergeant Jones!" "Present!" "Walton!" "Yee-haw!" Like nothing else, letters and packages from home lifted our sagging spirits.

Everyone receiving mail had something to talk about, and a well-stocked food package staved off starvation. It was a sad few days when one of us failed to receive either. Luckily, boxes of good-ies, and even love letters from wives and girlfriends were shared unselfishly by all members of the dorm floor. There were a few dreaded "Dear John" letters, but, on the other hand, many of our engaged soldiers, and even a few married ones, discovered the English lassie and broke off their relationships back home.

Food packages from our ethnic buddies were welcome taste diversions, and all the delicious morsels disappeared in minutes. Likewise, our Yankee colleagues greatly enjoyed the cakes, fudge, and Southern treats made in our loved ones' kitchens. Once in a while, rough handling by the post office broke open a package and much of its contents, sadly, were missing.

As the division settled down to a routine of hard training, we became part of Britain's defense establishment. The 5th Division was stationed in Iceland, and the 1st Big Red One Division left Britain and sailed for North Africa to fight Erwin Rommel in the desert campaign. The *Blue and Gray* remained, the only American infantry division in England.

It was 1942, and the low-water mark for the Allies was in the rearview mirror. The German Wehrmacht had overrun Western Europe, North Africa, and much of Eastern Europe. An invasion of Great Britain was possible, but unlikely. As 1943 arrived, the tide was shifting in the Allies' favor. The 29th Division kept its powder dry, staying ready and vigilant.

In July 1943, the personality of the division changed drastically when Major General Charles Hunter Gerhardt took command of the 29th from Major General Leonard T. Gerow, who was promoted to V Corps commander. During our early months in England, the *Blue and Gray* was on an accelerated schedule to become combat-ready. Passes and rest weekends were suspended until we were deemed battle proficient. Clearly, we now needed a rest.

To break the monotony and build friendly relations among us, General Gerhardt encouraged intercompany athletic contests and organized an armed forces exchange program. And, despite the official suspension of travel, he also arranged eight-day passes to London. Company A had the winning baseball team in all of the ETO, and Company D won the 29th Division touch-football championship and an eight-day pass to London. That football team boasted the best athletes in the company, many of whom died on D-Day or afterward in the war.

D Company's championship football team consisted of the following members: Technical Sergeant Marvin L. Mabes

(WIA-wounded in action), Staff Sergeant William R. Hurd, Sergeant Romeo B. Bily (KIA-killed in action), Staff Sergeant John B. Sink, Technical Sergeant Willard R. Norfleet (WIA), Sergeant Russell W. Jack Ingram (KIA), Private First Class Curtis C. Moore, Staff Sergeant Medron R. Patterson, Staff Sergeant Edward J. Fatula (WIA), Staff Sergeant Rufus B. Carr (KIA), Sergeant George D. Johnson (KIA), Staff Sergeant Phillip H. Hale (WIA), Staff Sergeant James Wright (KIA), Sergeant Edward D. Walton (KIA), Private First Class Walter D. Sink (KIA), Staff Sergeant Beverly T. Jones, Sergeant James W. Paulick (KIA), and Corporal Vittorio J. Crimone (WIA).

During this time, I spent a week on a British minesweeper operating in the English Channel and North Sea. Fortunately, all of the antisubmarine patrols I participated in were uneventful. Nevertheless, that week taught me that, despite all the discomfort and misery I had experienced so far, the American military had an easier time than the British. The rocking and rolling minesweeper frequently sent me to the head. The cold was awful, but the daily dram of grog kept the sailors happy, and helped keep us all from freezing.

The long hours and weeks of getting the 29th Division ready for war took its toll on morale. The men grumbled about the food and the lack of rest time, weekend passes, and furloughs. Then General Gerhardt came up with a solution which also gave him a chance to show off his combat-ready soldiers to the White House: first lady Eleanor Roosevelt was invited to inspect the troops and to speak at a Sunday morning church service. The general thought that having the first lady meet and mingle with the troops would excite and entertain the homesick soldiers.

For weeks, we readied the company area for Mrs. Roosevelt's arrival. Orders from top brass came like bolts of lightning, flashing and thundering down to regiment, battalion, company, platoon, and squad. Dry-run rehearsals took place from the colonel to the lowest private. Work crews were kept busy scrubbing and painting barracks, planting trees and trimming shrubs, polishing and waxing unfinished floors. Sandstones and flagpoles were painted or whitewashed.

Our uniforms were cleaned and pressed, we got fresh haircuts, we spit-polished our shoes and boots, we shined brass buttons and insignias—all to get ready for "Lady Eleanor's" inspection. Talk about building morale!

Ordinarily, on Sunday mornings we had the choice of going to church or catching up with personal chores. Every Sunday our captain would say, "Those not going to church, *fall out*! The rest of you, right face, for-*ward* march!" As he lined us up early for the much-anticipated event, many of us wondered, *Why in hell did she have to visit on Sunday, our only day off?* Many of the men, mostly Protestants, would have preferred an extra hour's sleep and were ready to fall out. But the skipper had other ideas.

First, to make sure we were immaculate, he gave an unusually strict inspection. Standing ramrod straight, he barked, "At-*ten*-hut!" He paused. "Those not going to church—" He paused again. "Right face! For-*ward* march!" Some of the men mumbled, "What the hell's he doing?" But nobody dared to leave. The entire company filed into church, all present and accounted for.

The chaplain welcomed and introduced Mrs. Roosevelt, inviting her to speak to her boys. In her high-pitched voice, Lady Eleanor expressed good wishes from President Roosevelt and the nation. Her brief message was cordial but uninformative. As she concluded her remarks, she asked us what she might do on our behalf when she returned home.

A private from one of the rifle companies jumped to his feet. He said very distinctly, "Mrs. Roosevelt, ma'am, wouldn't it be better for the taxpayers, and for our morale, to send one of us home rather than sending you over here?"

We almost choked. Mrs. Roosevelt was gracious, and we were all embarrassed, even though it was true that ninety-nine percent of us were fed up with cleaning, polishing, and sprucing up for one person. Yet Lady Eleanor's visit was not the reason for most of our malcontent, which had its roots in long, seven-day weeks of hiking and drilling, and our miserable living conditions. If Betty Grable had visited us instead, we probably would have had the same attitude. I felt sorry for the first lady, though, because she really wanted to cheer us up. And her visit did cheer us up for the moment, although her words would offer little comfort in the face of what was to come.

CHAPTER FOUR

THE 29TH RANGERS

COMMANDO TRAINING IN THE HIGHLANDS OF SCOTLAND

Although the United States *Lineage Book* makes no reference to the 29th Ranger Battalion, this unit was activated at Tidworth Barracks, England, on December 20, 1942, in compliance with a directive from ETO Headquarters. Volunteers were drawn primarily from the 29th Division, and because I did not believe the 29th would see action any time soon, I was one of the first to volunteer for this elite fighting force.

Oddly enough, our new ranger battalion appeared under different names. A memorandum from Capt. Cleaves A. Jones, Liaison Section, Allied Forces Headquarters, to Colonel Standman, Forces Headquarters, U.S. Army, stated that the unit referred to itself as the 29th Rangers. After all, most of us were from the 29th Division, and our mail came through APO 29, the 29th Division post office number. But the British called us the U.S. 2nd Ranger Battalion, which was understandable, as the 1st Rangers were the only other U.S. Army Ranger battalion at the time. The directive activating the force, issued on September 30, 1942, had also called the new unit the "2nd Provisional Ranger Battalion":

1. You are directed herewith to organize the 2nd Provisional Ranger Battalion from forces under your command. The provisional ranger battalion will be under your headquarters for administrative control, and will be attached to the Special Service Brigade (British) for training and tactical control.

2. The general purpose of the 2nd Ranger Battalion is identical to that of the 1st Ranger Battalion; it will be used as a training unit for a maximum number of selected officers and enlisted men of combat units to receive training and experience in actual combat, after which they will return to their organizations.

3. The 2nd Provisional Ranger Battalion will be organized as prescribed in T/O (table of organization) dated _____ consisting originally of a cadre of 3 officers and 15 enlisted men of the 1st Provisional Ranger Battalion and the remaining principally from the 29th Infantry Division. The 29th Infantry Division will be the principle beneficiary of the personnel trained in this battalion. Men and officers are to be rotated back to their original units after participation in an operation, sufficient cadre being retained to receive and instruct the replacements.

—By command of
Lieutenant General Eisenhower

This name confusion would continue into 1943, when General Gerow informed Major Millholland that several new battalions of rangers were to be trained in the States, including the 2nd Rangers. So our 2nd Provisional Ranger Battalion would become the 29th Ranger Battalion, Provisional (this was related in a letter from Millholland to historian Jermoe Haggerty). Regardless of what the new unit was called, its members consisted of ten officers and 170 enlisted men, formed around the cadre of 1st Rangers who had been left behind for medical reasons. The cadre of B Company, to which I belonged, was made up of British commandos and a Scottish Black Watch officer.

The concept of a commando unit, a lightly armed, quick-hitting shock force, was initiated by the British in 1940. Strict standards of selection and intense training formed the cornerstone of its success. In a circular sent by MO9 to the British infantry regiments in June 1940, ideal candidates would be able to swim and drive a motor vehicle, and be immune from sea and air sickness. In addition, volunteers were to possess "courage," "physical endurance," and "initiative"; be "resourceful" and "active," and display "self reliance, and an aggressive spirit toward the war."

The required skill set was wide, and readily displayed the dangerous nature of the tasks that rangers were meant to perform. According to the MO9 circular, a volunteer also needed to be an "expert marksman," to "become expert in military use of scouting," be able "to stalk" and "to report everything taking place day or night, silently and unseen . . . and to live off the land for considerable periods of time." During the interview process, some of us were also asked, "Have you ever killed a man? Could you stick a knife in a man—and twist it?"

Major Randolph Millholland of Company G, 115th Infantry, a thirty-six-year-old accountant from Cumberland, Maryland, was selected as battalion commander because he had just returned from the prestigious British General Headquarters Battle School at Durham, England. Major Millholland had no precedent as to the ranger table of organization and equipment, so he based the organization on the highly mobile pattern used at the General Headquarters Battle School from which he had just returned.

When the headquarters unit and Companies A and B were activated at Tidworth Barracks, I was assigned as a rifle squad leader in Company B. Standards of training and discipline were extremely strict. Millholland kept in mind Major General Gerow's guidance: "I want every unit and every individual ranger to stand out and to be easily recognized as such at a mile distant." From December until February, we trained vigorously in the Tidworth area. Our officers wanted all of us to be just as tough as our battle-tested commando instructors, and we were determined to pass the test.

In February 1943, I went North to Scotland with all the other ranger candidates for intense commando basic training. Our destination was the austere highlands British Commando Depot at Achnacarry House, near Spean Bridge on the shores of scenic Loch Lochy. Blue lochs shone between the low mountains and the desolate, craggy, waterlogged moors were full of green heather. Herds of wild deer roamed the wilderness in relative peace. But it also often rained, and our outdoor training subjected us to a constant, biting wind. The scenery was beautiful to the eye, but unpleasant to the skin.

The secluded camp, set in a hilly, evergreen forest, consisted of several plain, CCC-type barracks built of rough-hewn lumber that perfectly fit the surroundings. A Union Jack fluttered high above the rugged campgrounds. Another prominent feature was the mock cemetery, where tombstones displayed advisory epitaphs: "This man didn't keep the proper distance"; "This soldier failed to properly maintain his weapon"; "This soldier was nosy and set off a booby trap."

Inside, the barracks was plain and austere, with hard cots too short for my lanky frame and undersized stoves that died soon after lights out at 10 o'clock, leaving us just as cold as we had been at Tidworth. Numerous impromptu inspections highly encouraged us to keep our living quarters extremely clean and orderly.

Basic commando training was taught by battle-hardened instructors from Lord Lovatt's No. 4 Commando unit and a combat-tested Scottish Black Watch officer named Captain Hoar, who was B Company's senior commando instructor. There were reports that 1st Ranger officers and noncoms would also act as instructors, but to my recollection none were assigned to Companies A or B.

Captain Hoar, who was recuperating from wounds sustained in North Africa, was a prim, medium-sized, mustachioed military officer. His hatred of Germans was absolute and unconditional. One of his missions was to instill in us just how crafty and dedicated the subhuman Hun soldier could be. "This is not a bloody game. If you are not his equal, or better, you will not survive to go home." I determined to remember this and the captain's many other military dictums.

He and his noncom assistant instructors also dispensed heaping portions of very strict, colonial discipline. Our tutors justified this with, "It's better to find out now if you are unsuited." Within a short time, half of the candidates had thrown in the towel and returned to their units. Those of us willing to tough it out were proudly proclaimed "29th Provisional Rangers."

Training consisted of grueling speed marches, running the world's toughest obstacle course, mountain and cliff climbing, unarmed combat, boat drills, stripped-to-the-waist log PT (physical training) during the winter, and finding our way on the desolate Scottish moors with nothing but a compass and a map. Failing any of these could send a candidate packing, and I sometimes wondered if I had miscalculated my ability to do the task. I justified staying the course with the thought that someday the training might save my life—and I believe it did.

The obstacle course followed a five-mile climb up a steady grade. It had every diabolical obstacle a wartime British engineer could devise: negotiating ten-foot walls, log and rope bridges that crossed deep ravines, and rope swings over water hazards. A number of cadre acting as umpires were stationed along the route grading each squad's performance.

When man-sized targets popped up, we had to decide quickly whether to shoot—using live ammunition—or bayonet the thing. A bad shot or a wrong decision caused the umpire to deduct points or disqualify the contestant.

It was imperative that weapons be kept in good working order. Running over the muddy course could cause a weapon to jam, and this was grounds for disqualification. The entire squad was required to finish within a prescribed time limit. If an umpire judged a member "neutralized," that is, killed or wounded, his team had to carry him to the finish line. The last member of the team was timed, and if he didn't qualify, the entire team had to run the "black mile" on Sunday—the day set aside to wash clothes and to recharge batteries.

Nearby Ben Nevis, 4,406 feet high and the highest mountain in the British Isles, was an important climbing event. On one occasion, our instructors had us climb two gut-wrenching mountains in a single day. The slopes were so steep we had to be careful not to slide backward down the incline. Our instructors prodded us along and refused to permit any pauses. "Once you stop, you won't be able to restart," they cautioned.

Climbing those mountains was like crossing a desert and imagining a tempting mirage. Every step was difficult to make, but the illusive crest of the mountain seemed mercifully in sight. Then, just as the illusive crown came into reach, another "false crest" appeared—and then another and another still, until finally some of us did get to the top.

Captain Hoar, a career Empire soldier, carried a foot-long leather baton called a "swagger stick." It was more than decoration, or uniform British officer attire. During one of our routine speed marches, a candidate's leg began to cramp. Unable to continue the hike, he dropped out alongside the road.

Captain Hoar ordered him to his feet at once. The soldier, who knew he wasn't cut out to be a ranger, refused. That stick went into action around the shoulders of the "yellow-bellied-coward-that-wasn't-fit-to-be-a-ranger." I later saw the instructor rib-kicking a slacker who couldn't take one of the rigorous exercises. Both dropouts were sent packing in disgrace.

One British commando tactic designed to surprise the enemy was the speed march, which, along with stealth, supplanted infantry firepower. We traveled light: Browning light machine gun, Browning automatic rifle (BAR), grenade launcher, Garand M1 rifle or Winchester .30-caliber carbine, 60mm mortar, bayonet, cartridge belt, canteen, first-aid kit, and light pack.

The terrain around Fort Williams was so hilly that men sometimes complained that most of the hills went up. Nevertheless, the prescribed time for short hikes was seven miles per hour; for longer ones, it was five. We quickstepped uphill and double-timed down the other side. Near the end of each hike, and just before rounding the curve up the last hill to camp, Captain Hoar would bellow in his thick Scottish brogue, "Straighten up, mytees (maties)! Get in step!"

Camp was still a mile away when we heard the wail of bag-pipes in the distance. A pair of kilted pipers, standing at the entrance to camp, would greet us with one of the traditional highland tunes. This did wonders for our sagging morale. No matter how tired we were, the sound of bagpipes sent the adrenaline flowing, as we proudly marched into camp in step, with shoulders square and heads high.

In 1943, a group of senior officers, including Major General Leonard T. Gerow, commander of the 29th Division; Brigadier General Norman Cota; Brigadier Sir Harold Wehner; Brigadier R.

Laycock; and forty reporters and photographers, inspected the 29th Rangers at Camp Achnacarry. Almost all of the photographs ever taken of the 29th Rangers came from this inspection. The reporters were forbidden to refer to the unit by any name other than "a U.S. ranger battalion." Some of these photos have thus, at times, been captioned as the 1st or 2nd Ranger Battalion.

After completing basic commando training, we were rewarded with a pair of paratrooper boots and a three-inch felt patch sewn on an Ike (Eisenhower) jacket. The patch was rainbow-shaped, with a red background and blue lettering that spelled out "29TH RANGERS." These items set us apart from ordinary infantry, and we were very proud to show them off. As 29th Rangers, we thought there was no obstacle we could not hurdle, and we were eager to prove it.

My chance to do so came on my first eight-day pass to London after graduation. I was lounging at Rainbow Corner, a nonexclusive American Red Cross retreat for enlisted men and women. An American airborne corporal, who stood about 5 feet 8 and weighed about 160 pounds, swaggered over. I was also a corporal, and stood six feet four and weighed 205 pounds.

The cocky paratrooper looked up at me and sneered menacingly, "Mac, you in the 'troopers?"

I answered that I was not. I thought, *Hell, man, I'm in the 29th Rangers!*

He then said with authority, "Take those goddamned boots off!"

Surprised, I wondered if he wasn't juiced, even though it was too early for him to be drunk. He had a few buddies with him and I was alone. I decided he was not intoxicated with booze: he was a *paratrooper* with the 82nd All American Airborne!

His request lit my fuse. I said to him, with fire in my eyes, "Why don't you take them off me!"

He began a Geronimo charge, with fists flailing. I was ready.

Luckily, his buddies kept me from seriously hurting him. Later, the 82nd Airborne and the 29th Division teamed up in the great invasion of western Europe.

After A and B companies graduated, C and D companies followed them to Achnacarry for their turn at basic commando training. A and B Companies then were sent to Bude, Cornwall, a picturesque, prewar resort on the southwest coast of England. Before the war, Bude had been a summer resort with a beautiful sand beach and a nine-hole golf course. Our living quarters were in one of the former upscale ocean-side hotels.

Two men were assigned to each hotel room. My room faced the front overlooking the ocean. My roommate, also a corporal, was from Frederick, Maryland, and the 115th Infantry. His last name was Smith, and we called him "Smitty." The training here was tough, but the living quarters and food were excellent. The summer weather was pleasant, and swimming in the ocean became part of our training. The cliffs along the coast, we were to learn, were similar to those at Pointe-du-Hoc along the Normandy coast.

One evening, one of our ranger buddies was caught in a strong riptide. At first we did not realize how serious the situation had become. Rather belatedly, we interlocked hands to form a human chain. Being the tallest of the swimmers, I led the way toward the endangered soldier. The undertow had taken him several hundred yards out to sea. Almost immediately the chain broke, causing all of us to be swept out into the undercurrent. I swam out to the first fellow and tried to help him stay afloat.

Trying to swim against the current, he had become very tired, and inadvertently gulped a lot of salt water. I was also running out of gas. Thank goodness, someone had contacted the local Coast Guard. Buoys were shot from a cannon just in time to save us all from drowning. Even so, if we had not been in top physical condition, we might well have lost our lives.

During this period, the U.S. Army used our ranger battalion to field-test a variety of potential combat food rations. The winning selection ultimately became the official U.S. combat ration. Armies fight on their stomachs, so it is important that the meals be compact, filling, tasty, and nourishing. Each company was given a particular ration and asked to answer questionnaires about taste and hunger satisfaction. We all were weighed daily.

This ten-day ration-tasting ordeal separated many men from the boys, and served to prove our mettle as rangers. The four companies speed-marched an average of twenty-five miles a day for ten straight days. This alone was bad enough, but surviving on a skimpy combat ration was, indeed, a worthy ranger assignment.

Company A drew the canned C-ration for testing. The C-ration was tasty and filling, but too bulky, and hence was not the winner. Company B, my company, was given the new-issue K-rations. These were packed in flammable, waterproof waxed boxes that could be used to warm the meal and make coffee. Each meal added variety, but the biggest advantage was its compactness. Company C had the luxury of testing the tasty but bulky 10-in-1s. D Company combined 10-in-1s and chocolate D-bars. The K-ration Company B had tested, which filled the bill in every way, easily won the contest and became the official U.S. combat ration.

The first day of the test we speed-marched thirty-seven miles in seven and one-half hours. That averaged out to almost five miles an hour for thirty-seven miles. We were given a five-minute break every hour, and twenty minutes for lunch. I broke in a new pair of paratrooper boots that caused blisters to form where the bootlaces rubbed the bend of my feet.

After I had marched about twenty miles, the blisters broke and began to bleed. That night we tried to pitch tents on the windswept, soggy moors. The first thing I did was to wipe the gooey blood out of my boots. My feet were a mess. I couldn't get the tent pegs to hold in the mushy ground so I sat on a folded canvas half-shelter, and wrapped a blanket around my tired, aching body. No matter what I did, my legs cramped, and knots formed in my groin and calves.

I spent a miserable night, and when morning came very early the next day, I was far from rested. I had to prepare myself to be ready for the rest of the nine daily twenty-plus mile hikes or be washed out and disgraced. I persevered, but my weight dropped from 205 to 190 pounds in those ten days.

At the conclusion of the exercise, the battalion returned to Bude, looking worse than survivors of the Bataan death march. Bedraggled and very hungry, we limped over the last hill into camp. We showered and changed into clean, dry clothes and headed to the mess hall for breakfast.

It was an all-you-can-eat feast of powdered eggs, bacon, sausage, pancakes, syrup, jelly, bread, and coffee. I piled my mess kit high and found a quiet place to sit down. After a few small bites I was full. All of our stomachs had shrunk. In the following few days, however, we gained back most of the weight and soon began to feel almost normal again.

The rest period did not last long. The very next day it was back to the grindstone. Speed marches and climbing the steep cliffs along the shore made us visible to the townspeople, who seemed to like having us around. The 29th Rangers took part in the tactical maneuvers of May 27–29, 1943, involving the British 42nd Armored Division. On this occasion, the rangers completed a forty-mile flanking move in which we raided and destroyed the headquarters of a British unit, and captured its plan of attack. (This story is told in Lt. Col. Joseph H. Ewing's official history of the 29th Division, *29 Let's Go!*, which he wrote in 1948. He joined the 29th in 1944.)

During this time, the battalion also underwent night landing exercises in Dartmouth and Slapton Sands. All of this tough training gave us confidence. We became lean and mean, certain we were ready for anything. Our officers also were ready to take on the enemy. They were strong leaders who were educated, smart, and aggressively tough.

All of this tough training gave us confidence. We became lean and mean, certain we were ready for anything. Our officers also were ready to take on the enemy. They were strong leaders who were educated, smart, and aggressively tough.

After a few months at Bude we moved to Eastleigh, near Southampton in Hampshire. Private First Class John P. Kennelly, an Irish-Catholic from Waterbury, Connecticut, became my billet mate and friend. Many British housed small detachments of soldiers in private homes. This was much cheaper than building Nisson hut barracks. Our 29th Rangers adopted the British system. It was pleasant, but, in my opinion, less efficient.

Kennelly and I were assigned to billet with a sixtyish widow named Mrs. Brand. She generously shared her home and meager food rations with us. She knew we trained hard and were always hungry, and she gave up her scarce eggs, butter, cheese, coffee, and sugar for us. Like our mothers, she always waited up for us when we went out at night. Mrs. Brand knew about the consequences of war better than we did. When eventually it was time to say goodbye, we knew and she knew that we would never see each other again. Many, many times have I wondered what became of our wonderful substitute mother.

In the early summer of 1943, we conducted training exercises on the Cornish coast at Dartmoor and Exmoor. In September we moved to Dorlin House Commando Training Depot in the Argyle section of Scotland for additional land-sea training. During this period, a raid was planned to destroy a German radar station on the Ile d'Ouessant (also called Ushant), a small island in the Atlantic, just off the Brittany Peninsula. Ranger Lieutenant Eugene Dance of A Company, and eighteen enlisted men from the battalion were given the mission of destroying the Germans' primary radar station.

This radar station covered the Atlantic Ocean approaches to the English Channel and the Bay of Biscay. The nineteen men were to capture two German noncoms for interrogation and leave Major Millholland's helmet and pistol belt on the beach as evidence that American rangers as well as British commandos were involved. The organization of the raiding team was changed to a joint ranger-commando operation under the command of a British officer. The raiders left Falmouth on September 2 and successfully accomplished most of their mission—except all enemy troops were reported killed (as told in Ewing's 29 Let's Go!)

In August, B Company moved to Dover for an all-ranger one hundred-man raid, with orders to destroy the German coastal guns. We conducted dry runs, crossing the channel to within six miles of the coast, but the raid never took place. Two attempts were made, but adverse weather conditions forced the raiders to return to England, and the raid was canceled (Millholland letter to Haggerty). Although I was a member of B Company from beginning to end, I do not remember anything about this aborted one-hundred-man, all-ranger raid. I do remember training for an aborted night amphibious assault landing on the continent, but we were never told the object of the mission.

Occupied Calais, twenty-two miles across the Channel from our base in Dover, was defended by a strong contingent of German soldiers. Each side was capable of firing twenty-one-inch, 2,000-pound artillery shells across the Straits of Dover. When not in use, the huge coastal guns were wheeled by rail into sheltered caves.

Dover was thus a war zone. The city experienced cross-channel artillery duels, and German bombers flew over almost nightly on their way to London, Liverpool, Bristol, Coventry, Plymouth, and other densely populated targets. Antiaircraft batteries were stationed throughout the countryside and on top of downtown buildings. On nightly training exercises, red-hot shrapnel rained down from "friendly" antiaircraft guns, glowing white-hot. Occasionally, Jerry dropped his unspent bombs on the city before returning home.

All but essential civilians were evacuated from the coastal cities. Our landlady refused to leave her home, and so was allowed to stay. After the first blockbuster shell landed, which was usually at night, the sirens began to wail. Air raid wardens directed everyone into the nearest shelters, and underground shelters were filled to capacity every night. The market square in the city center was a favorite target, and became an uninhabited wasteland of rubble.

Kennelly and I were billeted near downtown. One night after the Lancaster bombers had raided the continent, one of them, mortally wounded, couldn't elevate above a nearby barrage balloon. The four-engine plane roared over our house and exploded less than a block away.

In 1943, everyone in Britain was either dancing or working stoically. The wartime philosophy was to live each day to the fullest, make no long-range plans, make every moment count, and postpone nothing if it could be done right then. No one ever complained. If one of us Americans dared to grumble about shortages or inconveniences, we again received the curt reply, "Mate, don't you know there's a bloody war on?"

I vividly experienced the result of this philosophy one night when we were invited to a special dance at the downtown armory. A Royal Air Force band played Glenn Miller and Tommy Dorsey-type music, and everyone was having a great time. Women from the British army, air force, and navy were all there, but the 29th Rangers were the only Americans present at the armed forces-sponsored festivities that evening.

Suddenly, the building began to shake and tremble, sending broken glass and plaster falling everywhere. "Surely," I thought, "the Heinkels are overhead and we are under air attack." The sirens screamed, but to my dismay, the music continued and the mostly British revelers kept dancing. And so they jitterbugged on, until helmeted, whistle-blowing wardens rushed in and ushered us all to safety. It was all very orderly, and very British.

Soon after, and without warning, it was announced that the 29th Provisional Rangers were to disband and rejoin their original units. A staff study prepared by Lieutenant Colonel L. W. Merriam for Brigadier General Norman D. Cota, Combined Operations, G-3 Section, September 25, 1943, advocated that the 29th Rangers be retained as a unit, either within the division or as army troops:

> "By absorbing the personnel within the division, the extensive training the battalion has had as a unit will be wasted. The proposal that if necessary the men can be withdrawn and reformed for a special operation does not appear very sound. To be an efficient organization the men must train and be together as a unit to assure proper teamwork and confidence in themselves and one another. In view of the training already received, it would be much more economical to organize this battalion as a separate ranger battalion than to organize and train an entirely new unit."

Colonel Merriam also recommended that if the authority was obtained to organize an additional ranger battalion, the personnel from the 29th Ranger Battalion should be transferred at a later date as individuals.

In late October, Major Millholland was summoned to London to army headquarters and was informed that the 29th

Ranger Battalion was to be disbanded along with the 1st, 3rd, and 4th Rangers. In spite of Major Millholland's plea, the War Department remained adamant, and the 29th Rangers were disbanded at Okehampton on October 15, 1943.

No solid reason has ever been given as to why the 29th Rangers were disbanded. There are many theories, but the official army explanation was that the War Department felt they could bring over better-trained ranger-type units from the States. It must be remembered that the original order authorizing the formation of this unit clearly states that the ranger battalion was to provide extra training and experience to selected men, who would then be sent back to their units.

The 29th Rangers were in existence less than eleven months—December 1942 to October 1943. During that short time we had come to exemplify what "ranger" means. Even though we saw no combat as a unit, we were a proud and disciplined group of men. Much of the credit must go to the British commando instructors, our battalion commander, Lieutenant Colonel Randolph Millholland, and battalion executive officer, Major Lloyd M. Marr.

Speaking only for myself, I believe it was a waste that the 29th Rangers were not used in combat as a unit. Nor was I ever asked or encouraged to transmit my ranger skills to members of my company or regiment. Even so, I am certain that my ranger training helped me to be a better combat soldier and leader. It also very likely saved my life.

On December 12, 1944, Major Millholland sent a letter to his daughter, Ginnie Schry, in which he wrote:

> Every boy should be made to play football and box and participate in all kinds of athletics, and above all the American should be taught discipline and decent living. Then he should be

given a year of the toughest kind of military training, not the kind that we know, but the kind I gave my Rangers.

God, but I wish I had those boys now; we would tear the Germans stringy. I hear of those boys now and then and although they are almost all gone now, they have done unbelievable things and are spoken of almost in a tone of reverence by officers and men alike who have fought with them.

They were men.

CHAPTER FIVE

ASSAULT TRAINING

THE GODFORSAKEN MOORS

The 29th Rangers disbanded on December 20, 1943, and I was sent back to my former platoon in D Company. The 1st Battalion's base camp was near Ivybridge, a small English village in Devonshire. I was glad to be rejoining my original heavy machine gun platoon, even though the 1st Battalion and D Company were undergoing intensive infantry assault training on the bleak, wet Devonshire moors.

Ivybridge was located less than a mile downhill from camp. As we approached the little town, an ivy-covered, humpbacked bridge crossed a rock-strewn creek that bounced off the moors. Many streams of clear water crisscrossed gently rolling hills covered by low shrubs and heather, and herds of wild ponies not much bigger than large dogs grazed in peace on the wind-swept heather and moor grasses. But aside from these pleasant images, everything else about the place was bleak. The land was good for nothing except raising sheep and training soldiers.

We used the camp as our home base, but spent most of our time hiking, training, and sleeping out on those barren, godforsaken moors. It was winter, and officers and men alike had to endure the harsh conditions. I never got used to the biting wind and cold weather.

There were no trees to take shelter from the wind and damp, drizzly fog. Large outcroppings of gray rock, called tors, were everywhere. The largest of the tors were labeled landmarks on maps, which helped us to orient ourselves. The ground held water like a sponge, and contained hard-to-see sinkholes filled with water that could easily swallow an animal, or even an unsuspecting soldier. Sergeant George Johnson accidentally stepped into one while toting a heavy machine gun tripod, and had sunk to his armpits before several of us managed to pull him out. Without help, he surely would have drowned.

The 116th RCT was in the initial stages of amphibious assault training. We were given endurance and strength tests, which we called "burp-up" exercises. All of us who finished the course were awarded the Expert Infantryman Badge (EIB) and an extra $5 in our monthly paycheck. The criteria for earning the EIB was running one hundred yards in twelve seconds (wearing heavy army shoes and clothing); doing thirty-five pushups and ten chin-ups; running an obstacle course within the prescribed time; and qualifying on the range with all small arms weapons. Failing to qualify could mean being transferred to noncombat duty.

While I had been detached to the rangers, the company transferred a few men deemed unfit for combat and replaced them with more rugged ones. Captain Schilling went on a recruiting expedition into the regimental rifle companies looking for large, tough men to carry the heavy machine guns and mortars—and he found them. George Kobe, Randolph Ginman, Bernard Latakas, Walfred Williams, David Silva, Stanley Borden, Dino Pettenuzzo, Joe Hawrylko, Ben Litwin, and Berdie Rooker were just a few of

Captain Schilling's hand-picked men, and they proved to be some of the best combat soldiers in D Company. Ginman, Kobe, and Silva, all privates on D-Day, were promoted to staff sergeants and machine gun section leaders. Rooker landed on D-Day as a private and a few weeks later was promoted to platoon sergeant.

Another case in point is Williams, my trusted number one gunner, the strongest man I ever knew for his size, and one of the bravest soldiers I ever served with. We called him "Fats," even though he was anything but fat. He enlisted in the army from Chicago and was nineteen years old, about five feet eight inches tall, and about 160 pounds. He had short-cropped brown hair and a short, wide neck, barrel chest, and narrow hips. I later learned he was Illinois high-school middleweight wrestling champion, and he looked the part.

Fats was assigned to my squad at Ivybridge, and I selected him as my number one gunner because he shot "expert" with the machine gun. He took his job seriously, learning everything possible about the gun and how to use it properly. During training, he once carried the fifty-one-pound machine gun tripod for the entire twenty-five-mile hike. He could do push-ups, sit-ups, squats, and figure eights forever, it seemed. He could do one-arm push-ups, using either arm.

Once I asked Williams how he got so strong. He replied that when he was very young, he worked out with an old iron cook stove, carrying the thing around his low-ceilinged basement to build up his stamina and muscles. He played all sports in high school, but his best sports were wrestling and football. He was probably the fastest runner in the company. He would have made a great leader, but Normandy claimed his life.

In November 1943, the 29th Division began amphibious assault training in earnest when the 116th Regiment moved to the assault training course located at a tent camp near Hampshire. The training site, at Woolacombe Beach near Barnstaple, was selected because it replicated the rugged coastline and deep, sandy beaches at Normandy. Transportation personnel, such as drivers and mechanics, also were instructed on how to waterproof all invasion vehicles.

The 116th Regimental Combat Team was the first infantry unit to take and pass the course. The army and navy built simulated mockup thirty-man landing craft, and hung ship-high cargo nets on cheap timber walls. We began with dry runs and more dry runs, until we graduated to wet-run loading onto actual landing craft, vehicle, personnel (LCVPs) and landing craft assault (LCAs) as we practiced assaulting English beaches. Thirty-man boat teams were trained to act independently in case a craft became separated or lost its leader.

Each boat team had unique experts who were trained for specific jobs. These specialists practiced until they were deemed competent at using explosives—TNT, bangalore torpedoes, and satchel and pole charges—and large, heavy-duty wire cutters. The hand-held explosives were also used for neutralizing bunkers. Each assault boat team was assigned Browning automatic rifles (BARs), heavy and light machine guns, and mortars. And of course they included the heart and soul of the infantry: riflemen and the indispensable medics. Combat engineers were later assigned to do most of the specialist tasks.

During December 1943 and January 1944, the 116th simulated an amphibious assault in "Operation Duck" on an English beach called Slapton Sands. The target beach was guarded by an armpit-deep salt marsh referred to on maps as a ley. The salty wash had to be waded before the team could neutralize the simulated enemy defense bunkers.

That salty pond ruined the careers of two D Company men, one of whom was a machine gunner in the 1st Platoon. When Captain Schilling learned the soldier failed to wade the ley, he demoted and transferred him. The soldier, devastated to be going to war with another outfit, landed on Omaha Beach with a different regimental company. He was later wounded in action, but he never completely recovered mentally from being transferred from D Company.

The other soldier was an ammunition carrier in my squad, Private Joseph Avolino. A recently drafted soldier who had not fully embraced the system, Avolino crossed the lake but lost a $6 machine gun water can in the murky water. Learning of the careless mishap, Captain Schilling screamed, "A water can! Slaughter, what in the holy hell's the matter with your squad?"

Looking toward 1st Platoon Leader Verne Morse, the Captain yelled, loud enough for everyone to hear: "Bust him to private! He pays for the water can, and make sure he learns to take better care of the equipment!"

For seven days I had to oversee the private's punishment. Both of us had to jog up a two-mile grade to an Englishman's private swimming pool. Avolino was instructed to wade through the cold water with all of his clothes and equipment—and a water can. The key to this exercise was Avolino's ability to hang on to the machine gun water container.

Avolino was a poor swimmer, and the water at the deep end of the pool was over his head. It was early March, and the water had a thin glaze of ice. He eased into the pool and sank to the bottom. I pulled him out of the frigid, slimy water and we both double-timed back to camp. I could hear Avolino's teeth chattering as we ran down the hill and into camp.

Each day after the run we had to prove to First Sergeant Obenshain that the private was wet all over. Sarge was usually very serious, but when he saw Avolino standing before him, dripping wet and shivering, he grinned sarcastically. "Must be nice to have a private swimming pool, eh, Private?" he said. I often wondered what would have happened if we had lost a machine gun. Captain Schilling was a tough taskmaster, but I am sure he was teaching us the importance of following orders.

We quickly learned the power that Captain Schilling held over our fates. During this exercise, even though there was a wooden footbridge that crossed the marsh, the Captain waded into the cold water, holding his carbine high above his head. He expected the entire company to follow him, but the machine gunner fell behind the company and stayed dry by stealthily crossing the bridge.

The company hiked all day, dripping wet on the cold and windy moors, and then slept that night in the same damp clothes. This was one of the most miserable experiences I remember as a soldier. Imagine sleeping on mushy, wet ground with the temperature hovering around forty windy degrees. Tent pegs were unable to hold in the soft ground, so we had to anchor the tent with weighted stones. Damp clothing, including our two wet wool blankets, which we paired with the blankets belonging to a buddy, made snuggling together a necessity.

During this time, we practiced climbing and descending ship-high cargo nets with full field equipment and shoulder weapons. After practicing on mockup landing craft, and climbing entangling rope cargo nets, we graduated to actual sea-going LCVPs (U.S. Higgins boats and LCAs, the British version).

We practiced loading and unloading dummy landlocked landing craft, exiting in columns of threes, peeling off left, center, and right, quickly getting across the beach, assaulting pillbox defenses, storming the top of the bluffs, and then digging foxholes in the prescribed perimeter of defense. Our job would be to hold on until more troops, armor, and artillery arrived.

On one of the many amphibious exercises, we were assigned to the ship that would transport us on D-Day, the HMS *Empire Javelin*. The British ship had a middleweight boxing champion on board who challenged 1st Battalion to a match. Someone shoved Fats Williams into the ring and he responded.

It soon became clear the sailor was in for a fight. He was skilled and quick, but Williams was throwing heavy bombs. Many of them missed, but when he connected they began to take their toll. Late in the second round Williams connected flush on the Englishman's jaw and knocked him out.

As April changed into May, the 116th RCT's amphibious assault training became more intense. The training course was preparing us for close contact with loud explosions, and teaching us what it feels like to be under live fire. I thought it was exciting to be crawling under barbed wire with machine guns firing live tracer bullets mere inches above our heads and rear ends. Accidental injuries and deaths were reported. It was unnecessary for the instructors to tell us to stay low to the ground. Strategically placed explosives boomed all around, which made them seem like the real thing. The exercises gave us confidence that we were ready to go to war.

A few weeks before D-Day, while climbing cargo nets, Sergeant Jack Ingram lost his footing and fell several feet, landing on his tail and fracturing a small bone. Ingram was a good friend of mine, and well liked by everyone who knew him. He had grown up in northwest Roanoke, and played all sports in high school. His father, who worked for the Norfolk & Western Railroad, liked to brag about his soldier-boy son.

Like the rest of us, Jack had worked hard and accepted untold hardships in order to be ready when the time came for the big show. After his injury, many of us thought he would not make it, but a few days before D-Day, he crawled out of his hospital bed and, remarkably, made the invasion. Ingram didn't have to go, but the popular squad leader wanted to be with his men and his company. He was not about to disappoint himself, the company, or his many friends.

One morning we spotted a few prominent spectators observing us as we were practicing small unit training. General Dwight D. Eisenhower, the supreme allied commander; General Bernard L. Montgomery, commander, 21st Army Group; Lieutenant General G. Omar Bradley, 1st Army commander; Major General G.

Lawton Collins, VII Corps commander; Major General Leonard T. Gerow, V Corps commander; Major General Clarence Heubner, 1st Division commander; and Major General Charles H. Gerhardt, 29th Division commander, along with their staff personnel were all there intently watching as we went through our paces.

After we finished the exercise, we formed up and marched in review past the commanders. Despite the fact that we had to march across a mushy moor, I believe we impressed the generals that we were ready for action. The parade halted and we remained at attention. General Eisenhower and his staff stiffly walked between the rows, randomly stopping to speak to a few of us. He looked up at me and halted.

"Sergeant," he asked in a snappy voice, "are you and your men ready to go?"

I straightened and replied with enthusiasm, "Yes Sir, we are!"

It later became almost routine to see these commanders at our training exercises. In France I saw General Eisenhower and his staff twice during the early days of the invasion. It was comforting to see the top brass near the action.

Other lessons we learned at the training center were how to probe for land mines with bayonets; properly don gas masks during poison gas drills; administer first aid; identify airplanes and tanks; use and detect booby traps; dig foxholes; survive unarmed combat; and use all infantry weapons. After graduation, we felt confident we were ready, but in reality, dry run combat can only prepare a soldier for the first hours of a real shooting war—a lesson we would soon learn too well.

Every day, troops and equipment streamed into our training area and the near vicinity. Tent camps sprouted like mushrooms. We spent much of our time away from Ivybridge, but on a few weekends we returned to base. One weekend, while we were away training, a battalion of black troops moved in across the hill from our camp. Over the months we had established a close relationship with the village and considered it exclusive 1st Battalion territory. We believed we had exclusive rights to the two or three pubs and the few pretty young girls.

An acrimonious rivalry soon grew up when black soldiers began to swarm into the bars every night and develop relationships with the local girls. The battle-fit 1st Battalion was itching for a fight. The fuse was lit when one of the prettiest girls in town was seen with one of the newcomers. I don't believe it would have been different if a white soldier from another unit had done the same thing. But this was 1944; blacks and whites were segregated in the army.

Fights broke out and a few men were severely wounded. It was a very serious problem, and it soon became apparent that the soldiers had to be separated. It was decided that every other night was off limits for one race or the other. To make matters worse, while black troops were in town, white soldiers acted as the MPs and vice-versa.

I was selected for MP duty one night and was paired with a rifle company soldier. Our job was to keep law and order and the white troops in check. Mainly we were to keep the all-white 1st Battalion from slipping into town. Animosity was high, so this was a crucial task. One evening, for example, Technical Sergeant John Stinnett, mortar platoon sergeant, had been stopped short of leaving camp with a loaded "Tommy" submachine gun. He reportedly said he was "going to clean the damn place out."

The night I was on duty, a mob of black soldiers began to leave town after the pubs closed at 10:30 p.m. There was not much doubt that they had been drinking. One of them, a large sergeant, was waving a semiautomatic pistol as he walked over in our direction. He was definitely under the influence, and was threatening our authority.

My partner and I backed into a doorway, and I ordered the sergeant to drop his weapon. He hesitated and I called again. He again failed to drop his gun. I fired my carbine into the ground near his foot. He dropped the weapon and, thankfully, the crowd dispersed. The crisis was over that night, but the problem persisted until we left Ivybridge for good.

On April 15, the battalion left the moors and our many Ivybridge friends. Our next destination was the invasion assembly area in Dorset, the prelude to opening the "second front." It was 6 a.m. sharp, but the sleepy-eyed townspeople were out in force, waving and cheering as we convoyed away.

Months earlier, when we had first arrived, we had gotten off to a very shaky start. The townspeople were not used to boisterous Americans who drank too much and chased after their daughters and sisters. In time, and with prodding from our commanders, we settled down, and the townsfolk came to refer to the First Battalion as their *lads*. Couples fell in love, and a select few received permission to marry, like Private Edgar B. Kiser of 2nd Platoon, who had fallen in love with an Ivybridge girl.

When the people turned out for our early-hour departure, some of them, especially the new brides, had tears streaming down their faces. Many of us were teary-eyed as well. As they lined the streets, hanging out of windows, waving and cheering, how did they know we were finally going to war when we didn't know for sure ourselves?

The battalion traveled 120 miles by motor convoy to a tent camp near Blandford, located near the headquarters of the 16th Infantry of the 1st Division. The 116th RCT was attached to the 16th RCT (1st Division) on D-Day, and this formed V Corps. Other units of the Big Red One were nearby. Training and preparation for the impending invasion continued at the Blandford camp. A heavily barricaded and guarded operations building in the center of the enclosure served as planning headquarters. All personnel involved in the preparation and planning process were sworn to secrecy as countless details were worked out.

The D-Day assignment for the 116th was finalized in April and May. Overstrength (supernumerary) personnel were assigned to each company as replacements, as it was thought that casualties could possibly be high. Exercise Fabius I, the last of the large-scale landing exercises, was held May 3–8. This amphibious maneuver included corps level troops (29th and 1st Divisions, plus attachments), and proved to be the dress rehearsal for the real thing. Some of the men remarked that the code name, Fabius I, stood for "Final Assault Before Invasion, United States Infantry."

Many of us thought that the dry runs would never end, but a blind man could see that something big was about to happen. Every field and vacant lot was piled high with materials of war for a great, impending battle. Tanks and other tracked vehicles, trucks, jeeps, personnel carriers, command cars, weapons carriers, and spotter Piper Cub airplanes with stripes painted on their folded wings were there. And so were artillery pieces such as howitzers and long toms, and gasoline, water, food, jerry cans, boxes, crates, drums—it was all there, in abundance.

Camped nearby were strange-looking and strange-talking soldiers wearing British uniforms, soldiers drafted from the worldwide British Empire. We were told that all assault troops would be incarcerated behind barbed wire and MPs would make sure that no one entered or left camp. A smart aleck remarked that if it weren't for the thousands of barrage balloons, the island would surely sink.

After we were briefed on where the 116th RCT was to land, and what the mission was, a strange thing happened that I still find hard to believe. It was reported that one of our officers allowed two truckloads of men to go to town for a few hours. The reasoning, we heard, was that he wanted to make this Sunday look as normal as possible.

Private First Class Richard Atkins of the mortar platoon and Private First Class Edgar B. Kiser, a machine gunner, both of D Company, decided to hitch a ride back to Ivybridge. Kiser had left his English bride without giving her a proper goodbye, and Atkins believed he, too, had prematurely left his Ivybridge sweetheart.

Both men had been briefed and knew the 116th's plan for D-Day. They thus were "bigoted," *Bigot* being the code name for the Overlord plan. Both men also knew they might possibly never see their women again. Neither of them was trying to get out of going to war. They simply believed they could catch a ride to Ivybridge and return to camp later that evening and nobody would be the wiser. A German spy would have killed for the top-secret knowledge these men possessed.

Everything went swimmingly until the next day when they tried to reenter the fence-enclosed compound. MP guards refused to allow them entrance without proper credentials. But good soldiers always find a way to accomplish their mission. Private First Class Atkins pleaded with the guard that if he could just talk to Captain Schilling, he would surely vouch for his credibility.

Unfortunately, both of them had been reported missing and declared AWOL.

First Sergeant Obenshain reported to Captain Schilling that the fugitives had returned and were ready to accept punishment. Schilling was infuriated. He snorted to the first sergeant, "Take the bastards out and shoot them! I mean it!"

After cooling off, the captain ordered Atkins demoted to private and transferred. Kiser was already a private, and it was unclear what his final punishment was. Private Atkins was extremely upset that he would miss D-Day, and begged the captain please to let him stay. Captain Schilling must have admired the initiative and determination of the two soldiers, for he reluctantly forgave Atkins and even selected him to be his personal radio operator.

Our preparations continued. All assault troops were issued new weapons, clothing, and equipment. Weapons had to be zeroed-in on the firing range. There were unlimited amounts of ammunition to be used for target practice. Bayonets and combat knives were honed to a keen edge. The men were honed, eager, and ready, too.

The food, for a change, was good and plentiful. On the menu were steak and pork chops with most of the trimmings. Often there was dessert, lemon meringue or chocolate pie. "Good God, they're fattening us up for the kill!" one of the wags exclaimed.

Officers became friendlier, and it seemed to me that the men were kinder to each other. First-run movies were shown all day in large tents. I remember watching *Mrs. Miniver* with Greer Garson and Walter Pidgeon, and other fine war films at the marshalling area. Spending two or three hours under a tent watching a war movie helped to divert our attention from reality. We also killed time by playing touch football and softball, boxing, reading, and writing letters. Many of the men prayed and read from the Bible several times a day.

Private First Class Francis "Skeets" Galligan, a New Yorker, organized a skit from the Broadway play and Hollywood movie *Yankee Doodle Dandy*. He portrayed George M. Cohan, the Jimmy Cagney character. Skeets had a squeaky singing voice, but was agile and a fair tap dancer. He sang and danced the show tunes and ended the dance routine by jumping high in the air and clicking his heels. For an encore, he portrayed a seminude hoochie-koochie dancer. Grinding his hips to the beat of a tight canvas cot, he elicited smiles and cheers from his captive audience.

Little did we know what would happen in just a few short days. High-stake poker games implied little regard for material wealth, and small fortunes were won and lost during our confinement. Money orders and other valuables were sent home for safekeeping. It was mandated that each of us buy a $10,000 government life insurance policy. Some of us joked that we should buy life insurance on each other. We were sure that with our training and skill most of us would survive.

Platoon briefings were held around a sand table model of the 116th RCT's sector. Captain Schilling and other selected officers had already been briefed about our mission. The captain briefly explained the overall D-Day picture, but concentrated on V Corp and the 116th RCT Omaha Beach objective. The captain mentioned that the 82nd and 101st Airborne would parachute behind the Utah Beach sector and seal the flooded causeways. I remember him saying that Carentan would be an important objective for the airborne. The 16th RCT was to assault and neutralize the eastern half of Omaha Beach; the 116th's assignment was to storm the western half.

We assembled in large pyramidal tents for intelligence briefings, updated each day as low-flying reconnaissance planes photographed laborers improving the beach obstacles and hard defenses along the Western Wall. The reconnaissance planes often caught the workers, who labored night and day, out in the open. We laughed to see them scattering for cover. Yet every day, we could see they were making steady improvement.

Lieutenant William Gardner, D company executive officer, presented our first company briefing. A U.S. Military Academy graduate, he was young, articulate, smart, tough, and aggressive, and possessed the qualities to become a senior military officer. He began by saying that the 1st Battalion would hit the Vierville Draw sector (Dog Green) of Omaha Beach. Using a pointer, he showed us topographical landmarks such as the Vierville Draw, St.-Laurent Draw, Pointe-du-Hoe (Hoc) and our guide point, the very important Vierville church steeple. The lieutenant had rigged intermittently blinking electric lights, which in the darkened tent were intended to simulate shell bursts.

Omaha Beach, a six-mile-wide stretch of sand and pebbles, was protected by bluffs and cliffs up to one hundred feet high. This sector was the most daunting of all the landing beaches. The tide was unpredictable and treacherous along the six-mile front that V Corps was given. The beach was fronted at low tide with four hundred to six hundred yards of golden, coarse sand. Men could climb the bluffs, but vehicles could not.

In order to advance the heavy equipment and weapons off the beach, it was essential to capture and hold four exit draws, or ravines. These were priority targets for the infantry. Heavy equipment and large vehicles had to be moved off the beach on a strict schedule. If the exit draws became bottlenecks, much of the heavy artillery and armor would be left stranded on ships at sea or vulnerable on the beaches.

The 1st Battalion, 116th, was given the most challenging assignment anywhere along the sixty miles of shoreline—the Dog Green sector of Omaha Beach. What made this landing site so daunting were the tricky tides and the four hundred to five hundred yards of flat sand that had to be crossed under murderous machine gun, mortar, artillery, and rifle fire. There were thousands of mines, miles of barbed wire, and dozens of concrete and steel bunkers connected by trenches and firing positions. The main exit draw was down the road from Vierville-sur-Mer, a small village of a few hundred people, mostly farmers and fishermen, that was less than a mile off the beach.

The Vierville Draw was designated D-1 on military maps and was paved from Vierville down to Omaha Beach. D-1 was the prime exit off Omaha Beach, so the Germans would vigorously defend it. To begin with, the Germans had laid a concrete wall to block the exit or entrance of the important exit ravine. Hard bunkers and machine gun emplacements were strategically placed so that every inch of the beach was covered by flat-trajectory grazing fire, or mortars firing high-trajectory plunging fire. These defenses were sited to work even in fog, darkness, or grass fire smoke.

The 1st Battalion, 116th, was assigned to land at Dog Green sector, using the prominent Vierville-sur-Mer church steeple as a guide. This landing site was just left of the D-1 draw, and several bunkers were able to crisscross the beach with machine gun grazing fire. Company A of the 116th was to land six landing craft at 6:30 a.m.

At the time we received our briefing, the Germans must have known something was imminent. Every night, the Luftwaffe flew over the assembly area. The 29th suffered its first casualties during an air raid. Company A had casualties while firing rifle grenades on the firing range. There was some shifting of personnel to make up for these losses.

The command post at Blandford Camp closed on June 1. All of the assault units moved to nearby transient camps in the marshalling area. Located in the vicinity of Dorchester, the camps were used for briefing the troops and forming soldiers into boat teams. Combat loading of assault transports followed.

On June 4, loaded down with equipment, we finally set off. Each man in the leading waves was laden with over sixty pounds of weapons, gear, and supplies. We were cautioned that what we carried would have to sustain us for at least three days. Marching in double file along the docks at Weymouth Harbor, we could see the ship that would take us to Normandy lying at anchor. We hardly noticed the few civilians and rough-looking dock workers eyeing our approach. I heard one of them say, "Give 'em hell, mate!"

As we struggled up the gangplank with our heavy burdens and onto the HMS *Empire Javelin,* D Company's Private First Class Curtis C. Moore, one of our jeep drivers, parked his vehicle along the street, waiting his turn to drive into the hole of the vehicle transport ship. He closed his eyes for a quick nap. He woke to find a small piece of paper pinned to the windshield of his jeep. Like all jeeps, it had the driver's name stenciled on it. The message read: "Good luck from the Moores of England."

Regimental Headquarters Company and the 3rd Battalion were loaded onto the USS *Charles Carroll* while the 2nd Battalion and various support units were to board the USS *Thomas Jefferson*. Like HMS *Empire Javelin*, both were amphibious assault troop transport ships with a troop capacity of about a thousand men, or a reinforced battalion. D-Day was about to begin, and *Festung Europa*—Fortress Europe, as the Germans called it—was about to be tested.

We were on a one-way mission to liberate occupied Europe. The 1st Battalion would land at the Vierville church steeple and assault and hold the Vierville exit draw of Omaha Beach. Meanwhile, the 2nd Battalion, one thousand yards to the east, would assault and neutralize the Dog White sector. The 3rd Battalion was to land behind 2nd Battalion in regimental reserve. Would Hitler's dream of world domination become reality? Would we overcome the beach defenses according to plan? Or would it be a bloody nightmare?

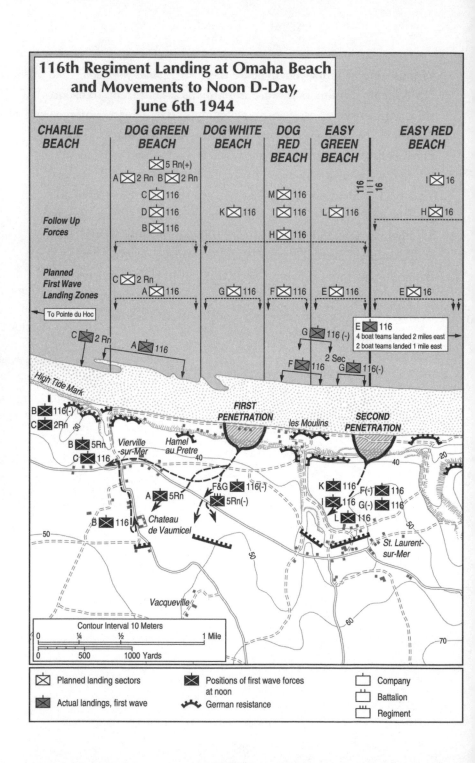

116th Regiment Landing at Omaha Beach and Movements to Noon D-Day, June 6th 1944

CHARLIE BEACH | DOG GREEN BEACH | DOG WHITE BEACH | DOG RED BEACH | EASY GREEN BEACH | EASY RED BEACH

5 Rn(+)
A 2 Rn B 2 Rn
C 116
M 116   I 16
Follow Up Forces   D 116   K 116   I 116   L 116   H 16
B 116   H 116

116 / 16

Planned First Wave Landing Zones
C 2 Rn   G 116   F 116   E 116   E 16
A 116
To Pointe du Hoc

E 116
4 boat teams landed 2 miles east
2 boat teams landed 1 mile east

G 116 (-)
2 Sec

C 2 Rn   A 116   F 116   G 116(-)

High Tide Mark

B 116(-)
C 2Rn

FIRST PENETRATION   les Moulins   SECOND PENETRATION

B 5Rn   Vierville -sur-Mer   Hamel au Pretre
C 116   40   F&G 116(-)   K 116   F(-) 116
A 5Rn   5Rn(-)   I 116   G(-) 116
B 116   L 116   St. Laurent- sur-Mer
Chateau de Vaumicel
50

Vacqueville

Contour Interval 10 Meters
0   ¼   ½   1 Mile
0   500   1000 Yards

Planned landing sectors
Actual landings, first wave

Positions of first wave forces at noon
German resistance

Company
Battalion
Regiment

CHAPTER SIX

THE D-DAY PLAN

116TH INFANTRY HITS THE WESTERN HALF OF "BLOODY" OMAHA

O n June 4, Weymouth Harbor was alive with activity—its job had begun, but *ours* had not. D-Day was scheduled for June 5, but a raging channel storm postponed the invasion for twenty-four hours. We were finely honed and mentally prepared for battle, but not, in reality, for what we would receive at "Bloody" Omaha Beach. Everything that possibly could go wrong went wrong. Weather was directly and indirectly responsible for most of it.

I don't recall what we did while waiting for the tempest to sub-side, but I vividly remember Captain Schilling's last pep talk. A howling topside wind caused the company to assemble below deck. The captain, smoking his usual Lucky Strike cigarette, stood about halfway up a steel stairway and leaned against the rail.

Captain Schilling had come up through the ranks of the Virginia National Guard. I remember seeing a 1935 photo of D Company at Camp Pendleton (summer camp) near Virginia

Beach, where the skipper was wearing sergeant stripes. He was all business around the rank and file, and he never condoned horse-play at any time. Suffering fools gladly or bending the rules was not his style. He disallowed company officers from fraternizing with enlisted men, and frowned on noncoms socializing with privates. Yet he would never ask anyone to do anything he wouldn't do himself.

Most of us thought Schilling was a stern taskmaster, but we also considered him a great leader. Private First Class George Kobe loved him as his second father. At Christmas 1943, Schilling had written personal letters to all D Company parents and wives, a kind gesture that made an impression on the big blond Yugoslav, who came from a Polish section of Chicago.

Mess Sergeant John B. Sink, to the contrary, had never forgiven the captain for an incident that occurred on the summertime 1942 Carolina maneuvers, when Schilling ordered the entire kitchen crew to make a grueling, all-night compass march in the stifling South Carolina heat and humidity. The fact that we had to subsist on one canteen of water each made it even worse.

I myself was far from Schilling's favorite noncom. Not yet fully matured into manhood, I was one of the baby-faced juveniles who were always getting caught playing stupid pranks. I gradually grew up—but it took a while. The captain never knew how I felt about him. There was no love lost between us, but I had great respect for him. I would have followed him to hell and back.

Assembled below deck in a medium-sized stateroom, most of us sat on our helmets on the floor to hear the words of our captain on this, our final meeting before D-Day. Men in the back of the room had to stand, and strain their ears to hear the skipper's words above the noisy diesel engines. The mood was solemn.

Schilling also was subdued. "Men," he said, "this is it, the real McCoy. The dry runs are over, the amphibious assault training has finally concluded."

Staff Sergeant Bob Slaughter somewhere in Germany, 1945.

Private 1st Class David Silva became a Catholic priest after the war. European Theater, 1946.

Left to right: (standing) Ed Walton, Pat Sibold, and George Johnson; (sitting) Vic Crimone, Dean Friedline, and Medron Patterson. Ivybridge, England, 1943.

Ed Walton(sitting at left), Romeo Bile (standing on left), and unidentified soldiers relax at their Nisson hut in Ivybridge, England, 1943.

Left to right: Dean Friedline, Ernest McCanless, Joe Walentowski, Sal Augeri, and Walfred Williams in Torquay, England, 1943. McCanless, Augeri, and Williams were in Bob Slaughter's squad on D-Day.

Left to right: Vic Crimone, Bill Hurd, Ed Walton, Pat Sibold, and Medron Patterson on the moors of England, 1943.

Left to right: (standing) Bill Hurd, John Stinnett, Pat Sibold, and Rufus Carr; (kneeling) Vic Crimone, Bev "Razz" Jones, and Ed Walton. Slapton Sands, England, 1943.

Left to right: James Richardson, Ernest Williamson, George Kobe, James Paulick, and Henry Brent in England, 1943.

Left to right: (standing) Ernest Williamson, Joe Trona, James Paulick, Frank Lutratio, Henry Brant, Randy Ginman, and James Richardson; (kneeling) Dewey Bishop, unidentified soldier, and Freeman Trotter. April 1943.

Above: Tech Sergeant Kyle Catron, Ivybridge, England, 1943. Wounded in action, July 16, 1944.

Left: Tech Sergeant Felix Branham at the Assault Training Center in 1943.

Brig. General Norman Cota, Assistant Commanding Officer, 29th Division (left), and Brig. General Charles D. W. Canham, Commanding Officer, 116th Infantry, get together somewhere in the European Theater, 1946.

1st Lieutenant Merle Cummings (left), killed in action, June 6, 1944. Tech Sergeant Marvin Mabes, wounded June 6, 1944. Ivybridge, England, 1943

1st Lieutenant William Gardner, Slapton Sands, England, 1943. Killed in action, June 6, 1944.

Sergeants Willard Norfleet (left) and Marvin Mabes in Westover, Maryland, 1942.

Private 1st Class George Deal (left) and Staff Sergeant Arthur Lancaster, Carolina maneuvers, 1941.

Tech Sergeant Edward
Fatula, Ivybridge,
England, 1943. Wounded
on July 6, 1944.

Lieutenant Verne Morris, 1st
Platoon Leader, D Company,
Ivybridge, England, 1943. Awarded
the Distinguished Service Cross.

Ralph Wheeler and Jack Ingram drying clothes in Ivybridge,
England, 1943.

Sergeant Russell Ingram, Fort
Meade, 1941. Killed in action,
June 6, 1944.

Sergeant George Johnson, Fort
Meade, Maryland, 1941. Killed
in action, June 6, 1944.

Corporal Jack Simms, Fort
Meade, Maryland, 1942. Killed
in action, June 6, 1944.

Sergeant William Lewis, 1st
Battalion HQ Company, 116th
Infantry, New York, NY, 1943.

Lieutenant Colonel Eugene Meeks, NATO Headquarters, Germany, 1946.

1st Sergeant William Pressley, Company B, 116th Infantry, London, England, 1943. Awarded the Distinguished Service Cross.

Captain Walter Schilling, Fort Meade, Maryland, 1941. Killed in action, June 6, 1944.

Major John Sours, Fort Meade, Maryland, 1941. Killed in action, June 6, 1944.

Ernest McCanless (left) and Curtis Moore in Torquay, England, 1943.

Sergeants Odell Padget (left) and Robert Sales, Company B, 116th Infantry, Normandy, France, 1944. Both were later severely wounded.

Private 1st Class Emmett Journell, Fort Meade, Maryland. The last man in Company D to be killed in action—April 24, 1945.

Left to right: (standing) Willard Norfleet, Bill Hurd, Reece Bower, Aaron Bowling, and Marvin Mabes; (kneeling) Harry Ferris, Medron Patterson, and John Biggers. Fort Meade, Maryland, 1941.

Company D, 116th Infantry, European Theater football champions, London, England, 1943.

Sergeant Phillip Hale (right), clowning around in Ivybridge, England, 1943. Wounded in action, June 6, 1944.

Staff Sergeant Jimmie Hamlin, Ivybridge, England, 1943. Wounded on June 6, 1944.

Members of Company D, 116th Infantry, pose for a snapshot as the war winds down. Lieutenant Gerry Orglar is at parade rest, right rear. Germany, 1945.

D Company's first reunion, Roanoke, Virginia. Memorial weekend, 1982.

29th Division veterans, led by Bob Slaughter, march down the famous Champs-Élysées in Paris, June 6, 1994.

Left to right: Bob Slaughter, Joe Dawson, President Bill Clinton, and Walter Ehlers (Medal of Honor recipient) at Omaha Beach commemorating the fiftieth anniversary of D-Day, June 6, 1994.

Bob Slaughter (at right) and other American veterans parade through Saint-Lô, Normandy, France, on the sixtieth anniversary of D-Day, June 6, 2004. Parents offered their children as escorts.

Bob Slaughter and President George W. Bush at the National D-Day Memorial dedication ceremony, Bedford, Virginia, June 6, 2001.

National D-Day Memorial invasion scene. For more information, visit the National D-Day Memorial Foundation's website, www.dday.org.

We understood his message, and, to a man, we were ready to go. We knew there was a tough job to do before we could go home and resume our lives. It was a relief to know that we were finally going to do something to shorten the war. The seemingly endless repetitive training on the soggy moors of southern England, day after bloody day, was finally behind us.

One of the men said, "I'll be damned glad to go over there and get it over with." I suppose he spoke for us all. We believed that going into battle couldn't be much worse than spending another winter on the godforsaken moors and going through more tough assault training exercises. We were very, very wrong. Not in a hundred years could we have visualized what it would be like to lose our limbs or eyesight, and see our best pals being blown to Kingdom Come. Nor could we imagine being killed ourselves.

Captain Schilling took a puff from his cigarette, straightened, and said, "I am proud to be leading you men into battle. This is what we have been working so hard for these many months. I know I can count on each of you to make us proud. The German is well trained and will fight like hell to protect his homeland."

He then reminded us that there would be twenty-two pillboxes protecting the Vierville Exit Draw, but only one or two of them were expected to be manned. Intelligence had reported that the sparse defenders in the Dog Green sector would be second-rate soldiers: Slovakian, Polish, and Russian conscripts. It was doubtful that they would be fanatical defenders of the Third Reich. "And, too," he said, "when they get a taste of our navy and air force, they will be ready to quit."

The captain concluded: "Get across the beach fast, and gain the high ground. Dig yourselves a perimeter of defense, and get ready for the counterattack." At the end of Schilling's remarks, I don't remember anyone hooting and hollering, but we were as ready as we would ever be.

Many 29th Division officers and men had turned out first-rate; going into D-Day, numerous officers of the 116th, battalion commanders and above, were regular army, graduates of the U.S. Military Academy or military schools. On the company level, our leaders were as follows: Sergeant Robert F. Bixler (Shamokin, Pennsylvania) was 1st Squad leader; I had the 2nd Squad; Sergeant Aaron J. Bowling (Roanoke, Virginia) had 3rd Squad; and Sergeant Dean L. Friedline (Gray, Pennsylvania) the 4th. Staff Sergeant Edward J. Fatula (Gray, Pennsylvania) had the 1st Section, and Staff Sergeant Kyle H. Catron (Roanoke) led the 2nd Section. Technical Sergeant Willard Norfleet (Roanoke) was 1st Platoon Sergeant, and 2nd Lieutenant Verne Morse (Pennsylvania) was 1st Platoon Leader.

I, for one, was confident of my ability to inflict harm on the enemy, and I believe my fellows in Company D fully shared the same sentiments and credentials. Most of us had been training for three years with the .30-caliber Browning machine gun, M1 Garand rifle, .45-caliber Colt pistol, and the Winchester M1 carbine. We knew how to shoot these weapons with reasonable accuracy or more, and could assemble and disassemble them blindfolded. As for me, I shot "expert" on the firing range with the heavy machine gun and M1 rifle, and qualified with the carbine and pistol. This nine-teen-year-old sergeant had also served as an instructor on two thirteen-week basic training assignments teaching 20ish privates army basic training—and had been detached for eleven months with the 29th Ranger Battalion. I don't recall where I slept the night of June 4 and 5, but I remember lying on a cot in a small stateroom. I removed my shoes and leggings, which I set under my cot, and slept in my woolen uniform. Some of the men talked about being home for Christmas.

Despite being tired, I had a hard time falling asleep. There were so many things to think about. In training, we had no difficulty negotiating the twelve-mile ride to a beach in our small landing craft. But I worried that we might not land on our sector of the beach. I don't remember thinking of home or family that night. I just wanted to get some sleep.

Finally, when I did drift off, my sleep was short and fitful. Not being overly worried about being killed or maimed, I truly believed that the landing area would be so softened by shelling and bombing from the navy and air force that it would nullify most of the opposition. It just didn't occur to me that we were going to hit major resistance at the shoreline.

As I remembered, we were jolted awake about 2 a.m. by the clanging of the ship's general alarm bell. Our English breakfast consisted of chunks of well-done meat swimming in white gravy, light bread, and coffee. I wasn't hungry, but I forced it down. After eating we went to our sleeping quarters and strapped on our gear, readying to embark on the "Great Crusade," as General Eisenhower called it. It would be the largest air, land, and sea battle ever fought in world history.

Before 4 a.m., Company D and other soldiers of the 1st Battalion prepared to transfer from the *Empire Javelin* to the six thirty-man landing craft that were hanging by davits along both sides of the ship. I parted the blackout curtains and stepped out on deck. It was pitch dark, windy, and unusually cold for June. The cold, windblown spray was like a damp slap to the face.

Loaded down with gear, we awaited orders for our squad to board one of the British LCAs hanging on the port side of our ship. We were anchored about eleven miles off the Normandy shore. As I gazed over the bow, the French coastline looked like a brilliant sunrise. It wasn't the sun! American B-24s were dropping their calling cards on elusive targets, obscured by the improving but still-dreary weather. Exploding bombs from Allied planes and German antiaircraft artillery created pulsating streaks of orange that reflected off the low clouds. A steady, monotonous droning overhead was assurance that more of the same was on the way, as squadron after squadron of medium and heavy bombers painted a strangely beautiful, multicolored skyline over Normandy.

I knew that sleeping German defenders were being jolted out of their comfortable sacks. If the Nazis' infamous Western Wall held, we would have to postpone our victory celebration for God knew how long. If the Western Wall cracked, Germany and the Axis would lose the war. It all depended on three divisions of widely scattered and disorganized allied paratroopers, five divisions of weary and seasick infantrymen, and some very brave onshore and offshore airmen and sailors.

Friends mingled on the deck of the *Empire Javelin*, shaking hands and wishing each other good luck, good hunting, and so forth. I remember finding Sergeant Jack Ingram, who was getting his gear together. A machine gun squad leader in 2nd Platoon, he had assembled his men while waiting for orders to load into his squad's assigned landing craft.

"How are you doing, Jack?" I asked, referring to his back injury. He said with supreme confidence, "I'm doing O.K., Bobby. Good luck. See you on the beach."

A few short hours later, Jack was out front, leading his 4th Squad, 2nd Platoon, across Omaha Beach, when an enemy MG42 cut him down. A healthy back might have made the difference.

Another Roanoker, Sergeant George D. Johnson, one of my neighborhood friends and former classmates, came by. We had both joined the National Guard in August 1940. "Are your men ready to go?" he asked in a serious tone. I couldn't imagine why he had asked me the question like that, but I answered with conviction, "They're ready."

Each of us was given a letter signed by General Eisenhower, the same message broadcast over loudspeakers by Eisenhower himself to all Allied assault troops: "You are about to embark on the Great Crusade," it famously began. I shoved a pen and the Eisenhower missive into the hands of a few men standing nearby, who autographed my copy. I wrapped it in plastic, folded it neatly, and tucked it into my wallet. This piece of paper was carried with me throughout the war, and became one of my most treasured possessions (see Appendix IV, pages 282–283).

The D-Day planners were overly optimistic, and their overconfidence spilled over to some of the men. Just before loading, Sergeant Robert Bixler ran his hand through his blond wavy hair, and said to me in jest: "I'm going off that damned boat with a comb in one hand, and a pass to Paris in the other!"

Looking back, however, it seems as if Omaha Beach was doomed from the beginning. Combat engineers riding with the infantry in the early waves disarmed the mined obstacles and marked the cleared lanes with white tape. This plan was reasonably effective. But what Captain Schilling and the SHAEF (Supreme Headquarters Allied Expeditionary Force) planners did not know was that the German 352nd Infantry Division, a crack, up-to-strength outfit hardened by battle on the Russian front, had moved up to the defenses all along the Omaha Beach sector. Further, these troops were not softened up as we expected. Poor weather and heavy smoke from grass fires caused the navy and army air force to drop their loads inland rather than chance hitting friendly troops.

Aerial bombardment of the beach had been ruled out because large craters would hinder vehicular traffic from crossing the expanse. We thus relied on the navy to create cover for the infantry by saturating the beach with cordite-induced foxholes. The rocket-firing landing craft, tank-rocket (LCT-Rs) launched hundreds of banks of rockets, almost simultaneously, toward the beach. I vividly remember watching in horror as the boats launched their salvoes from too far out. Someone yelled, "There go our foxholes!"

Because of bad weather and low visibility, the air force and navy failed to hit the German beach fortifications. Another ploy that failed was lashing 105mm artillery pieces to barges. The plan called for the 111th Field Artillery to fire in support of the landings, but nearly all of the artillery pieces went down in the very choppy seas. The artillerymen, left without their big guns, became infantrymen.

The use of new and secret duplex drive (DD) amphibious (or floating) tanks was also a miserable failure. Equipped with canvas flotation devices, the strange-looking Sherman tanks were to float to shore firing 75mm guns and .50-caliber machine guns. Floating a thirty-two-ton Sherman in high seas was ludicrous. Nearly all of these odd, minibattleships sank in the rough seas before they got within range of the beach, taking many of their occupants down with them. And what was the army thinking when it overburdened its front-line assault troops? The infantry soldier was asked to carry over sixty pounds of gear, which was to sustain him for at least three days. A canvas assault vest was designed specifically for this amphibious operation, with four pockets in the front and two large ones on the back. The bulky vest was meant to carry toilet articles, extra underwear and socks, rations, a raincoat, an entrenching tool, hand grenades, a bayonet, cigarettes, matches, and anything else the soldier had room for. On his belt he carried a canteen of water, first aid packet, trench knife, and compass. On his back were two or three bandoleers of ammo.

Heavy weapons companies—D, H, and M—carried additional burdens. The heavy machine gun is broken down into three parts: the tripod (fifty-one pounds), the receiver (thirty-four pounds), a box of 250 rounds of ammunition (over twenty pounds)—ammo carriers usually carried two boxes—and a two-gallon water can that had to be carried full of water. The 81mm mortar is also broken down into three parts: the base plate, bipod, and tube. These weighed about thirty pounds individually. Squad members not carrying mortar parts carried mortar bombs in heavy canvas bags. Such overburdening was a terrible, inexcusable mistake. It slowed us all, drowned many, and was the cause of numerous other deaths.

CHAPTER SEVEN

ROUGH RIDE TO HELL: OMAHA BEACH, DOG GREEN

THE BAPTISM OF COMPANY D
AND THE 1ST BATTALION

Each man on our thirty-man boat team climbed over the railing of the *Empire Javelin* into our assigned seats on the LCA. We were then lowered into the sea by winches held by davits. The always-rough English Channel was much worse than usual, making it very difficult to disengage the ship. Our craft immediately began taking on water as its flat bow slammed into seven-foot swells that sloshed over the front and ended up in our laps. It wasn't long before all hands were ordered to bail water with battle helmets. It was to be a long, miserable ride. Yes, I actually looked forward to getting ashore.

Our boat circled around and around until the other five had lowered to the water. This maneuver, called "Piccadilly Circus," was designed to slow our departure until the entire six-boat wave had formed a straight line. 'Round and 'round and 'round we went, getting colder and wetter as the icy, briny water poured into the boat. Finally, the last landing craft in our wave caught up, and the wave commander signaled for us to proceed to the beach.

The roar of the engines made it hard to talk or listen. Besides, there wasn't anything more to be said. As far as I could tell, no one on our boat seemed reluctant to go. We were well aware that the road back home was through Berlin.

Others were undergoing, or soon would experience, similar conditions. Roanoker Captain James D. Sink, commanding officer of the 116th Regimental Headquarters Company, for example, vividly recalled that those aboard the *Charles Carroll* also rose "about 2 a.m. while the ship was still in motion, and had an early breakfast. The anchorage, some twelve miles out, was reached about 3 a.m. The navy sounded general quarters as the anchor dropped.

"Going out on the open decks in the dark, we could hear aircraft off in the distance as they flew toward the Cherbourg Peninsula. Flashes of light in the sky and the roar of the distant artillery indicated enemy antiaircraft fire. The wind was coming up and the waters were beginning to run rough when Colonel Charles Canham, commander of the 116th Regiment, left the *Charles Carroll* in his free boat (an LCVP), about 5:30 a.m. H-Hour was scheduled to be 6:30 a.m."

Sink's account also testifies to the difficulty caused by overloading the men, and problems of radio contact which later occurred. He himself

" . . . experienced difficulty in loading Landing Craft, Mechanized (LCM)-10-2-DG, which came alongside the *Carroll* from another ship at 6 a.m. As loading over the side involved considerable hand-carried equipment, it was necessary to change loading stations to the leeward side of the ship and go over the side on a chain ladder, which gave better footing. This change in loading caused some delay in departing for the rendezvous area.

"The craft proceeded slowly through the rough seas to the control ship, a British landing ship, the *Prince Baudouin*, to be told that our wave had departed and to return to our parent ship for instructions. This order was complied with and the *Carroll* ordered us to proceed to land on our own. Meanwhile, H-Hour had come and gone. Significantly, the many radios in the various command nets reported promptly on time to the net control stations aboard the LCM when radio silence was lifted at H-Hour. It was unfortunate that most of them would go silent upon landing and not be heard from further on D-Day."

While Captain Sink was loading up, our landing craft had performed the last circle in the "Piccadilly Circus," and was heading in to shore. Until almost daylight I rode in that craft—wet, shivering, and cold, but not seasick. All of us had been given Dramamine tablets and brown paper puke bags, along with sparse instructions. I had never been seasick in my life, and believing I was immune, I gave my puke bag to someone who had already filled his. We still had a long way to go. My stomach was feeling almost up to par, but I couldn't control my shivering. Tucked into my assault jacket, I found a folded plastic gas cape, designed to protect the upper torso from blister gas, and pulled it over me to block the wind and sloshing spume.

Oxygen depravation under that cape shortly caused me to feel deathly seasick. I held my battle helmet with both hands and puked my insides out, and then threw the contents over the side of the boat. By scooping up water from the bottom of the boat, I was able to wash out the helmet. I heaved and vomited until there was nothing left in my stomach. It seemed that everyone on the craft was sick, and the sour odor just made things worse.

All of the men suffered from conditions in the crowded landing craft. Captain Charles R. Cawthon, commander of 2nd Battalion Headquarters Company, memorably described the angry sea: "Blowing spume had soaked us before we hit the channel. It seemed we would surely swamp, and life belts were inflated. Not only our persons but also reels of telephone wire, radios and demolition packs were girded with these in hope that if they were lost in the surf they would float ashore.

"The expansion of perhaps a hundred belts added to the bulk already crowding the craft, and so we rode, packed in an open can, feet awash in water and altogether cold, wet, and miserable. It seemed that we were slamming into waves with enough impact to start any rivet ever set.

"After about an hour of circling, the control launch passed a signal, and the craft carrying us—the second wave of 116th RCT—peeled off into line and began battering through heavy seas toward Normandy; thirty minutes ahead was the first wave; twenty minutes behind would come the third.

"For the next hours the line pitched and rolled toward Normandy, and gradually a lighter horizon, as we closed with the dawn of June 6. There was no attempt to talk above the roar of the engines, wind, slamming of the waves, and the laboring of the bilge pump that managed to keep up with the water washing in.

"We stood packed together, encased in equipment, dumb with the noise, and with the enormity toward which we were laboring. I recall offering no prayers and having no particular worries other than whether we were coming in on Dog Red sector."

As the sky lightened, I watched as large and small landing craft, transports, and men-of-war emerged from the misty darkness. The smoking and burning French shoreline became more defined. At approximately 5:30 a.m., the huge guns of the Allied navies began the greatest cannonade in the history of the world.

Imagine seven battleships, two monitors, twenty-seven cruisers, and 164 destroyers, firing five- to eighteen-inch guns, over and over. The engine noise from the LCA, a howling wind, and crashing waves failed to muffle the booming of the navy artillery. I couldn't help wondering what it was like on the other end—but I was just wondering, not sympathizing. Sympathy for the Germans was in short supply that morning.

Knowing the navy and air force were dishing out misery by the ton gave us confidence that we would walk ashore, gain our objectives, and be home by Christmas. The lopsided First Act seemed to help moderate the miserable chill and the dreadful seasickness.

A few thousand yards from shore we rescued three shivering, water-soaked survivors from a landing craft or floating tank that had swamped and sunk. I don't know what outfit they were from or how long they had been in the water. The lucky three were grateful to have been rescued, but in reality, their ultimate fate just might have been postponed. We left their mates, with Mae Wests inflated, bobbing in the turbulent waves. Riding low in the water, our boat was already filled beyond capacity.

About a mile to our starboard side, the ancient but still virile battle wagon USS *Texas* was turned broadside so it could aim and fire all of its ten fourteen-inch guns toward the dangerous six-inch gun batteries at Pointe-du-Hoc. We cheered as the Texan boomed and belched fire and smoke in the direction we were heading. A few seconds after the orange fire and white smoke, the roaring boom-boom-boom! was followed by coveys of 2,000-pound missiles whining to their calculated destinations. We could actually see the projectiles spiraling as if thrown by a gigantic quarterback.

Unfortunately for us, not long after the battleship lit the fuses that fired her ten-gun salvos, a mountain of water came roaring over to toss us around like a cheap cigar box. Twin-bodied P-38 fighter-bombers flew close support, but they could do nothing to smooth those gigantic ocean waves.

The sea was so rough and the currents and wind so strong that the six LCAs carrying Company D became separated as we approached Omaha Beach. We had followed at an interval behind Companies A and B, respectively, but smoke from the bombardment and the foggy mist obscured our view of the preceding companies and the coast.

Our own boat became even further separated from the rest as we got closer, and the coxswain fought to miss obstacles amid the waves and tidal currents of the shoreline. At this point in my war, I myself was not the least bit worried about what the Germans would do to us.

About 150 yards from shore—despite the warning from someone behind me to "Keep your head down!"—I cautiously peeped up. I could see that the craft about twenty-five yards to our right and a couple of hundred yards ahead were targeted by small arms. Fiery tracer bullets skipped and bounced off the ramp and sides as they zeroed in before the ramps fell. I said to anyone close enough to hear above the bedlam: "Men, we're going to catch hell. Be ready!"

Then it began to happen. Enemy artillery and mortar shells sent great plumes of water spouting skyward as they exploded in the water. Near misses rained us with seawater. I suddenly became very worried about what Jerry could do to us.

How in the hell did those sonsofbitches survive what we thought was a carpet-bombing and shelling of the beach? At Slapton Sands we trained with live explosions, but these were far more frightening. This time they were shooting to kill every one of us.

We expected A and B Companies to have the beach secured by the time we landed. In reality, no one had set foot where we touched down. Smoke and fog had prevented our coxswain from guiding on the Vierville church steeple. This, plus strong tidal currents had diverted us about two hundred yards to the east of our intended landing. Mortar and artillery shells exploded on the land and in the water as we approached. The telltale screech just before impact and explosion made the incoming artillery even more terrifying. Even worse, they seemed to land in clusters.

The craft slowed as we scraped a submerged sandbar, which kept us from a dry landing. Everyone wanted to get the hell off that rocking boat, but the coxswain had trouble dropping the steel ramp. When it finally slammed and splashed down, the front of the boat began to buck like a wild stallion, rising six or seven feet, turning slightly sideways, and then slamming down again. Over and over, it went: rise-turn-slam! rise-turn-slam! The boat and the ramp became enemies in and of themselves.

The first man to exit went off about midramp. The craft surged forward and crushed the poor fellow to death. Everyone who followed went off at each side or the rear. I was about fifth from the front on the left; Platoon Sergeant Willard Norfleet led the right side. Bullets and shrapnel notwithstanding, it was especially hard and dangerous to exit the front of that boat. Many of us simply had to wait our turn.

My turn came, and I sat on the edge of the ramp waiting on the down cycle, when the ramp would allow me a clean getaway. I must have sat there for two or three ups and downs, causing a bottleneck that endangered those behind me. So I jumped off and moved away from the crazy, erratic landing craft. Luckily, I didn't see anyone else get hit by the ramp.

I was now struggling in water up to my armpits. Luckily for me, at six foot five, most of the time my head was above water. Later, as I crossed the beach, my height would be a detriment, making me a larger target. Meanwhile, as I tried to get to shore, shorter men grabbed my clothing to keep their heads above water. Suddenly, as fear replaced seasickness, I was no longer cold. Most of all, I feared I would drown after being shot. Snipers hiding in the bluffs hit quite a few men. But most of the damage came from rapid-firing automatic weapons.

In every war since gunpowder was invented, soldiers have experienced the dreaded feeling of being under live enemy fire for the first time. It was demoralizing to hear good men scream as bullets ripped into soft flesh and others scream as the fierce, flooding tide dragged the nonswimmers under.

Almost everyone dumped their heavy assault jackets and weapons, as getting to dry land became the prime objective. For some reason, most likely the earlier incident with Private Avolino losing a water can, I kept my jacket and its contents. It was extremely hard to shed the extra weight, and a weak swimmer could drown before inflating his life preserver. I had to inflate mine to get ashore even though I was a pretty good swimmer.

Especially if you were hit and going under, it was extremely tough to shed the sixty to one hundred pounds of weapons and equipment in time. I remember helping Private Ernest McCanless, who was struggling to get closer in. He still had one box of precious .30-caliber machine gun ammo. I remember him shouting to me, "Slaughter, are we going to get through all of this?" I didn't know how to answer him, so I didn't say anything. To tell the truth, I thought we were all going to die.

A body with its life preserver inflated floated by. The face had already turned a dark purple. At first I thought it was Private Richard Gomez, who had a dark complexion. But I later found out that Gomez had survived the day. The fellow I saw was just one of thousands who died. There is no way to be sure if I had known him. Many of our company were hit in the water and drowned, good swimmers or not.

I came ashore surrounded by the screams of men who had been hit and were drowning under their ponderous loads. All around me, dead men floated in the water, along with live men who acted as if they were dead. The Germans couldn't tell which was which. The flooding tide washed everyone in.

I finally washed in to the water's edge and took cover behind a log bipod obstacle. I looked up and saw a large round teller mine tied to its top. It was suddenly clear that this was not going to be the easy "walk-across-the-beach" operation we had thought it would be. Jerry was either very clever or very lucky. No one thought he would give us this kind of opposition coming off the landing craft at the edge of the water.

At that moment, we sorely needed our officers and senior non-coms, but many of them were already wounded, dying, or dead. Tracer machine gun bullets raked the beach and, as we got closer, the puffs of white smoke changed into accurate target patterns along the shoreline.

Lying at the edge of the high water mark, I watched a GI trying to cross the beach. He had a hard time running. I believe he was from the craft to our right. An enemy gunner cut him down and he staggered and fell to the sand. I can still hear him screaming. A well-marked medical corpsman moved quickly to help him. He was also shot. I will never forget seeing that medic lying next to that dying soldier, both screaming for help. Within minutes, as I watched, both men fell silent and, mercifully, died.

I saw men vomit at the sickening sights, and others cry openly and unashamedly. All of us had to find it within ourselves to get across that sandy no man's land. This is where the army's strict discipline and rigorous training took over. Individual pride had a lot to do with it, too.

The tide was rushing in and later waves were due. I couldn't retreat, and I couldn't stay where I was, so I signaled my depleted squad to follow. Before disembarking, I had stripped the plastic from my rifle, designed to protect it from salt water and sand, and fixed my bayonet. I wanted to be ready. For what, though, I wasn't sure.

It was a bad mistake.

I gathered my strength and my courage, and then I just came up out of the water and started running. I ran as fast and as low as I could, to make myself less of a target. I had a long way to go: three hundred to four hundred yards. I was loaded down with gear, and my woolen clothes were soaked and heavy. As I ran through a tidal pool six or eight inches deep, I began to stumble, which caused me to accidentally fire my rifle. Luckily, no squad members were in front of me when it went off. I caught my balance and kept on running. I ran and ran for what seemed an eternity, and finally made it to a five-foot-high sea wall to take cover and catch my breath.

After I fired my M1, it jammed. To clean it, I slipped out of my assault jacket and spread my raincoat, only to discover bullet holes in my pack and coat. Suddenly overwhelmed with fear, I became weak in the knees. My hands shook as I tried to wipe sand from my weapon. I had to catch my breath and compose myself.

I believe I was the first from our craft to reach the sea wall. Following me were Private First Class Williams, Private Augeri, and Private McCanless. Augeri lost the machine gun receiver while struggling to get ashore. Williams was still carrying the fifty-pound tripod, and McCanless had a box of machine gun ammo but nothing from which to fire it. We were pinned down over halfway across Omaha Beach without a weapon capable of firing. At that point we were essentially helpless. I felt like a tasty morsel on a giant sandy platter just waiting for the Germans to chew us up.

At the sea wall, I could hear the firing of concentrated enemy machine guns over to the right where Companies A, parts of B, and our own D were landing. We didn't know who was catching all that hell. Finally, I cleaned my rifle and organized the squad as best I could, although many of them were missing. Then we went up over the sea wall and, fortunately, made it to the base of the bluff.

About midday, we met a few machine gunners from H or M Company who had a machine gun receiver but no tripod. By combining our assets, we finally had a workable offensive weapon. We had been watching a German 88mm, considered the best field weapon of the war, firing from a pillbox up on the bluff. We set up the gun in the best position possible, which was behind an exposed sand dune.

Williams was determined to get even with those square-headed bastards. The gunner pulled the bolt handle, sending a bullet into the machine gun's firing chamber. He then squeezed the trigger, sending a burst of .30-caliber bullets at the concrete and steel bunker. I watched as a string of fiery tracers ricocheted around the opening of the gun emplacement.

The gun jammed after a few bursts. I couldn't believe it when I saw Williams stand over the machine gun, trying to eject the jammed cartridge from the chamber. "Fats, for God's sake, get down!" I screamed. He looked over at me and smiled. He and Augeri picked up the gun and tripod and moved to another location.

That was the only time that day that we were able to use our gun. I'm sure we didn't draw much blood, but it helped vent a bit of anger and frustration.

By midmorning we had worked our way to the base of the hill. Men from other units began to gather. The regimental commander, Colonel Charles D. W. Canham, appeared from down beach with his right arm in a sling and clutching a .45 Colt semiautomatic pistol in his bony left hand.

Canham didn't look like a soldier, but he sure as hell was one. He was tall and thin, wore wire-rimmed glasses, and had a pencil-thin mustache. He yelled for the officers and noncoms to help him get the men across the beach and up the hill: "Get these men the hell off this goddamned beach and go kill some goddamned Krauts!"

In a nearby sentinel pillbox, a lieutenant colonel taking refuge from an enemy mortar barrage yelled out to Canham, "Colonel, you'd better take cover or you're going to get killed!" Colonel Canham screamed his reply: "Get your ass out of there and help me get these men the hell off this beach!" The officer did what Canham ordered. (See Canham's D-Day instuctions in Appendix IV, pages 279–280.)

Later, we joined with eight or nine men from Company B who were being led by First Sergeant Bill Pressley. He was looking for a cleared path through antipersonnel mines planted on the slope of the bluff. There were many *"Achtung Minen"* signs to warn the public of the danger of mines, their message reenforced by a skull and crossbones.

There was, however, a path marked by white tape that seemed safe to use, one of the paths cleared by German work crews. A dead naval officer was lying facedown at the base of the bluff. Strapped to his back was a large backpack radio. We followed Pressley and his contingent up the path to the top of the hill.

A strange sounding *zoop-zoop-zoop* came from a battery of German nebelwerfers, the rocket-firing six-barrel mortars aptly nicknamed "screaming meemies." The battery was being fired from fixed concrete positions about 200 to 300 yards to our right front. We could actually follow the missiles' high trajectory to their targets down the beach. What a sight that was! But how could a dozen men armed with .30-caliber weapons neutralize a battery of screaming meemies and a battery of armed German soldiers?

"Simple," said Pressley. "We'll get that radio off the dead officer." I don't remember who fetched the radio, but it was the sergeant's good idea. We hoped the radio was workable, and that we could make contact with its source.

Pressley flipped a switch, and the radio came to life. After extending the antenna, he was soon talking to someone miles away out on the English Channel. He calmly told the destroyer that the ship's liaison officer was dead and that he had a target for them. He described nearby landmarks and asked them to fire a test round, which they did.

We heard the report of the cannon and then the whine of the six-inch shell go over and explode hundreds of yards away. We didn't actually see the first two or three explosions, but after a while, one came within our sight. It was now a matter of time and, I suppose luck, that he would find the range. We could hear the ship fire its salvo: *boom-ba-ba-boom! Boom-ba-ba-boom! Swish-swish, ker-whoom! Ker-whoom!*

The ground trembled as the exploding shells saturated the area to our right front. Some of those explosions came too close for comfort, but they put that nebelwerfer battery out of action and earned Pressley the coveted Distinguished Service Cross. There is no telling how many lives he saved that day.

Later that afternoon, we still hadn't gotten farther than the top of the hill. A few German bicycle troops appeared, riding down the road parallel to the beach as if on a Sunday outing. If that were the case, we surely ruined their picnic with a few rounds of well-placed rifle fire that separated many of them from their vehicles.

After that, we began to think about defending against the expected counterattack that we were told would take place in less than twenty-four hours. To bolster our defenses, we took turns making special trips back to the still-dangerous beach in order to find more automatic weapons, ammo, and supplies.

When it was my turn to go down, I was horrified at what I saw. The debris-strewn beach was a disaster area. The incoming flooding tide brought with it the bodies of hundreds of our proud regiment. Scores of our men with bloodstained shirts rolled in the surf among helmets, assault jackets, gas masks, and M1 rifles.

At the edge of the water I saw a burning landing craft, tank (LCT) that had been trying to deposit a Sherman tank down its ramp. The tank was also burning and abandoned. From our perspective, the battle looked hopeless.

As I later discovered, one company of the 116th Infantry had fared even worse than we had in D Company. As the ramps splashed down, the 180-man A Company, led by Captain Taylor Fellers, was cut down like wheat under a slashing scythe. Because this first-wave team beat the smoke and fire, they landed precisely where they were supposed to land, and were decimated in mere minutes. Ninety-one of the 180 men in the landing party died, and most of the others were wounded. We found out later that it was that concentrated machine gun fire we had heard to our right when we were at the sea wall that nearly wiped them out. The next day, only about fifteen soldiers from Company A were able to continue the fight.

Company B, led by Captain Ettore Zappacosta, had landed at 7 a.m., following Company A at the draw. It, too, was cut down, execution style. Captain Walter Schilling's D Company followed B at 7:10. We sustained at least seventy-two casualties. Company C, led by Captain Bertier B. Hawks, came in at 7:20 and fared somewhat better, because C Company drifted to the left of the Vierville Draw. The 2nd Battalion, 116th, landed companies abreast: E, F, and G, with H in reserve.

It was a far cry from the unarmed pillboxes, "second-rate soldiers," and POW conscripts whom we were told would likely surrender at the first opportunity.

While scouting for D Company survivors near the Vierville Draw, I saw a regimental intelligence officer armed with a carbine, interrogating a German prisoner. The prisoner was on his knees with his hands behind his head. He was rather small and frail looking. I was surprised he was not wearing the usual square-shaped battle helmet. Instead he wore a gray, billed cap.

The lieutenant asked the prisoner, among other things, where the minefields were. The soldier, wearing a single inverted stripe on . his sleeve, answered only with the accepted Geneva Convention requirement of name, rank, and serial number. We had been instructed not to take prisoners for the first two or three days, so I expected the officer to eventually shoot the prisoner.

Again the interrogator screamed, "Where are the damned mine fields?" Again, he received the same reply: name, rank, and serial number.

The lieutenant's carbine barked, but the bullet was aimed at the ground between the prisoner's knees. The arrogant German looked straight at the officer and said with a smirk, *"Nicht hier."* He pointed between his knees. *"Hier!"* He pointed to his head. This told me something about our adversary.

116

ROUGH RIDE TO HELL: OMAHA BEACH, DOG GREEN

After dark, what I believe was an enemy Me-109 fighter plane flew over the entire Allied fleet, from right to left, just above the ships' barrage balloons. Every ship in the English Channel opened fire on that single airplane, illuminating the sky with millions of tracer bullets. Somehow, he flew over the fleet and circled back unscathed.

It was almost 11 p.m. before it got dark, due to double daylight saving time, "the longest day." That night, we got into our perimeter of defense on top of the hill and close to a copse of scrub trees. We had been on the go since 2 a.m., and I had never been so tired in my life. I asked Private First Class George Borys if he would stand first watch for a half-hour. I promised to take the second shift if I could first catch a short nap. We had dug shallow foxholes in the hard shale because we didn't have enough energy to dig deeper.

Borys, nicknamed "Churchill" because he was a bit chubby, said he would take the first watch. Not until dawn's early light of June 7 broke over the Normandy coastline did our squad awake from a sound sleep in our shallow slit trenches. We found out later that German soldiers were dug in less than twenty-five yards away. Borys, feeling sheepish, said he didn't remember going to sleep.

June 6, 1944, was unlike any other day of my life. Yet at the time, I failed to realize its full significance. I was too busy trying to keep my squad and myself alive.

Combat deaths are ugly and sickening. A bullet or piece of red-hot shrapnel tears flesh, gristle, and bone into gruesome wounds. A few hours in the sun causes a body to swell grotesquely and turn dark purple. The stench is unbearable. Such deaths were tragic insults to all those handsome young GIs just beginning their lives, who would not fulfill their dreams.

Many of those killed were, like me, barely teenagers when they enlisted, just starting to grow to maturity in the army. Those comrades and I spent many happy weekends and furloughs together, soaking up culture and drinking bitters. We shared living quarters, read each other's mail, and, more significantly, shared the misery of training in the most extreme of elements.

The 116th Infantry lost from eight hundred to one thousand men on D-Day and D Company lost at least seventy-two. Of the dead, twenty of them were from my hometown of Roanoke. Five of nine of our officers were killed, including Captain Walter O. Schilling (who was from Roanoke), 1st Lieutenant William Gardner, 1st Lieutenant Merle Cummings, 1st Lieutenant Vincent Labowicz and 2nd Lieutenant Alton Ashley. There were twelve noncoms killed, including these Roanokers: First Sergeant James H. Obenshain, Staff Sergeant James L. Wright, Sergeant Russell W. "Jack" Ingram and Sergeant George D. Johnson, Corporal Jack R. Simms. Add to the list of the dead twenty-three privates, including Roanokers Private First Class Charles R. Milliron and Private First Class Walter D. Sink. The company had thirty-two men wounded, many of them severely. And yet our nightmare had just begun.

Before the invasion, the 29th Division numbered about fourteen thousand, and replacements poured in as men were killed or wounded. By the time we took Saint-Lô six weeks later, it was said that the 29th was really three divisions: one in the field, another in the hospital, and yet a third in the cemetery. We endured those unbelievable hardships so we could participate in D-Day, which we knew would be huge, deadly, and unforgettable. Yet we couldn't fathom the terrible odds of surviving just one day fighting in the hedgerows of Normandy.

CHAPTER EIGHT

FROM OMAHA TO SAINT-LÔ

ENTANGLEMENT IN HEDGEROW COUNTRY

The second day broke with sun and clouds. I was still unable to answer the penetrating question that McCanless had asked me at the water's edge. Would we eventually get through all of this? We had no communication or news of other sectors. I was confused, totally exhausted, and still in shock at the terrible carnage that had been inflicted on us.

Moreover, I was very worried about the prediction that a German counterattack was expected to take place that day. We were without communication, heavy weapons, armor, or leaders higher than green lieutenants. The vaunted naval ships with guns pointed shoreward and fighter planes flying overhead were little help, because we had no liaison with them.

What a way to begin a war! All our training, conditioning, and planning were wasted by a voracious grim reaper on the crimson sand of Omaha Beach. When the navy's rocket missiles were prematurely launched, sending most erroneously into the water, thousands of fish were killed, but Jerry, poised in his concrete bunkers, was left ready to fight. As somebody said, "a few old women with brooms could have swept us back into the channel."

Without adequate radio communication, rumors flourished. Remnants of 2nd Squad had become separated from the company, and it was rumored that they were dead. When the official casualty report became known, the shocked survivors went into deep denial, then accepted the facts, and finally shed tears. I myself vowed never to take a prisoner.

The 29th Division's D-Day objective was Isigny, a town approximately twelve miles from our landing site, and 2nd Squad's immediate objective was finding our D Company brothers and 1st Battalion. As we moved inland, our group of stragglers began to grow and join other disorganized groups. The fifty or so stragglers, less than two platoons, were from B, C, and D Companies; A Company had been decimated. They also included men from the 2nd and 5th Rangers, artillerymen, engineers, medics, and one or two soldiers from 2nd Battalion.

It was comforting to have men from other units carrying a serviceable weapon and professing a willingness to fight. I have to admit that I felt vulnerable and lonely during the first early hours in Normandy. We were taught to keep a distance from one another to lessen the target, but we found it much more comforting to be near a friend. No one wants to die alone.

Almost as soon as we left the coastline and turned inland, we were greeted with the *bocage* country of the Cotentin Peninsula. The Norman countryside above the bluffs was a series of lush farms and villages, divided into acre-sized plots with hedgerows typically separating each plot. Our English amphibious assault training courses had been thorough to the "nth" degree with boat drills and beach-clearing operations, but SHAEF commanders failed miserably to prepare ground troops for the hedgerows.

These borders had begun centuries earlier, as Norman farmers cleared the plentiful deposits of alluvial debris that glaciers had left on the land, using the stones to surround their fields. Wind-blown soil helped many kinds of foliage to grow out of the acre-long hedgerows, forming walls two to four feet thick, and three to six feet high. Local houses were usually one- or two-story structures with stucco and timber siding and thatch or tile roofs. Affluent farm manors usually had a barn and outbuildings, and were surrounded by high stone walls. As we soon would discover, the Germans used both the manor houses and hedgerows to great tactical advantage.

We received sporadic incoming mortar and small arms that sent Sergeant Willard Norfleet and me diving into a large bomb crater. Minutes later, as I urged Norfleet to "get the hell out of here," we moved just in time to see a ball of fire and smoke from a 90mm mortar shell hit the center of the crater.

Clearing out of that crater just in time is only one of many seemingly miraculous tales of survival I could recount. Sergeant Dean Friedline of 1st Platoon, for example, was hit in the chest by a multicolored "dum-dum," or wooden bullet, that shattered a block of TNT he carried in his vest pocket. Amazingly, he was only bruised, and lived to tell about it. Then there was the 2nd Battalion officer who had been shot through both cheeks, barely missing his teeth, while shouting orders—a story kept alive by the famous war correspondent Ernie Pyle. Captain Charles R. Cawthon, 2nd Battalion Headquarters Company commanding officer, wrote in *Other Clay* that he collected shrapnel from two separate wounds. As all of these tales illustrate, it takes good sense and a lot of luck to survive infantry combat for very long.

As our diverse group of volunteers followed the road into the coastal hamlet of Vierville-sur-Mer on June 7, all the civilians and most of the German defenders had already evacuated the town, leaving a rear-guard contingent to slow our advance. Up ahead we could hear German snipers firing, and an occasional burp gun

121

outburst. The column took cover along each side of the road, and waited for someone ahead to eliminate the obstruction.

Waiting for the outcome, many of us smoked K-ration cigarettes or just tried to rest. I was lying on my back catching a catnap when, directly across the road, a muffled explosion was followed by a whiff of white smoke. A soldier at the heart of the action let out a shrill scream. Walfred Williams bolted across the road to offer help to the stricken private. There was very little anyone could do but deaden his pain and watch him die.

The private had accidentally pulled the pin on one of the many hand grenades hanging on his belt. The grenade blew away most of his buttocks and portions of his back. A jolt of morphine helped to calm him until, mercifully, he died. Word spread that the heat from the sun had ignited the pineapple grenade. Because of this rumor, many confused men discarded their precious hand grenades.

Our column resumed its march along the coastal road and into the outskirts of Vierville. The tiny village overlooked the English Channel from the heights behind the beach. Our British coxswain had been instructed to guide by the prominent Vierville church steeple, which usually can be seen on a clear day above the D-1 Draw off Omaha Beach.

Although the frontline village of Vierville suffered little damage, strangely enough, the first roadside dwellings we saw were ruined. As we approached, enemy rifle fire increased, and incoming shots sent us to the leeward side of the road. We quickly realized that our enemy targets would not be easy to locate.

We fired in the direction of the sound, but skillful German camouflage and smokeless powder made hitting the bull's-eye a lucky shot. After a brief exchange of gunfire, white flags appeared, followed by three or four shaken gray coats with their hands over their heads, yelling, *"Kamerad!"* Even though we had been instructed to take no prisoners for the first few days, they were marched back to the beach for intelligence interrogation. After what they had done to us the day before, it wasn't hard to hate the square-headed German bastards.

After the brief encounter at Vierville, our rabble-like group followed the coast road about seven kilometers southwest to Pointe-du-Hoc. The force grew as other stragglers joined us. Putrid-smelling dead cattle with bloated bellies littered the lush green fields of the once-beautiful countryside. Even worse was the nauseating sight of dead American and enemy soldiers, mingled with wrecked German vehicles, artillery pieces, self-propelled half-tracks, and all kinds of equipment strewn along the narrow two-lane roadway.

Unrolled, multicolor-coded communication wire lay in ditches alongside the road. The scenery clearly informed us that the air force and navy had had a field day. Later, we saw entangled dead American paratroopers hanging by their harnesses from trees. I am not sure whether they were shot while descending or after getting snagged. A foul odor hung in the air.

And paratroopers were not all we found in the trees. As we departed Vierville, leaving the road and traveling cross-country, we began to receive accurate sniper and incoming artillery fire. A rifle company lieutenant grabbed some "volunteers" and went after the obstruction. After a few BAR bursts, the sharpshooter-artillery spotter was brought to military justice. Cleverly hidden by camouflage in a fixed artillery observation post in a tree, that lone shooter was responsible for delaying our progress for over an hour, and lost us several good men. It became clear that the dedication and courage of the enemy was going to make for a long, tough war.

B Company's Bob Sales said it best: "D-Day was the longest day. But there were many, many long days in Normandy, hopping those damned hedgerows and getting men killed. We lost good men every single day." A disproportionate number of the losses occurred among the much-needed replacement soldiers who began to join our much-depleted ranks soon after the beachhead was secured.

Many of them had been civilians only a few weeks before. On one occasion, after dark, a shaken replacement crawled up to my foxhole and stammered, "I-I-I'm l-l-l-looking for a S-S-Sergeant Slaughter!" I answered that I was Slaughter. He said that he had been assigned to my section.

I assigned him to one of the squads and he was told where to dig a foxhole. That was the last time we saw that young man alive. I never learned his name. Replacement turnover was rapid and disheartening. Before a replacement learned the ropes, even though it usually didn't take long, he often became a casualty. We didn't have the manpower to quickly and adequately teach the newcomer all he needed to know.

On a good day, we were able to capture two or three hedgerows. Mostly it depended on the strategic importance of the position. After each battle, there were fewer of us left for the next one. If the hedgerow was contested, it sometimes took all day and many casualties finally to gain a few yards of land.

Before the confusion was settled, Jerry often tried to regain the prize, and sometimes succeeded. Hours later, after the field was secured, the medics collected the wounded amid artillery and mortar fire. We often could clearly hear the moans, groans, and screams of the wounded on both sides. The dead were collected later.

Prior to H-Hour of the battle, artillery and heavy weapons saturated the defensive hedgerows. D, H, and M Companies supported rifle companies with heavy .30-caliber machine guns and 81mm mortars. Machine guns fired rapidly from the corners of the line of departure, pinning the defenders. When orders were given to go over the top, machine guns either ceased fire or fired over the heads of attacking riflemen.

Machine guns and mortars were prime artillery and mortar targets, and my section lost seven machine guns in less than three months of hedgerow fighting. One problem was that a water-cooled heavy machine gun produced smoke that made it necessary to move the gun to an alternate firing position. The number one and number two gunners moved the eighty-five-pound tripod and gun attached. After firing a few bursts, the barrel became extremely hot, which made it impossible to touch barehanded. If shrapnel or a bullet punctured the gun's water jacket, the gun became inoperable.

Universally, we foot soldiers—infantry, armor, artillery, engineers—could not say enough good things about the Allied Tactical Air Force. The Ninth Air Force P-47 Thunderbolts, P-38 Lightnings, P-51 Mustangs, and medium bombers, B-24 and B-26, all flew close support and made our job easier. These spunky pilots risked their necks, and we appreciated it. As a result, Jerry hated clear days, and we hated cloudy ones.

At one point, ground fire hit a low-flying P-47 as it strafed ahead of our marching column. The pilot skillfully lined up his fighter plane on a straight stretch of dirt road just ahead of us, and clipped some foliage as he made a hard crash landing. As I walked past the wrecked airplane, its nose buried in the road and its gasoline gushing into the ground, infantry medics were extricating the moaning pilot out of the tight cockpit. They told us that the poor guy's back was broken. But we were thankful for small miracles in those days. The pilot had managed to miss us, and, luckily, the plane never caught fire despite the river of gas that poured out.

Another vital weapon that helped to even the score was the flimsy spotter monoplane. These slow, kite-like craft hovered like hummingbirds over frontline positions, directing artillery on German armor, mortar, or artillery positions. Spotter planes also acted as the all-seeing eyes of the infantry. The observation plane could spot a tank or troop buildup, warn the friendlies on the ground, and then direct artillery on the target or call for an aerial strike.

Early on the morning of June 8, the Vierville defense force was relieved, and we joined the 2nd and 3rd Battalions, 116th, and a few rangers at St. Pierre. Our mission was to rescue a few beleaguered rangers at Pointe-du-Hoc. The destroyer USS *Ellison* supported the effort by throwing 140 rounds of eight-inch missiles on the Point.

The 1st Battalion moved out cross-country and made contact with a few besieged rangers without opposition. By noon, Pointe-du-Hoc was cleared of German opposition. 2nd and 3rd Battalion, 116th, and the rescued rangers moved westward toward the port city of Grandcamp-les-Bains.

The 3rd Battalion was held up by machine gun and mortar fire at a bridge over a stream near the port city. The attack was suspended while the British cruiser *Glasgow* hammered the tough enemy position with a one-hour barrage. Later that afternoon, K and L Companies moved through the rangers and attacked astride the road leading into the channel port.

The attack again stalled. Technical Sergeant Frank D. Peregory, rifle platoon sergeant of Charlottesville's K Company (Monticello Guard), and a former National Guardsman, 116th Infantry, single-handedly worked himself up the hill and dropped into the trench that surrounded the position. With rifle, hand grenades, and bayonet, he killed eight of the enemy and captured thirty-five. He was directly responsible for the capture of the strong point, and ultimately for Grandcamp itself.

Six days later, Peregory was killed in action at Couvains. For his "conspicuous gallantry and intrepidity at the risk of his life above and beyond the call of duty," he was posthumously awarded the Medal of Honor.

While the 2nd and 3rd Battalions and Frank Peregory were fighting at Grandcamp, the 1st swung around, bypassing the seaport town, toward the heavy artillery positions at Maisy. My squad and several infantrymen were following a creaky Sherman tank half-concealed in a sunken dirt road. There were three- and four-feet-high hedgerows on the right side—the enemy's side—of the road. Tanks drown the sound of incoming artillery and send clouds of yellow dust skyward. These tend to draw enemy artillery fire the way spring apple blossoms draw honeybees. Even so, foot soldiers and tankers feel mutually protected by each other's presence.

We began receiving sporadic mortar fire and an occasional 88mm round. The Sherman created stifling dust, so I lagged a bit to escape it. Suddenly, an earthquake explosion shook the ground twenty yards ahead, and a fireball sent death and destruction in all directions. A hidden teller mine had blown the tank and all the tankers inside to smithereens. A squad or more of infantry had been crouching around and behind the splintered hulk. I was near enough to feel the heat and blast of the explosion.

The explosive energy from that hidden teller mine sent the 45-ton Sherman tank into the ditch on its side. This scene echoed the bloody, grotesque carnage of D-Day. One minute they were healthy young men, and the next minute they were bloody arms and legs wrapped around bloody torsos. We found body parts and shoes with the feet still in them twenty-five yards away. We couldn't help but get sick and vomit. I thought I was getting used to seeing men killed in every gruesome way possible, but that teller mine explosion was one of the most horrific things I have ever witnessed. This was war in the hedgerows, and it was not pretty. After that I kept my distance from road-bound tanks.

We met little opposition at Maisy after a prolonged naval shelling. There were isolated snipers and sporadic mortar and artillery, but it was mostly ineffectual. After this operation, the 116th Regiment went into a much-needed 29th Division reserve.

To be in division reserve does not mean languishing safely miles behind the front. Reserve troops are subjected to artillery and mortar fire, must stand guard duty, and must patrol nightly. While in reserve, the regiment was resupplied with replacement soldiers, weapons, and equipment. Later, the army post office got organized enough to distribute months-old letters and packages from home.

But before I had a chance to remove my shoes or shave, we were ordered back to hell. We headed off toward Couvains, a village typical of many Norman farming communities.

The sight of another terrible death that occurred at this time haunts my dreams to this day. My squad and I were digging a machine gun emplacement behind a scrubby hedgerow. We had just finished fixing the camouflage when I happened to see a junior officer with field glasses scanning the front. I could tell he was a newly arrived replacement. His uniform and equipment were relatively new and unworn.

The sharp report of an 88mm fired from nearby sent me diving. At the same time, the high explosive missile hit the lieutenant's upper torso. The 2nd Squad and I were splattered with gore as the spotter was blown backward, minus his head. Number two gunner Private First Class Sal Augeri vomited, and I nearly did, too.

The dreaded German sniper was almost as highly respected as the 88. Sharpshooters gave no warning, taking careful aim with sniper-scoped Mausers. The receiving end would hear the sharp crack and instantaneous whine of the bullet. If you heard the report of the bullet leaving the muzzle, it wasn't for you.

German snipers nearly always aimed for the head if it was visible and in range. Most infantrymen never removed their helmets except when they shaved. I confess that I slept in mine. The 8mm bullet could easily pass through the helmet, through the head, and out the other side with enough energy left to do more damage.

I saw men get hit between the eyes or just above the ears, which killed them instantly. If the bullet missed the helmet, the entry hole was usually neat and showed only a small trickle of blood. But after the steel-jacket bullet hit the helmet or skull, the bullet flattened, causing the exit wound to shatter the other side of the head away.

The 1st Battalion advanced toward Couvains from the west, double file, marching cautiously down a sunken dirt road just wide enough for a horse cart. We were flanked by hedgerows four to five feet high, and covered with a canopy of overhanging foliage. Intermittent mortar and artillery rounds were coming in ahead, which kept us on our toes. German communication trenches two feet wide and three feet deep were dug along on both sides of the road. These shallow ditches protected enemy communication wire from being cut by artillery.

As we moved closer to town, the foliage overhead thinned enough to reveal the steeple of the Catholic church, the first edifice we saw as we approached. The closer we got to the steeple, the more accurate the 88mm and mortar fire. Suddenly, the banshee scream of an 88mm shell sounded as if it had my number written all over it. *Sh-boom!*

I dove headfirst into the left ditch, losing my helmet and almost my neck. Somehow the exploding shell missed hitting anyone; we were keeping a space between men. Picking myself up to brush off my uniform, I saw a strange and shocking sight. On the edge of the ditch lay a German forearm. Part of the uniform sleeve was there, with the elbow, arm, hand, and all fingers intact. I wondered what had happened to the rest of that poor bastard. I never did find out.

I climbed back on the path, shaken but unscathed. Within minutes, I had another surprise. As I approached an opening on the right side of the hedgerow, I heard someone moaning. Crawling carefully through the opening, I came face-to-face with a young German paratrooper, who had been hit by a large chunk of shrapnel. He had a very serious upper thigh wound, and his left trouser leg was bloody and torn.

This was my first encounter with the enemy up close. The German paratrooper is a fierce and fanatical warrior, easily distinguishable by his round helmet and baggy smock. My first reaction was to put him out of his misery and keep going.

I believe he knew what I was thinking. He begged tearfully, *"Kamerad, bitte"* (Friend, please). He was an impressive-looking soldier, about nineteen years old—my age. He was as filthy as I was, with long, brown, stringy hair. I had always thought most German soldiers had short, blond hair. He had an athletic build—about five feet ten inches tall and about 180 pounds—and a handsome face.

I suspended the promise I had made at the beach about not taking prisoners. I thought, *That was then, and this is now.* I just couldn't shoot a wounded human being at point-blank range. I made sure he didn't have a weapon hidden on him. Then I tied his belt around his upper thigh, which stopped the blood from gushing. I gently swabbed the dirt from his wound and applied sulfa powder. His wince turned to a forced grin.

He was in pain, so I gave him a shot of morphine and a drink of water from my canteen. Then I gave him one of my Lucky Strike cigarettes, and lit it for him. As I left, he smiled weakly and said in guttural, broken English, *"Danke. Gott bless. Guten luck."*

That changed my thinking about taking prisoners. I still hated the enemy, but I couldn't kill one at close range, especially if his hands were up. I sent one of our medics to finish what I had started. I hoped the German would recover and that his war was over.

The column scattered in a Couvains apple orchard, waiting for Lieutenant Patterson Moseley (D Company 1st Platoon leader), a rifle platoon officer, and Technical Sergeant Norfleet, who were scouting the source of the incoming artillery and mortar fire. Someone ordered a retaliation counterbattery artillery barrage, but due to the imponderables of war one of the rounds fell short, killing one man and wounding three.

"Friendly" shrapnel hit my friend and platoon sergeant, Willard Norfleet. Not only was the wound painful and bloody, but it severed a vital nerve in his favored right arm. The sergeant's days at the helm of his platoon were over, and became the subject of nightly nightmares and useless operations. At least he went back home to safety in Roanoke with his loyal wife and child.

Veteran 1st Platoon soldiers were now becoming casualties of war. We lost two more of them in that lethal apple orchard on the outskirts of Couvains. A *Wehrmacht* sniper put an 8mm bullet between Sergeant Romeo B. Bily's eyes and killed him instantly. Private First Class Tony Carusotto was also killed there. The snipers were deadly, but the 88s were much more frightening. The slightest movement caused a sudden, *boom-swoosh-boom! Boom-swoosh-boom!* And then: "Medic! Get me a medic! Please, hurry! Get me a medic! Oh my God, please hurry!"

These hits told us that an enemy artillery spotter was observing our every move. The serene-looking little stone church with centuries of headstones around it housed a deadly enemy who was aiming straight at us. We knew he had to be in the church steeple.

We called for artillery support, but the 105mm high explosive couldn't neutralize the belfry. After several tries, 1st Battalion engineers fixed TNT explosives at the base of the tower. An ear-splitting *ka-whoom!* sent rock and mortar flying and the enemy artillery observers to their deaths.

I returned to Couvains in 1993 and found the church had been renovated. The caretaker was working in the garden of the cemetery. I told him about us blowing the belfry with explosives. He said that residue of TNT had been found when the church was rebuilt.

On July 1, 1st Battalion was holding defensive positions along one of the ridgelines approaching Saint-Lô. Private First Class Walfred Williams and I were making improvements to our shared foxhole. Sporadic artillery and mortar rounds kept us digging. The swish of a 50mm mortar bomb and its aftermath explosion persuaded a visitor to dive into our hole, causing our two-man slit trench to become overly crowded.

I noticed a white cross stenciled on the officer's helmet. "Sergeant Slaughter," the chaplain said to me, "I have bad news. Your mother requested, through her local pastor, that I break this to you personally. Last May, your father died of a massive aneurysm while being treated at the University of Virginia Hospital."

That was how I found out my forty-nine-year-old father had died. My mother had asked her pastor, Dr. Robert Lapsley of Roanoke's First Presbyterian Church, to write to the chaplain, and that the chaplain tell me. Speaking for the battalion, the chaplain said, "Wish we could give you a few days off, but you know how short of men we are."

I replied that I would be all right, and that I understood. But my 19-year-old mind couldn't fathom at the time that I would never see my father again. My mother had not told me that he was in failing health. Who would look after her, a stay-at-home mother, and my three siblings still at home? There was no time to grieve properly until later, when Saint-Lô was liberated and we were off the line.

Our battalion position was on the forward slope of a hill that graded down to a deep ravine. Section Leader (Staff Sergeant) Roy McKay and Sergeant Charlie Cawley's machine gun squad, with a squad of riflemen, was protecting the right flank of our defensive line. The enemy was dug in on the rise across the ravine, and the fields were checkered with acre-sized hedgerows.

Cawley's squad, among other defenders, was dug in on a hedgerow perpendicular to the front. This put Sergeant McKay's two machine guns and several riflemen in a precarious position. Jerry had an excellent view up the hedgerow and could bring enfilade-grazing fire if anyone ventured even partly out of his hole.

I was heating a cup of coffee when Captain Thomas Murphy's runner rolled into my foxhole, out of breath. The runner told me that Captain Murphy wanted me to report, at once! I couldn't imagine what he wanted, but I grabbed my rifle and we both ran back to the company command post (CP).

The CP was a few hedgerows behind the front, secluded in a sunken, canopy-covered road. I didn't know Captain Murphy because he was formerly from H Company, and had just taken over our company after Captain Schilling was killed on D-Day.

The captain told me that Staff Sergeant McKay had just been killed and I was to take over McKay's 2nd Section. He warned that the position was dangerously exposed, but extremely important to the integrity of the battalion's defense. He ordered me to go quickly and be careful.

I followed a sunken, one-lane dirt wagon path and found the battalion aid station directly behind our right flank position. The aid station was somewhat protected by the covered section of the road. The aid man in charge was an old 29th Ranger buddy nicknamed "Cheesy" Quinn. We didn't have time to catch up on old news, but he did warn that my destination was a hot spot. He said that snipers had killed at least two men that day, July 5.

I rolled to the sunken road hedgerow and ran bent-over for about twenty-five yards until I found Sergeant Cawley's foxhole. His entire squad was taking refuge in their holes. I saw no one guarding the hedgerow flank.

I warned Cawley that we had to have someone keep an eye on the flank. It worried me that Jerry might sneak up on the other side of the hedge and toss a potato-masher grenade at us. Sergeant Cawley said with conviction that, by damn, neither he nor any of his men were going to expose themselves.

I knew I had to show some leadership right then, as I had just taken over a new job with new personnel. I let it be known that I would never ask anyone to do something I wouldn't do myself. I slowly raised my head over the hedgerow, as I had done many times, panning left to right, right to left.

Suddenly, no more than ten or fifteen seconds later, *WHAM!* My helmet flew off and I fell forward on my hands and knees, landing on the floor of Cawley's slit trench. The force from the steel jacket bullet against my forehead felt like a healthy swing from a Louisville Slugger baseball bat.

My ears rang and I saw a zillion stars as blood gushed over me and pooled on the ground. The shot came from left to right and downward. The slug had entered the bill of my helmet front and exited through the liner, cutting the plastic liner strap. Either the shattered steel jacket or a piece of my helmet had glanced off my skull. I knew I was going to die.

Cawley was over me with eyes as large as saucers, and his mouth gaping. Like me, he was in shock. He froze.

"Charlie!" I screamed. "Get me a medic! Get me a damn medic, Charlie!"

Cawley didn't move a muscle.

"Never mind, I'll get him myself!" I said.

I retraced my path over the hedgerow and into the sunken road where the aid station was located. Corpsman Quinn quickly cleaned me off and assessed the damage. He happily pronounced that I was very lucky. The bullet had merely grazed my forehead. The corpsman stitched the wound and bandaged my forehead. Both of my eyes swelled and partly closed. I spent four days at the regimental CP until the swelling subsided.

That was where I first tasted Calvados, the brandy from the Calvados region of Normandy. The 116th Regimental Band members were helping to evacuate wounded soldiers, and one of them, Melvin "Bub" Proffit, a drummer boy from Roanoke, offered me a drink from his canteen. It was a warm day and I was thirsty. The drink smelled like apple cider, so I took a big swig. The fiery French country brandy burned my insides all the way down and took my breath away, making it impossible for me to speak for several seconds. Bub thought it was hilarious.

The next mission of the 116th Regiment was to capture and hold the high ground overlooking the strategically located city of Saint-Lô. Jerry knew the importance of this communication hub to the final breakout of the Cotentin Peninsula. Strongly entrenched, the Germans were dug in on the dominating high ground along a ridge road leading to the hamlet of Martinville, called Martinville Ridge. Among ourselves, we called it "the Ridge of Death." (See map in Appendix IV, page 284.)

I rejoined the 2nd Section in time for the great battle for Saint-Lô. We jumped off after dark. The white bandage around my forehead and partly under the helmet seemed to illuminate, which made me an easy target. Mortar Sergeant George Kobe later said he couldn't believe it when he saw me with that white bandage around my head and black, swollen eyes.

Jerry pounded the 116th all day and two nights with blockbuster 155mm and 105mm artillery. Near misses caused enough concussion to make our ears ring and our heads ache. The pounding rounds of salvo after salvo of earth-shaking artillery were relentless and frightening.

During the bombardment, I shared a long, shallow slit trench with one of the first D Company replacements, Private Lewis Cass Leigh from Chevy Chase, Maryland. We nicknamed him "Junior" early on, because of his boyish looks and demeanor. Junior was from an affluent family and had volunteered into the army upon graduation from high school. He didn't look like the type that could last very long in brutal combat.

Our slit trench was covered with wooden sheathing and topped with a roof of piled dirt. Like thousands of other infantry soldiers subjected to such heavy bombardment, Junior and I were a pitiful sight. Fine yellow dust sifted through the cracks of the roof and stuck to our sweaty skin and eyes. If the dust had been black, we would have looked liked very tired coalminers. The yellow dust turned to mud around our swollen, bloodshot eyes. When nature called, we had to answer in the safety of our slit trench, lying down.

All of the training and experience in the world could not have prepared us for this kind of harassment. Those boxcar-sized shells sounded like they were flip-flopping end over end and screeching straight for our hole. This went on hour after hour, all day and through the night. Many good soldiers cracked. And who could blame them?

On the morning the shelling finally stopped, the hilltop land-scape was unbelievable. All of the vegetation had been stripped and the ground looked like a pockmarked moonscape. Leigh, despite my earlier doubts about him, seemed relatively OK. He had passed the ultimate test and become a hardened infantryman, albeit a baby-faced one. I, too, was unhurt and very thankful to be alive.

After brushing myself off, I inspected nearby foxholes. Some had taken direct hits, with ugly results. Other near-miss craters contained dead GIs, lying together as if asleep. To my shock and sorrow, in one of these craters, I found Private First Class Walfred "Fats" Williams, my trusted number one gunner, and an old friend from Roanoke, Sergeant Aaron J. "Ajax" Bowling—my buddy from the incident in Savannah, Georgia. They looked dusty and disheveled, but could have passed for two GIs sleeping late. I'm sure that Walfred Williams didn't believe there was a German sol-dier or weapon that could kill him, and I didn't think so either. But he died on that Martinville Ridge of Death on July 18, 1944, and part of me died with him. I grieved over Ajax Bowling as well.

That night, Jerry hit the right flank with some enthusiasm, a small counterattack, which forced both of my machine guns back to the hedgerow where I was staying. During this brief encounter, one of my gunners, Private First Class Junior Leigh, was hit in the leg with shrapnel.

By the time we took Saint-Lô, the 29th Division had been in the line for forty-two straight days: the 115th and 116th regiments since D-Day, the 175th since D plus 1. The long bouts of front-line duty had been taking their toll. It was extremely rare for an infantryman to go unscathed for very long. Many 29ers were wounded two, three, or four times fighting through the hedgerows of Normandy. All of us were praying for the "million-dollar wound," which missed vital organs, bone, and nerves, but would give us a long stay in an English hospital, sleeping under clean, white sheets and (at least in fantasy) in the care of a beautiful nurse.

Meanwhile, battle fatigue and self-inflicted wounds had become serious problems. At least once, nearly all combat soldiers, if they are honest, consider shooting themselves in order to get out of the hell of battle. Self-inflicted wounds, however, are considered disgraceful and, if proven, a court-martial offense. Nevertheless, many respectable KIA and WIA reports were, in reality, self-inflicted or "friendly fire" accidents.

Land mines and booby traps were also common ways to be killed or wounded. Hearing the news of who had gotten hit was always hard, and every day, new faces replaced seasoned infantry men. It was easy to distinguish a new arrival from a veteran. The "old-timer" could be eighteen or nineteen years old, but if he had survived a week at the front he was considered old. And we all looked it.

On a diet of K-rations, we all lost weight. Our ribs, shoulder blades, and Adam's apples stuck out, and our filthy, ragged uniforms hung like worn-out drapes. Our eyes were blood-red and sunken, and we had bleeding sores on our exposed skin. Ordinarily, these would be telltale signs that a man needs a month's rest. But we all knew there could be no rest until Saint-Lô was taken.

Knowing that there was no immediate end in sight drove some fellows over the edge. A few good soldiers who couldn't take the pounding day after day committed suicide. This was the case of Stanley Koryciak, a nineteen-year-old private, born and raised in Chicago. He was a tough, athletic little soldier. He made the D-Day landings and had fought well through the hedgerows. But everyone has a breaking point. His squad reported that Stan, who had seen many of his close friends killed or severely wounded, had begun to act strangely. He cried often, especially during incoming artillery barrages, and sometimes his crying reached the point of hysteria.

Instead of the usual disciplinary action for similar behavior, he was sent back to the kitchen area for a break from the action. Many of us thought that a few days of rest, a couple of hot meals, and a warm bath might rehabilitate him. But he was in more pain than any of us realized. Why couldn't we see that he had reached his limit?

Private Koryciak found a cook's Springfield '03 rifle, removed his shoe so he could pull the trigger, and blew the top of his head off. One of the cooks heard the shot and ran to his tent. Stanley Koryciak had had enough of the constant fear, the filthy grime, the ear-shattering explosions, the putrid smells, the excruciating pain, and the maiming and deaths of close friends.

Stan Koryciak died on July 2. The record book shows he was killed, a nonbattle casualty. In my book, Private Koryciak died an American hero.

CHAPTER NINE

SAINT-LÔ
AND BEYOND

THE MAJOR OF SAINT-LÔ

A t the end of June, Major Thomas D. Howie, formerly 116th Regimental S-3, had been elevated to 3rd Battalion commander. Colonel Philip Dwyer, who replaced Colonel Charles Canham as 116th Regimental Commander, ordered Major Howie's 3rd Battalion to proceed posthaste into the flattened city of Saint-Lô on July 17.

"Major Howie got on the phone to report to Colonel Canham, and I could tell by the conversation that he was telling the colonel that Major Bingham was in no position to help with his battered battalion," wrote William H. Puntenney, newly promoted to 3rd Battalion executive officer, in his personal journal. "Major Howie informed the colonel that our 3rd Battalion was ready and able to proceed into the city. Canham evidently told Howie to go ahead. Major Howie ended the conversation with, 'See you in Saint-Lô.'

"I looked at my watch and it was 8:20 a.m., ten minutes until we moved out in our attack. Our command group was spread out along a hedgerow at the north edge of the orchard. There were several slit trenches at the base of the hedgerow that the Germans had dug. I was standing about fifteen feet away from our two radio operators, who were adjusting their SCR-300 backpack radios, getting ready to go. Howie and I were standing together talking when at least six mortar rounds landed in the orchard. The sound was deafening and shrapnel seemed to be [flying] everywhere.

"I saw Major Howie fall to the ground and I knew he had been hit. I got him under the arms and pulled him into one of the (formerly German) slit trenches. His body lay across my lap and I noticed that Captain Shuford, our artillery liaison officer, was also in the trench. Howie, bleeding from the mouth, was trying to breathe. I opened his shirt and could see several large shrapnel wounds to his chest. He gasped, 'Bill, I'm hit bad!' He then slumped lifeless into my arms."

The main force of German defenders finally withdrew from the battered city, leaving a rear echelon contingent to delay our advance. During the mop-up operation, General Gerhardt asked one of his staff, "Where's Tom Howie?"

"Sir, Major Howie is dead!"

The general snapped, "Damn it! I know that! Where's his body? I want you to take his body into Saint-Lô." The general reasoned that the victory belonged to the dead as well as the living. Major Howie represented the legions of dead who helped to liberate the city. So it was that Major Howie's body was laid in state atop a pile of rubble that once was the wall of Saint Croix Church, and the major was forever promoted to "immortal hero."

On July 18, the decimated 1st Battalion, 116th, staggered off the battered ridge into Saint-Lô. I remember seeing Major Howie's flag-draped body propped up against a pile of debris, and being told who it was. That day, July 18, I viewed it as just another of the many hundreds of war deaths since D-Day. Yet, I will never forget that special and highly symbolic flag-draped image of "The Major of Saint-Lô."

Whenever XIX Corps needed an attack dog to go after the most stubborn objectives, it seemed that "Uncle Charlie," as we called General Gerhardt, yelled our battle cry: *"29, let's go!"* The dreaded briefings predicted the always-heavy casualties. We kept praying for the coveted "million-dollar wound" or the speedy demise of the Axis. By then, death was commonplace; my D Company and 1st Battalion seemed to be approaching one hundred percent casualties.

One of my strongest memories of Saint-Lô was how emaciated our 116th Infantry looked after forty-two truculent days at the front. The fierce battle for the piles and piles of rubble was over. The battered 116th Infantry was finally relieved of frontline duty on July 19. We began our withdrawal into corps reserve, five or six miles to the rear. No American soldiers had endured more than the survivors of the D-Day invasion and the dogged battles for the Norman hedgerows.

Many of the survivors, including myself, were still wearing the same ragged and grimy uniforms—woolen trousers, shirts, leggings, shoes, underwear, and socks—issued at the marshalling area in England. It was mandatory that we keep our uniforms buttoned, but many of us no longer had any buttons left to fasten. Eating K-rations and chocolate D-bars for weeks had caused our uniforms to hang from our bodies like loose, tattered rags. Shaggy, dusty hair, haggard faces, and sunken eye sockets gave evidence that we had about reached our limit.

But at last we were going back for a much needed rest. Many of us were scraped, scratched, and bloody, but thankfully we were still alive. The 116th trudged back to a semblance of civility, a respite that promised warm showers, hot food, a few hours of extra sleep, and a change into dry, clean clothes.

The remnants of the 1st Battalion, 116th Infantry, reduced from 1,000 men to less than a full company of 150 to 200 men, slogged back through territory we had fought over a few short days before. Along the way, we saw abandoned war wagons, some still smoldering, with their long guns pointing cock-eyed. Painted on metal turrets were hateful black crosses and gray, wavy camouflage. Small-arms ammunition was strewn about, showing that our P-47s had been active and accurate. The smell of rotting flesh permeated the air.

The gut-wrenching spectacle of the depleted, emaciated battalion moving to the rear, staggering like intoxicated zombies, is still indelibly printed on my memory. I was one of those unwashed, ragged infantry soldiers, wearing all the same clothing I had stepped into prior to D-Day, but I had no mirror to see myself. We were dirty, khaki-clad bags of bones toting weapons and ammunition, slung on bony shoulders or carried in our hands. We had been through bloody hell, and we looked the part.

Curtis Moore, one of our jeep drivers, remembered asking Private Joe Boriski, a member of my machine gun section, what it was like up there at the front. Boriski, who had spent most of his life digging bituminous hard coal in the deep mines of western Pennsylvania, was good at digging foxholes, and he was used to dirt. But at that moment, he could only shake his head. His hands were trembling and he couldn't speak. Sometimes enough is enough, and he had had enough. Joe Boriski's combat days were over. We never saw him again.

The chance to recuperate and regain our sanity came not a moment too soon. Platoons lined up to take showers and get a change of clean, reconditioned clothing. New weapons were available to anyone who requested them. As usual, I had a hard time finding a decent uniform that fit my large frame, but I didn't care. Mail was distributed and copies of *Stars and Stripes* were given out. Haircuts and shaves helped to change our appearance and morale. Smiles and silly banter returned.

The battalion settled into an assigned bivouac area, where we learned a hard lesson about digging in. All foot soldiers are taught to dig foxholes under any battlefield condition—static or fluid, temporary or permanent. It is smart to continue making improvements to the hole as long as the position is occupied. We dug machine gun, BAR, and mortar defensive positions around the forested perimeter. The rifle and machine gun squads dug two-man foxholes near the defensive gun positions. Pup tent half-shelters were pitched over each hole and camouflage material was finally added. But extreme weariness persuaded a few men to sleep first and dig foxholes second.

Late in the afternoon, a single ME-109 fighter plane flew over the battalion bivouac area. We were marching at close-order drill, because our leaders believed it best to keep us busy so we wouldn't lose our combat edge. The plane flew in low, just above the trees. Gunning its engine, the airman departed without strafing or dropping a bomb. It all happened so fast that we didn't have time to duck for cover.

After dark, Jerry returned to ruin our rest with barrage after barrage of accurate long-range artillery. Nineteen men from D Company became casualties and had to be evacuated. On day two, the regiment ordered a full schedule of training exercises: close-order drill, hedgerow tactics, weapons firing, and arms inspection. Every man in D Company began to grumble out loud, but at least we were still alive.

On July 25, Operation Cobra was launched west of Saint-Lô. This bold operation was designed to break out from the hedgerow tangles and help launch General George Patton's 3rd Army tanks into the plains toward Paris and the German border. The 116th, still in reserve, sat on a sunny hillside to watch the massive air strike. Reportedly one of the largest strategic air assaults in military history, it began with 550 fighter bombers flying over in military formation. If that wasn't enough, formations of 1,800 B-17s came next, unloading ton after ton of block-buster bombs on the shell-shocked German defenders.

We hooted and hollered as rockets and bombs descended, feeling very glad it wasn't happening to us. We had seen massive B-17 bomber formations before, but this one kept on coming, almost darkening the sky. First came the fighter-bombers, then the mediums, and finally wave after wave of B-17 heavies. It took over an hour and a half for all the aircraft to fly over.

We watched the bombers release their tons of ordnance, carpeting a seven-mile front. The ground underfoot shook, even at our distant position. As in any war, there were catastrophic miscalculations: 111 Americans were killed, including Chief of Army Ground Forces General Leslie McNair, and 490 more were wounded. But the crack German Panzer Lehr Division, the main defender of the Periers-Saint-Lô battlefront, fared much worse.

Over seven glorious days of rest and relaxation, the color in our faces slowly returned. Most good things must end, however, and this one ended abruptly. The news we didn't want to hear arrived like the shock of a thunderbolt, when Lieutenant Verne Morse, 1st Platoon leader, called the platoon noncoms together for the dreaded announcement.

It was a simple briefing: "Men," he said, "we're going back up. Assemble the platoon." Every one of us gulped. We all knew what he meant. "Make sure the four .30-caliber machine guns are in good working order, and that extra ammo, grenades, spare parts, bedrolls, rations, water, etc., are loaded on weapons carriers trailing the column. Any questions? OK, let's go!"

We broke camp and assembled at the road. Regimental Service Company furnished two-ton troop-carrying trucks to ferry us to the combat zone. Trucks, engines running, were already spaced in the required thirty-five-yard intervals.

Darkness was descending despite a partial moon that helped to illuminate the sky. Orders were given to "en-truck and no talking or smoking." A cigarette would help to ease frayed nerves, but a lighted match might prove fatal. Platoon officers made sure everyone was on board, and seated on fold-down wooden benches.

Signals were passed up to the lead vehicles that all was ready to move out. So far, no Jerry surveillance plane had spotted the convoy. Not a single whisper was uttered from anyone on our truck. Our adrenaline was now pumping overtime. "Please," we all were thinking, "let's get this thing over with."

Finally we inched forward, making sure to keep the interval. The rough road bounced us around for a short distance before we were let out. After orders to de-truck, we stood up and climbed out the rear. Words can't describe the feeling at that moment. We were going back to death, destruction, and fear. We were all painfully aware that many of us would soon be wounded, and others of us would soon be killed.

Chapter Ten

SHRAPNEL WOUND AT HILL 203

HOW THE ENEMY BECAME MY FRIEND

N o one had to tell us that we were now in the combat zone. In the distance ahead, the sharp flashes of light and sound of faraway thunder seemed like an approaching storm. But we all knew what it really was.

At the rest area, our weary and depleted ranks had been replenished somewhat by undertrained replacement soldiers, who brought the company's strength to about sixty percent of what it had been. Imagine you are a replacement soldier assigned to the 29th Division at the front. You are newly drafted and given six weeks of basic training. You probably are not given the chance to actually fire a weapon. After disembarking a troopship in England or France, you join other replacements. The group is assigned a package and loaded onto trucks. You are aware that you will replace a soldier who has been killed, wounded, or injured in battle.

Arriving at your destination after dark, you are assigned a platoon. You are scared to death, because you know that replacement casualties are extraordinarily high. All of this was easy to see on the faces of these new replacements. And even though we all faced the same possible fate, I felt sorry for them.

The night of July 25, as our weakened column shuffled by a large cow pasture used by XIX Corps heavy field artillery batteries, we saw several 155mm howitzers behind makeshift breastworks. The guns' short barrels were tilted up, sending death and destruction about three or four miles ahead, straight in the direction we were going.

This was the moment of truth. We were now within enemy artillery range. The late hour made our eyelids heavy, but jolts of adrenaline kept us alert. As our column trudged toward the thunder and light, the firing brought out a lot of bad nerves.

One of the recent replacements, walking a few feet ahead, began to utter strange phrases under his breath. He walked a few feet in silence, and then let out some more odd words. It was clear he was having trouble facing what lay ahead. He raised the volume a decibel for all to hear: "When it gets too tough for the men up front, it's getting just right for me! I can't wait to get a goddamned German sonofabitch in my [rifle] sight!"

I thought at first this fellow had gotten into some hard cider. There was an interval of silence, and then he upped the tempo and sobbed, "They march us to the front like prisoners! Why don't they just shoot us now and be done with it!" The poor fellow then fell into a heap on the dusty road. Lieutenant Morse ordered him loaded on the ammo jeep and evacuated. Before we had received one shot of angry fire, that soldier became a nonbattle casualty.

The reconditioned 116th Infantry Regiment was replacing elements of the 35th Division, whose ranks were as ragged and depleted as ours had been a few days earlier. The transition took place after midnight. The relieved were glad to see us but had nothing to say. One of them, when asked how bad it was, just shook his head, like Joe Boriski had. I knew exactly what he meant. We still

had to dig gun emplacements, work on our individual holes—
unless we could find one already dug—and then catch a nap before
the dreaded early-light attack order.

During the confusion of the transition, we were surprised by
two or three low-flying Jerry airplanes investigating the situation.
The sudden roar of twin-engine planes, flying just above the trees,
scared us out of our lethargy. The lead plane dispersed parachute
flares, turning darkness into daylight. I could plainly see the wing-
markings and the silhouette of a German JU-88 as it raked us with
.50-caliber machine gun fire, up and down the row, and plastered
the field with grenade sized antipersonnel bombs.

I will never forget it: *rat-tat-tat-tat-tat*, *rat-tat-tat-tat*, up and
down our hedgerow. Then, as suddenly as they appeared, they were
gone. The flares slowly burned out. I never knew if there were any
casualties from that surprise attack. All of this took no more than
ten or fifteen minutes, but it sure ruined our sleep.

The allied armies were slowly punching their way out of
hedgerow country and into the good tank flatland. But a formidable
obstacle loomed in the way before we could turn General George
Patton's 3rd Army loose. That obstacle was the hill-protected
medieval city of Vire.

Three prominent hills—code named Hills 203, 251, and 219—
overlook the city and the Vire River that runs through it. Hill 251
and Hill 203 controlled an important transportation hub and market center. The city was crucial militarily: five roads led in and out
of it, and the allies needed to control all of them.

The challenge would prove to be as difficult as the battle for
Saint-Lô. The 1st Battalion, 116th, would earn an Oak Leaf Cluster
to its Presidential Unit Citation, for taking the daunting Hill 203,
one of the three hills overlooking Vire.

It was Hill 203 where I also would be wounded.

On July 31, the 116th Infantry was ordered to attack Moyen, a
small town on the outskirts of Vire, important because of pockets of

German armor. All three battalions of the 116th jumped off at 5 a.m., August 1, with the 1st Battalion out front. The three battalions ran into strong resistance from tanks and self-propelled artillery of the German 2nd Panzers, but managed to push the panzers out of Moyen. The 1st Battalion next swung southeast toward Vire. The enemy held Hill 257, one of the dominant hills overlooking the approaches to the city.

On August 6, we got word that all five exits and approaches to the city were sealed. I heard that two of my buddies, Sergeants George Kobe and Randy Ginman, had been wounded and evacuated.

As the battalion approached Vire, we had to cross a wooded, lightly defended hill, designated as Hill 219. I remember seeing Captain George Boyd, ex-first sergeant of D Company. He now was leading H Company of the 2nd Battalion, smiling and saluting those of us he recognized. Everything seemed all right.

It was the lull before the storm.

1st Battalion's mission was to capture the heavily defended and strategically situated Hill 203. The Germans were well entrenched and had excellent observation from its heights. The constant artillery and mortar barrages made life miserable, both for those of us approaching and for the poor people who lived in the city. But we first had to neutralize the high ground before the city would be safe to occupy.

The 1st Battalion's mission was the most daunting of the three; the 2nd Battalion was to take Hill 251, and the 3rd to follow the 2nd, in echelon formation to the left rear. As we moved into the jump-off position, we immediately came under heavy artillery and mortar fire. Wounded men screamed for medics. The attack grew worse. More men screamed.

We crossed the initial point on time, only to discover a terrible obstacle. Down a hill, directly ahead, our platoon had to traverse a crossroad. Very accurate German artillery was zeroed in, and hitting near the center, right where we had to cross. We tried to estimate how long it took for Jerry to reload between salvos—a desperate gamble that several men would lose.

D Company was burdened with equipment and heavy weapons. Squad Leader Sergeant Cawley timed his sprint safely, but fifty yards on the other side he was hit by shrapnel to the thigh. I stopped to help him. His trouser leg was filling with blood. I cut his right pant leg away and used his belt for a tourniquet. A gaping hole had been torn in his right upper thigh. His face was ashen and twisted in pain. I knew that if I didn't quickly stop the bleeding he would go into shock. I plunged a syrette of morphine into his thigh above the tourniquet, then offered him a cigarette and a drink of water. He seemed to be stabilized, so I left him and ran toward the platoon to get help.

Mortars bombarded us from three sides as we followed a small, rocky stream that coursed down the steep hill. The forward slope of Hill 203 was straight ahead. When I finally caught up with the platoon, I was out of breath, and hurriedly told Staff Sergeant Robert Bixler, the other section leader, about Cawley's wound.

Still puffing from the run, I didn't hear the whispered warning of the 50mm mortar bomb until it was too late—*swish-sh-sh-sh!* Landing about eight feet behind me, it killed a man farther away and wounded Bob Bixler and me. I felt the red-hot fragment just over my right kidney. It didn't hurt right away, but I had a hard time standing. I called for a medic. The time was about 4 p.m.

My newly arrived platoon leader, Lieutenant Joe Barron, applied first aid and comfort before he had to move on. It was late afternoon and the battlefield was heading up the hill. Mortar shells continued to pummel the rocky slope, so I crawled over to the creek bed. Bixler was farther away and stayed where he had fallen, likely because he was hurt worse than I was.

I lay there for what seemed a long time. Just before dark, a medical   jeep, with two litters mounted on the hood, struggled to climb the rocky streambed.

One of the corpsmen yelled, "Anyone over there?"

I answered, "Yes, over here!"

The corpsman left the motor running as he came to help me. He cut my shirt off and changed the bloody bandage. I showed him where Bixler was lying. He and the other corpsman strapped me, and then Bixler, to the two stretchers affixed to the hood. A 90mm artillery round exploded forty yards away, and that quickened their pace. In reverse gear, the driver bolted down the rocky path. It was the roughest ride of my life, but neither Bixler nor I complained. Within forty-five minutes, we rolled into the newly erected 45th Evacuation Hospital.

Accessible to the fluid front lines, the facility was a makeshift tent hospital that prepared the newly wounded for the journey to a well-equipped general hospital in the British Isles. There was not enough room for all the wounded to be under shelter, so most of us lay in the open, on stretchers on the ground. Hundreds of moaning, groaning men were tended by doctors, nurses, and corpsmen in a scene reminiscent of the wounded in the movie *Gone with the Wind*. It was dark outside, and the light inside the operating tent was subdued. I wondered how long those doctors and nurses had been operating on patients and when their shift would end.

I was finally lifted into one of the operating tents. A nurse cut my filthy clothes off and scrubbed my back with antiseptic. A GI doctor placed a mask doused with ether over my nose and mouth. He told me to start counting backward, starting with one hundred. Instead of counting, I inhaled as deeply as I could. The tent spun around and around and around.

A few hours later I woke with a tremendous pain in my stomach and a very parched mouth. I asked the nurse for a tall glass of orange juice. She politely told me that I couldn't have anything to drink because there was a chance my stomach was punctured. Instead, she gave me a damp piece of gauze to suck on.

I was segregated to the abdominal ward, where many of the patients had colostomies and were much worse off than I was. My wound had come from a small piece of shrapnel just over the right side of my kidney. In order to find out how much damage was done, the surgeon had performed an exploratory operation, which made a four-inch incision just to the right of my navel. Abdominal cases were kept in the evacuation hospital for ten days before they were shipped off to England, so I lay there and waited.

In the adjoining bed was a thirty-six-year-old German prisoner, Fritz Reinhardt, who had a gunshot wound to his stomach. He had served on the Eastern Front before he was transferred to Normandy to bolster the Western Wall. Reinhardt was a very likable fellow, and the two of us learned to communicate, thanks to an army nurse who lent us a German-American dictionary. He told me he had been a noncombatant, an ambulance driver, who was wounded by an American at Vire. He had been transporting wounded Germans when a GI leveled his weapon.

I knew that the Geneva Convention forbids killing noncombatant medical personnel, so I asked him if he had been wearing the universally accepted Red Cross marking. He answered with much emotion, "Ja, ein grosses Rotes Kreuz!" using his hands to draw a cross that covered his entire body. German medics wore white smocks with large red crosses that covered their front as well as their back; their white helmets were also marked with red crosses. I had no answer for him on that one. It was a terrible shame.

Reinhardt told me he was married and was worried to death about his wife, who was living in Hamburg, where severe firebombing had destroyed much of the city. I don't remember if he said he had children. We both knew that his service was over, and we both hoped someday he would be reunited with his wife. We also knew that my service was *not* over, and that I would be going back to fighting his countrymen. We did have one thing in common. Fritz told me that he was not a Nazi, and he thought that Hitler was insane. I agreed with him on that.

It was a strange crossing of paths, because under different circumstances we might have been friends. Now that I am at the point where I am frequently interviewed about my military experience, I always try to mention both the German paratrooper I met at Couvains and Fritz Reinhardt, especially if I am speaking to the German media. I would love to know what happened to both of them, but to my regret, I have never received any news of either one.

CHAPTER ELEVEN

RECOVERY AND RETURN

REPLACEMENT DEPOT SYSTEM

I recuperated from surgery at an English hospital in August and September and part of October. Two days after arriving, I was up walking to the bathroom. A few days after that, the hospital staff had me doing light calisthenics and a regimen of physical therapy.

It is one thing to visit a wartime army hospital, but something quite different—and much worse—to be a patient in one.

Lawmakers would consider armed conflicts more carefully before rattling the proverbial saber, if they were forced to visit an amputee, abdominal, burn, or plastic surgery ward.

I recovered in a ward dedicated to abdominal wound patients. A bullet or piece of metal shrapnel puncturing the stomach can cause a lifetime of embarrassment and misery. The aftermath of a gut wound is either death or eternal marriage to a colostomy sack. The stench in that ward was predictable. It was tough to share quarters with seriously wounded patients. At night the moaning and groaning—and sometimes screaming—made it hard to sleep. Many of the men there died.

I remember one particularly sad loss. Swarthy Tony from Brooklyn was the third-floor clown. The shift nurses fell in love with him because he kept the ward laughing with his teasing and practical jokes. But one night his cherished laughter came to an awful end.

On a Saturday night, with a skeleton crew on duty, Tony began to complain of a sharp pain to the gut. A floor nurse was paged and, after several tries, she arrived. By that time Tony was screaming as two orderlies quickly wheeled him to the emergency room. Two hours later Tony was dead of gangrene poisoning.

Facial disfigurement was terrible and more devastating to the patient than any other kind of wound. A few men had lost arms or legs, either partly or completely, and as a result some of them became so-called basket cases. Even so, and it's sad to say, some severely maimed men were actually happy about their condition, because they were going home. Their combat days were over.

Soldier-patients thirsted for news of the war and events back home. Mail and packages from home were weeks and sometimes months late in getting to Great Britain or the front. We read stale news printed in *The Stars and Stripes*, the GI periodical, and old newspapers and magazines. The only way we found out about the 116th and D Company was from recently wounded 29ers at the hospital. We tried to follow the army's movements across France as it prepared to invade Germany.

The medical teams had perfected an efficient system after the wounds were treated and the rehabilitation begun. Within hours after the stitching and bandaging, we were up walking around. Some patients resisted the accelerated rehabilitation process, but they soon learned that they couldn't buck the system. Many were sent to frontline duty with wounds that clearly hadn't healed.

Army doctors worked tirelessly to rehabilitate the less seriously wounded in order to recycle them back to duty. As one of them, I wanted to return to my old unit instead of being sent to another infantry division. I often thought about my buddies, and wondered what had happened to them. I wondered how many of them had been hurt or killed, and how many were lying in hospitals like I was.

Weeks later—I found out on August 12—General Norman Cota, assistant 29th Division commander, left the 29th to become 28th Division commander. I also heard that the 29th Division on or about August 16 had been happy to say *au revoir* to the Normandy hedgerows. The proud Blue and Gray Division already had left more than a cemetery full of dead and several thousand wounded lying in French, English, and American hospitals, but this was only the beginning. Many gravediggers and medical personnel would stay busy for almost another year or so, as the official battle toll continued to mount.

I found out by the grapevine that the haggard 29ers were being sent to the Brittany Peninsula. Their mission was to capture the fortress seaport of Brest, France's second largest seaport. Brest harbored Germany's vaunted Atlantic U-boat fleet, which operated from concrete and steel submarine pens situated along the harbor. The 29th Division had a tough time dealing with the 2nd German Parachute Division, plus nearly fifty thousand other defenders at Brest, but the besieged enemy garrison finally surrendered on September 18. On September 24 and 25 the Blue and Gray, mission accomplished, motored to the war zone at the French-German border, which is where I joined them at Aachen.

After I was discharged from the hospital, life went into a steep decline. At that time, there existed a unique system of replacement centers to integrate onto the lines new arrivals from the United States and just-released combat veterans like myself from hospitals in France and Britain. Those of us who endured this ordeal will never forget it.

After we left the hospital, the route back to the front took us through the replacement center at Litchfield, England. This was our last stop before shipping across the Channel and back to

Germany. Our introduction to Litchfield consisted of a cold shower that shocked us into remembering what we had forgotten about real soldiering. We had heard about the center's commandant, the infamous Colonel Killian, long before we were subjected to his brutality. Killian treated all soldiers who passed through the depot, be they returning combat soldiers or convicted felons, identically—as animals.

Litchfield did indeed house a number of incorrigible American soldiers who had committed felonies and lesser crimes. There also were soldiers who refused to go back to frontline duty. Under Killian's command, the prison staff and guards treated all prisoners harshly: guards had orders to shoot any prisoner who even looked out the iron-barred window of his cell. This order was just one of the reasons that, after the war, Colonel Killian was arrested, court-martialed, and convicted. These were rumors I clearly could not substantiate. I did read about his court martial and conviction but not about details. I believe his name was Colonel John Killian.

Rehabilitated wounded veterans were integrated into their units at Southampton and Portsmouth with green troops arriving from the States. It was easy to spot the new arrivals because they were mostly lower-grade enlisted men. These replacement soldiers had new uniforms, shoes, haversacks, and helmets, and they carried pristine Garand M1 rifles. Because the seaport harbors were overextended, we transferred to landing craft from the troop transport. This time we descended with cargo nets; the channel was choppy as usual. In one horrible accident, one of the new arrivals lost his grip, fell from the net, and was crushed flat between the transport and the landing craft. Yet another soldier's mother would be sent the dreaded telegram that her son was KIA.

After crossing the channel to Le Havre, we were transferred to rail "40-and-8s" boxcars for the journey east. In use at least since World War I, the boxcars were so-called because they could hold forty men or eight horses. They were, however, loaded far beyond their capacity, with over forty men plus equipment squeezed into each boxcar. Straw was scattered on the floor for sleeping, but there was no room for anyone to stretch out. K-rations were again on the menu.

As we neared our destination, the hard life of combat, as we old-timers remembered it, was imminent. Memories flooded our brains: the thundering cacophony of artillery barrages, the screeching of incoming shells, the explosions and ground tremors, the sharp crack of enemy rifles, the pop and crack of bullets break-ing the air, the dreaded *brrr-brrr-brrr* of German machine guns. And the putrid smell of death. We all remembered.

As we neared the end of the line, most of us dreaded the reunion with danger. We were saying goodbye to sweet-smelling sheets, caring nurses, hot prepared food, warm showers, and clean clothes for goodness knew how long. It was time to focus on our mission while trying to stay alive, and sometimes the focus was blurred.

It was disheartening to be with young, undertrained men who didn't have the slightest notion of what they were in for. Some of them were eager to get into the fight and were actually looking for-ward to it. Most of them were scared to death. So was I.

Our narrow-gauge train huffed and puffed across the green French countryside, but the slightest grade was often too much for the heavy load. Sometimes the orders were passed back to us: "De-train! Help push!" All hands rolled out of the boxcar to help push the overloaded train over the grade. Once, while resting a few min-utes, we raided a boxcar at the siding loaded with cases of American chocolate (D-bars). Each of us liberated a few cases of the bitter-sweet Hershey bars. D-bars and cigarettes were excellent for barter-ing with French civilians. One bar was worth two hundred francs, about two dollars. American cigarettes were worth even more.

We spent one night at a tent camp replacement depot, or "repel-depel," in a wooded area near Rouen, the birthplace of Joan of Arc. I grabbed my mess kit and headed for evening chow. On the way, I passed an American prison compound with a twelve-foot-high barbed-wire enclosure around it. The GI-clad inmates were a rough-looking bunch, and I suspected most of them were likely felons.

As I walked by the enclosure someone yelled, "Hey, Slaughter!" I went over and was surprised to discover an ex-Company D private who had punched the late First Sergeant Obenshain in a dispute at Ivybridge. Obenshain had chastised him for a rule infraction and got a fist in the face. For this, the soldier was court-martialed and missed the invasion.

That day, as we talked through the barbed-wire, the private told me he had also been caught stealing GI gasoline and selling it on the black market. Then he asked me to help him break out of the compound so we could become rich together. I told him I had a better idea: that he come along with me and rejoin his buddies in D Company. He didn't answer me, but I'd be willing to bet he thought it sounded like a bad idea.

The rail tracks skirted the suburbs of Paris, but I would have to wait forty-one years for a good look at the beautiful French capital. No Eiffel Tower, no Notre Dame, no Arc de Triomphe—what we saw that day, from the open door of our crowded boxcar, were the ugly slums of Paris.

Despite their poverty, the people were happy. As we passed, the newly liberated French waved and threw kisses. We returned the favor. We threw D-bars and "calgume," or chewing gum, to the mademoiselles and children. If only for a moment, we were able to forget our destination and dreaded mission.

We finally arrived at the end of the line and transferred onto two-and-a-half-ton trucks for the last leg of the long journey. I found Company D and the 116th Infantry near the German border city of Aachen. The 1st Battalion was attached to the 30th Division, and its mission was to close the gap in the line and to link up with the 1st Division.

My combat reindoctrination at Wurselen was fierce. The Germans used their sixty-ton Tiger Royal tanks that fired 88mm missiles. It was house-to-house, street-to-street fighting. Banging and whamming, the artillery came from both sides, and squeaky-wheeled Tigers and Panthers rumbled down the narrow streets, firing into windows and doorways. We had no answer to those mammoth tanks—our hand-held antitank weapons were useless.

I remember seeing an elephant-sized tank that had free rein of the street, firing at will. We radioed Battalion Antitank Company for help. Three men rolled a 105mm howitzer into position and we watched it fire from thirty-five yards point-blank. The high-explosive shell did little damage to the turret, but it did disable the tank track. After dark, we heard tank-retrievers hooking up and pulling the Tiger away. Within hours, that menace was back in action, blasting our basement dwellings.

Aachen has been the site of many battles over the centuries. The great Siegfried Line, built to counter the French Maginot Line, was another obstacle we confronted, with its dragon-teeth antitank obstacles, and underground steel and concrete fortifications. Zigzag trenches connected to underground bunkers, barbed wire, mines, and booby-traps, all intended to stop an invading army. The plan's fatal flaw, though, was that all of its guns were in fixed emplacements facing west toward France. We merely flanked the positions or by-passed them. One night we slept in one of the impregnable undergrounds. A Jerry plane dropped a large high-explosive bomb on our boudoir, and it hardly interrupted our sleep.

Soon after, the November Offensive began.

The 1st Battalion, 116th, was bivouacked in woods waiting for orders to move back to the front lines to help launch the wintertime offensive to gain the Roer River, and then the Rhine. The weather had turned cold and the clouds hung low. We were assembled in a wooded area awaiting Major General Charles H. Gerhardt's memorable battle instructions.

General Gerhardt had joined the division while I was with the 29th Rangers in July 1943. He was a short, wiry, bald-headed man, who spoke in a high-pitched, staccato stream of words. Shortly after his first meeting in England with the senior division commanders, Gerhardt said to them, "A year from today one out of every three of you will be dead, and the toll will be higher if senior commanders don't know their stuff and get out of their chairs."

The general came to the 29th Division from the 91st Infantry Division, but his entire career had been with the horse cavalry. Like his father before him, he was a U.S. Military Academy graduate. A stickler for strict military discipline, Gerhardt caused the career of many 29th Division senior officers to come to a screeching halt. The least infraction of a rule, or the wrong answer to one of his questions, was enough to send a colonel or major packing.

One of the important standard operating procedures (SOPs) that every member of the 29th had to remember, word for word, was the correct rifle sight picture: "Top of the front sight in the center of the peep sight, bull's eye resting on top of the front sight." If you left out one word, you were wrong. Another SOP that had to be memorized precisely was the correct trigger squeeze: "With the second joint, finger well through the trigger guard and thumb alongside the stock." Another favorite was, "All 29th Division soldiers, officers and men, must keep their helmets buckled at all times." And, most of all, General Gerhardt brought to the division the battle cry, "29, let's go!"

The day the battalion was to receive the general's battalion orders, we assembled twenty minutes early in formation to await his arrival. Another of Gerhardt's edicts was: "Being on time is late. Fifteen minutes early is on time. Any time after on time is *not tolerated!*" The general sped into the assembly area fifteen minutes early and his jeep screeched to a halt. He invited the companies to come closer and sit on the ground. We were to leave our helmets on and, of course, our chin straps buckled.

He sprung onto the hood of his Jeep, which he had named "Vixon Tor" after one of the rock outcroppings on the southern English moors. His leap was as graceful as a ballet dancer's.

The former West Point quarterback began his speech by saying that we were entering the Huns' homeland and that the light could now be seen at the end of the tunnel. He cautioned that we could not ease up in any way and that we were not to show the bastards any mercy. Uncle Charlie was not a spellbinding orator, but he tended to stir the troops, especially the officers.

He continued his spiel with instructions on how important it was to take care of the equipment. The Browning Automatic Rifle (BAR) was heavy to carry and many soldiers found ways to ease the burden. Gerhardt said, while gesturing, "I've noticed that BAR men have removed the bipods from their rifles. Bipods are there for a purpose and I want them back on, understand?"

A proud rifleman from B Company raised his BAR over his head, showing the bipod clearly in place.

The excitable Gerhardt quickly answered, "Soldier, tell me, are you a private or private first class?"

The soldier reluctantly replied, "I'm just a private, Sir!"

General Gerhardt turned to B Company's commander and said, "Captain, promote that man to private first class and make sure the order is on my desk first thing tomorrow morning! Understand?"

Weeks later, the battalion had taken its objectives and had earned a well-deserved turn at regimental reserve. The general was in the area and was, again, addressing the battalion. Gerhardt snapped at the B Company commander: "Captain, I don't remember seeing the order to promote that private to private first class! What the hell is the reason for that?"

The captain snapped back, "General, Sir! The private was killed in that first day's battle!"

General Gerhardt turned to the captain and replied, "Very well, Sir, that's okay if he's dead! Mighty fine! Mighty fine! Carry on!"

This exchange gave us a good sense of the stuff that Gerhardt was made of.

Shortly thereafter, progress slowed quite a bit. We now were up against fanatic German defenders who knew the territory and took advantage of fighting from fortified bunkers, stone houses, factories, zigzag trenches, and even sports stadiums. German sappers laid thousands of antipersonnel mines.

As we crossed plowed or open fields, unsuspecting GIs stepped on or snagged trip-wires, springing dreadful Z mines. Tripping one of these "Bouncing Betties" caused it to spring waist-high and spray maiming shrapnel all over the upper torso.

Late one evening, while crossing a frozen beet field, I felt my clumsy boot snag on what I thought was a vine. I tried to kick though the snag, but instead unearthed a hidden Bouncing Betty Z mine. Thank goodness the explosive mechanism had frozen. If the mine had detonated, I would have surely been killed.

Fighting and dying in Germany was different than in the Normandy hedgerows. It was easier to fortify homes and industrial structures for comfort and protection than to dig foxholes along hedgerows. So that was how we spent the winter of 1944 to 1945—fortifying and fighting. Sometimes we fought from water-filled trenches the Germans had previously dug. Whenever possible, we slept in the basements of German row houses, where there was usually straw for bedding.

By late November, XIX Corp was fighting for the Ruhr Valley, Hitler's former industrial workshop. Factories and mines, now dormant, had once turned out hardware and fuel for the mighty Nazi war machine. The industrial revolution had transformed this once-lovely part of Germany into an ugly eyesore, especially in the winter. The landscape was marred by tall, sooty smokestacks, and heaps of coal, coke, and slag; the water and air had been fouled by the mining and steel industries. But the Third Reich needed the Ruhr, and so did we. The weather had deteriorated into a constant overcast, which produced a cold rain, and then mud. All of this hampered the effectiveness of the air force and the armor. But weather never stops the infantry.

CHAPTER TWELVE

A LONG WINTER INTO SPRING

GUARD DUTY AT THE FROZEN ROER RIVER

From November 1 to 18, 1944, the 116th was stationed in a rehabilitation area near Markstein-Hofstadt, Germany. We received refresher training in the fundamentals of river crossing, pillbox assault, tank-infantry-tank destroyer coordination, close-order drill, and the care and cleaning of equipment. For rest and rehabilitation, men were rotated for a few hours back to the regimental rest center at Sittard, Holland.

We slogged our way to our next location, where we occupied enemy-dug communication trenches. The zigzag trenches were about three feet deep with several inches of cold, muddy water in the bottom. Our defensive positions were silhouetted on a hill against the skyline, making it extremely dangerous for a soldier to raise his head out of the hole. There we stayed, pinned down in those muddy trenches from dawn till dusk, sitting on one ammunition box with our feet on another.

After dark on November 17, we moved off that precarious hill and waited for orders to move out. The immediate objective was down a tree-lined road that led into the German town of Setterich.

I was leading one of the machine gun sections in a ten-yard spaced column of twos. A hail of rifle bullets from the woods sent me to the ground. I dove headfirst into a muddy beet field, and ended up crawling behind a ten-inch-high mound of unharvested purple sugar beets. The rest of the column went into a shallow ditch on the other side of the road. I was left alone in the muddy field. (See map in Appendix IV, page 285.)

It was getting to be late afternoon, and I was afraid my platoon would leave me there. If I raised my head or made the slightest movement, a burp gun about twenty-five or thirty yards away sent a string of white tracers that popped and cracked around my head. Slowly scooping mud and dirt with my bare hands and fingernails, I managed to dig a shallow slit trench that gave me slight protection. I lay there praying for nightfall. About forty minutes later, it was dark enough for me to crawl out of that mud hole, shaken but grateful, and I got back with my unit.

The entrance to Setterich was well defended by some determined gray-coats with heavy and light machine guns, mortars, and rifles. The 1st Battalion's B Company, following orders to lead the attack across an open field leading into the outskirts of town, was caught in the field and suffered severe casualties. The attack stalled and the rifle company had to pull back and regroup.

Company B's commanding officer, Captain William B. Williams, ordered Platoon Sergeant Robert L. Sales to get ready to take out the German obstruction the next morning before first light. It was still pitch dark, but Jerry was able to light the sky with flaming parachute flares, which were shot into the air to pop open into daylight and gently float to the ground. That's exactly what happened when the groggy platoon of infantry tried to tiptoe across that wide-open field. Jerry opened up with his entire arsenal, killing ten more of Sales' platoon and wounding several others.

Three tanks from 2nd Armored supported the attack, but a hidden teller mine disabled one. Sergeant Sales pleaded for one of the tanks. He knew the position of a German MG42 that had done damage to his platoon, and he wanted to get it. At first he was refused, but finally he was given permission to use one of the tanks to help root out the machine gun.

Sales squeezed into the turret of the tank and was directing the tank's gunner, when suddenly, *ka-WHAM!* A high-explosive missile hit the turret of the Sherman and severely wounded Sales, blinding him in both eyes. He was quickly evacuated.

The next day, November 19, two battalions abreast—1st on the right, 2nd on the left—were ordered into Setterich. Bitter house-to-house fighting slowed the 1st, while the 2nd quickly advanced. With Company A leading the way, 1st Battalion joined 2nd Battalion east of town and buttoned up for the night. After a long night of fighting, the town of Setterich finally fell.

After Setterich was in Uncle Charlie's back pocket, the 116th's next objective was to clear the West Bank of the Roer River. We knew it would not be easy. The desperate Germans were fighting from predug trenches, factory buildings, sports arenas, swimming pools, and high rock walls. Thousands of mines and booby traps were set and ready for us.

November in Germany is always wet and cold, and 1944 was the wettest month in memory. A steady drizzle of foggy rain and heavy downpours turned the back roads and battlefields into quagmires. Antitank and doughboy-type defensive trench bottoms were filled with cold, muddy water.

I don't know if the miserable weather made us more cynical, but those of us willing to take foolish chances took unfair advantage of our newly won status. Looting for souvenirs had been forbidden and strictly enforced in France. Officers were supposed to enforce the no-loot edict. But even so, no one I knew thought stealing valuables from the enemy would be wrong or uncivilized.

Back in Normandy, or on any battlefield in history, it was legal to search and take from the enemy, dead or alive, anything of value: watches, rings, jewelry, money, food. If killed or captured, we could expect the same treatment from our adversaries—and sometimes from our comrades. Our own rear echelon medical personnel sometimes robbed wounded soldiers blind. American bodies were robbed on the battlefield. I once watched a ghoulish soldier bayonet-chop a dead man's finger to get his wedding band. Of course there were exceptions to the looting. But for the most part, few watches and rings were sent home or buried.

Things were taken from the homes and property of civilians, too. Early in the Rhineland campaign, any German civilians who were able to evacuate the danger zone did so. Whatever was left behind in their houses or barns was fair game for GI looters.

One day, an innovative and very hungry D Company cook spotted a grazing heifer behind a farmhouse. The brown-and-white yearling was roped and led into a farm outbuilding. Machine Gun Squad Leader Scott, a city boy, shot the animal between the eyes. As the .30-caliber rifle barked, the heifer's knees buckled. The calf lowered its head and staggered around the room, spraying sticky red goo over everything and everyone. Another shot from Scott's rifle sent all of us out the door and away from that bloody mess. The heifer again stumbled to its knees and continued to spray blood around the room. An ex-farmer boy roped the calf's hindquarters, and, with help, hoisted the four-hundred-pound animal over the transom.

He surgically cut the jugular vein with his sharp trench knife, which intensified the bloody shower around the room. The calf kicked and butted and bellowed. It became clear that we might have to settle for bland K-rations. Finally, after what seemed an eternity, the poor animal died.

When other members of the company saw the bloody men, they thought they had been wounded and screamed for the medics. But when the butchers explained what they had done, and when the kitchen grilled the juicy beefsteaks and fixed a side order of French fries, everyone forgot the mess. It was a rare wartime treat.

But, even in that little town, it was hard to forget reality for long. Nazi propaganda and inspirational slogans, such as "Heil Hitler" or "Alles fur Deutschland," were everywhere, painted on brick walls and buildings. Yet it was impossible to find a German civilian who admitted to being a Nazi or fan of Hitler. "Nicht Nazi! Nicht Nazi!" was the universal answer. Many civilians pointed fingers at houses across the street or explained that a neighborhood Nazi had just left town.

Most Germans respected authority and were eager to please. And, of course, their need for food and other amenities motivated them to cooperate with us. GIs often traded rations for favors of one sort or the other.

Soon afterward, the 1st and 2nd Battalions, 116th, were ordered by the high command to relocate in the vicinity of Baesweiler. Company A, with a section of D Company heavy machine guns and an 81mm mortar section, was ordered to Schleiden to occupy a defensive position in the 175th Infantry sector. Enemy counterattacks partly isolated Companies F and G. Company C was ordered to replace Company G in the line; the remainder of the 1st Battalion was alerted for possible action.

A force of fiftysome enemy infantrymen tried to infiltrate our lines in the sector occupied by Company K. But they were repulsed with an artillery barrage, leaving them with many casualties.

Then it was on to Koslar, a battle that was stubborn and costly. Many areas of the region were very well defended, and it took many days and many casualties to clear the West Bank of the Roer. Among the major obstructions were the Sportzplatz, Hasenfeld

Gut, and the Swimming Pool. The 116th finally wore the defenders down, and on November 28 Koslar capitulated.

A Norway Clipper blew nasty weather down to further harass the European battle zones, making life miserable for soldiers on both sides of the war. For weeks the Germans surreptitiously prepared for a major counterattack. By taking advantage of the foul weather that grounded the Allied air force, Germany assembled a formidable army of heavy artillery, armor, and well-equipped infantry.

As December 16 broke, a low fog bank and falling snow hid the beginning of the great German counteroffensive. Great panzer armies rolled through the deep Ardennes Forest in Belgium on their way to Antwerp. Hitler's winter offensive (forever called "the Battle of the Bulge") was a last-gasp effort for a lenient peace accord with the Allies. This effort diverted attention from the 29th Division sector and suspended the inevitable Roer River crossing.

The overextended 29th Division was left to defend the Roer River sector while other elements of XIX Corps repaired the Bulge. Five battalions of the 29th Division had the task of defending twelve miles along the Roer River's western front.

After the all-night stint of outpost duty, we lived in relative comfort during the daylight hours in the basements of riverfront homes. We kept busy by making improvements to our machine gun defensive positions. The heavy guns were positioned so they could fire from ground floor windows. We cleared trees and other obstructions from the fields of fire, set antipersonnel mines to prevent infiltration, and laid barbed wire in the no man's land.

In the beginning, we coexisted with the enemy across the river in a live-and-let-live arrangement. As we approached the Christmas season, after dark Jerry entertained us by singing Christmas carols to the accompaniment of an off-key piano. We didn't share the same Christmas spirit. We rudely retaliated with Yuletide mortar rounds at the direction of the singing. Jerry would then reply with mortars and artillery. We finally decided, unanimously, that his singing wasn't all that bad and stopped shelling the chorus.

At times, the watch on the Roer was entertaining. One afternoon a large, fully antlered stag gracefully bounded between the American and German outpost lines. Jerry was the first to see the deer and fired at him. Our side also began to shoot.

The agility and grace of the stag's reaction was amazing. I loosened the swivel on one of the machine guns and began traversing, firing freely at the quick-moving target. Both sides then began to fire everything in our two arsenals. I am happy to report that the deer ran through that hail of gunfire unscathed. The final score: deer, a perfect 10, Yanks and Jerry, 0.

Most of the German civilians, if they were able, had evacuated the war zone. However, rather than sleeping upstairs in their beds, we preferred the safety of dank basements, where we slept on heaps of dirty straw.

One night, I shared my bed of straw with an unwelcome stranger. I was comfortable and almost asleep when I felt something move under my right shoulder. I was tired and I thought whatever was there would go away. But the visitor made itself at home by crawling over me. I jumped to my feet and lit a kerosene lantern. Lo and behold, there looking me in the eye was the biggest black rat I had ever seen in my life. He was seeking the warmth of my body, and I didn't have it to give.

"*Enough is enough,*" I thought. I grabbed my blankets, moved to the second floor of the house, pulled off my filthy clothes, and climbed into a nice, soft German bed. It felt great to lie down in a real bed, and that night I didn't even care that it was dangerous. Jerry threw a few mortar shells, but I ignored them and slept like a baby.

Outpost guard duty was a dreaded chore that befell us too often. Changing of the guard had to be performed after dark. We

almost tiptoed as we made the rounds patrolling or traveling to outpost duty. The single-cart dirt path was under German surveillance
during daylight and was zeroed-in night and day. Intermittent mortar and artillery rounds kept us alert as we traveled the road. It was
never safe to use the path, even at night. We were told, emphatically, that when a Very light pistol shot was fired, we were to freeze
in our tracks. We did as we were told.

On November 26, our side began experimenting with antiaircraft searchlights as antipersonnel weapons. These powerful sixty-
inch, 800-million candlepower units were trained directly at the
Germans' position, blinding them. They were also used to good
advantage to reveal the nocturnal movements of enemy troops.

The outpost line, sometimes called the listening post, had to be
manned day and night. By continually improving these important
positions, we made them more comfortable and less vulnerable to
attack. We stockpiled ammo, food, and drink so that, if we were cut
off, we might survive until help came. There were too many casualties, but nothing like Normandy. The weather was raw and uncomfortable, but it was December in northern Germany, and we
expected it.

I spent my third Christmas overseas in Germany's Roer River
Valley. As Christmas drew near, the 29th Division Headquarters
was making plans for a proper turkey feast for the troops. Before
and after the holiday, 29th soldiers were rotated from frontline duty
over two or three days. It was a welcome Christmas present.

A strange and foolish thing happened that Christmas, though,
and it could have been a disaster. One very cold afternoon, 1st
Battalion was trucked a couple of miles behind our post at the front.
Two or three inches of fresh snow lay on the ground. D Company
de-trucked in a sparsely wooded area about five miles behind the
frontline. The kitchen trucks were already in place and the cooks
were ready to serve up the food. There was also alcohol: Uncle
Charlie found out IX Army had liberated a gin distillery at

Steinhagen, and he made sure we had an ample supply of schnapps and gin to complement our feast.

The Christmas dinner was served buffet-style, which in the army means one big pile of food. Two thick slices of turkey, topped with a heaping spoonful of mashed potatoes and giblet gravy, peas on top of that, candied yams on top of that, and a slice of pumpkin pie thrown on top of the whole mess. Each soldier then got a bottle of German schnapps and a bottle of Steinhagen gin—a big mistake. I sat on a tree stump and ate my pile of Christmas dinner. After eating, we all popped the corks and took big slugs of schnapps and chased it with gin. It didn't take long for the liquor to do what it does to most people.

In fifteen minutes most of D Company was staggering around, firing weapons in the air: fifty or so uncontrollable drunks shooting tracer bullets. I have to wonder what Uncle Charlie was thinking by giving liquor to armed and worn-out soldiers. Maybe he thought we were mature enough to handle it. If so, he was wrong.

To make matters worse, the Luftwaffe chose to spoil our Christmas party. When the JU-88s came in, I was leaning against a tree stump, vomiting my head off, too sick to take cover. A squad of Hitler Youth with baseball bats could have whipped our butts. Luckily, the attack only scared us. No one was hurt, unless you count all the bad hangovers the next day. I always wondered if General Gerhardt found out about the drunken Christmas party and, if so, who was blamed.

During this time, the Ninth Army provided rest areas in Holland for war-weary combat troops. The towns of Heerlen and Maastricht were equipped to give exhausted soldiers warm showers, hot food, a change of clothes, and two hours to buy souvenirs to mail home. The whole thing lasted about four wonderful hours.

I was among the lucky guys chosen for one of these 240-minute vacations. My group was lined up and loaded onto a two-and-a-half-ton truck headed the short distance to Maastricht. We de-trucked at an obsolete manufacturing facility that had been converted into a rest center. The hot showers were unforgettable. I can't describe how wonderful the warm, soapy water felt running over my filthy, tired body.

After drying off, we selected clothes from tables of reconditioned, second-hand—but clean!—woolens. We could also choose underwear, socks, and shoes if we needed them. It was like being let loose in an army department store, and everything was free. The clothes, the showers, the food, and the whole break made a noticeable positive difference in everyone's morale. When I returned to duty, I felt as if I really had been on a vacation.

From January 1 to 31, 1945, the 116th was still located along the West Bank of the Roer River. The 116th relieved the 2nd Armored Division, and it had two battalions up and one battalion in reserve. As the New Year began, materials furnished by the 29th Division's 121st Engineers bolstered the regiment's defensive positions. Laying barbed wire, booby traps, and mines as well as clearing fields of fire helped to fortify our defenses along the Roer. On February 3, my 20th birthday, the 116th Infantry Regiment celebrated the fourth anniversary of its induction into federal service. In celebration, the regiment fired every weapon at its disposal for fifteen minutes, right at noon, at all suspected enemy targets.

Three days later, the 29th crossed the Roer River and attacked Julich. The operation was originally scheduled for January 10, but the Germans had opened the floodgates upstream and flooded the riverbanks, which meant we had to wait. After a thirteen-day delay, the 175th Infantry smashed across the river at 4:45 a.m. and hit relatively light resistance.

The 3rd Battalion, 116th, was attached to the 175th and in reserve. Its mission was to mop up after the initial assault. K Company was ordered to attack the citadel, an ancient, thick-walled, moated fortress. The streets of Julich had to be cleared of debris in order for the armor to support the attack on the citadel fort. With the aid of 155mm self-propelled guns, the citadel fell to the onslaught of the task force. It was a meaningful triumph, symbolic of the ultimate Allied victory over Hitler's strongest citadels.

The large Nazi flag that flew over the citadel was captured and is now residing in Bedford, Virginia, at the archives of the National D-Day Memorial.

The 29th Division's whirlwind offensive eastward and northward across the Cologne Plain was brought to a highly successful conclusion on March 1. Assault units of the 116th, cooperating with the 175th Infantry in what was widely considered a superbly coordinated attack, wrested the great industrial community of Munchen-Gladbach from enemy hands. This was the largest and richest city within the bounds of Germany proper that had not yet been struck by Allied troops.

I remember the ease with which we captured Giesenkirchen and Holz, and then it was village after village. We were moving so fast that the German merchants were still conducting business, and customers were in the stores and on the streets when we arrived. Nobody had had time to leave. Five or six men in my section ordered a meal from the menu at a fancy restaurant. We also were given shaves and haircuts, a welcome perk of victory.

My section and I also became very wealthy for a short time. In Holz, a city between the Roer and Rhine Rivers, we entered town unannounced late one morning while the townspeople were bustling at market and conducting business in the street. Jerry had fled ahead of us, and we had not been contested at all since Julich. The people of Holz were surprised and frightened to see armed Americans in their uncontested town. There was no war damage as far as I could see.

We passed a small savings and loan bank with its doors open for business. A couple of tellers were at their stations, and one or two customers were inside as well. I couldn't believe that the safe's door was wide open; neat stacks of brand-new reichsmarks sat in plain view.

We didn't hesitate. After all, this was war, and we were the victors. While members of the section waved their M1s in the air, each of us traded our haversack contents for stacks of new reichsmarks. I wasn't sure that the thirty-five or forty pounds of paper money in my haversack was worth anything. Even so, I had a guilty feeling stealing it.

I carried my "guilt-pack" for a few days until we were fired upon by an enemy ambush. I was so laden with reichsmarks that it was hard for me to find cover fast enough. I realized that staying alive was better than being a wealthy corpse. I searched for someone to give my thousands of reichsmark notes to, and found an elderly couple that I thought could use the money. They seemed surprised and happy to get it.

I had never thought to send some of the money home, as other members of the section had. And for some reason I didn't keep one reichsmark note, not even for a souvenir. After the war, as I struggled to make a living, more than once I asked myself, "Couldn't I have kept just a few hundred dollars' worth of notes?" But I consoled myself by thinking that I made that one old couple very wealthy very fast.

On March 31, at 3:30 a.m., the 116th formed a combat team and moved to the area of Bruckhausen. The team consisted of Company B, 121st Engineer Battalion; 111th Field Artillery Battalion; Company B, 104th Medical Battalion; Company B, 554th Antiaircraft Artillery Weapons Battalion; and 29th Infantry Special Troops. A vehicle accident that injured eighteen enlisted men slowed our movement across the Rhine, but we made it.

The dangerous phase of the war was not quite over for the 116th Infantry. The regiment was reinforced with attachments from 121st Engineers; 898th Field Artillery, 275th Engineers; Company B, 747th Tank Destroyers; Company B, 821st Tank Destroyers. With

Company B and a platoon of Company D, 747th Tanks, the regiment prepared to attack across the Dortmund-Ems Canal.

On April 4, after a thirty-minute artillery barrage, the 1st Battalion, 116th, jumped off at 1 a.m. The 2nd Battalion was on the left. The sides of the canal were perpendicular and thirty feet high, and it was about thirty-five yards wide. The water was partly drained but still about three feet deep, making it necessary to use scaling ladders for crossing the canal. Three feet of muddy water was no obstacle for the infantrymen, but wading the frigid water was damned uncomfortable. German artillerymen and mortar crews had the crossing sites zeroed in.

The 1st Battalion encountered resistance and ran short of ammunition. A supply was flown by Piper Cub plane, and the attack continued. Company B passed through Company A and advanced seven thousand yards. But one thing made this attack noteworthy: we took many enemy prisoners. The stiff enemy backbone we had seen earlier was beginning to bend.

CHAPTER THIRTEEN

MY WAR ENDS

IT AIN'T OVER WHEN IT'S OVER

On April 7, the 116th Infantry Regiment was assigned occupation duty in the vicinity of Walstedde. Our mission was to process thousands of liberated Allied prisoners of war and displaced persons. We were also given orders to control the potentially volatile civilian population. This included surveying civilians, house to house.

I rapped loudly at the front door of a middle-class home in Walstedde. An aristocratic-looking young man, about thirteen years old, answered. He was dressed in short pants with knee socks and a fancy starched shirt and bill cap. I could tell he despised the "inferior" American GI.

Jokingly, I said that my men and I were looking for Herr Adolf Hitler and that when we found him, we would hang him from the nearest lamppost.

I will never forget the *Jugend's* emotional reply in perfect English: "No, no," he shook his head, gesturing emphatically with his hands, "That will never be! *HE IS OUR FÜHRER!*" I found the incident amusing, but it also showed me just how deeply the Nazi movement had penetrated German society.

On March 31 and April 1, the 29th Division had crossed the Rhine River on engineer-constructed bridges. I worried that crossing the Rhine would be another Omaha Beach bloodbath, but it turned out to be uneventful. The 29th was now attached to the 75th Division, with the mission to clean up the collapsing Ruhr pocket. The Germans had established an outpost line in defense of Dortmund, and the 75th was preparing to attack in their direction, in an operation that involved crossing the Dortmund-Ems Canal. Two other canals bound the 116th zone of attack. The Lippe Canal, the main obstacle for the infantry, also presented major problems for vehicles.

Enemy resistance was sporadic but disconcerting. We had to reckon with civilian Nazi sympathizers and pockets of organized resistance. And no one wanted to be the last fatality of the war.

Infantry soldiers have to deal with all kinds of obstacles, often while under fire. All the bridges across the Lippe were blown, so we had to use scaling ladders to cross. Platoon Leader Lieutenant Gerald Orgler was with my section when a half dozen accurate mortar rounds scattered those of us trapped between the thirty-foot walls of the canal.

I heard someone scream, "I'm hit!" It was Private First Class J. T. Hendrix from Valley, Alabama, a big, 180-pound machine gunner in 2nd Squad. Hendrix, I knew, was nearest to an explosion that had bounced off the wall of the waterway. Shrapnel had torn part of his foot away, causing a nasty, bloody wound. There was three feet of filthy water in the canal, which would guarantee infection, so he was given first aid immediately.

Lieutenant Orgler was about twenty pounds lighter than Hendrix, but he threw the gunner over his shoulder like a sack of flour. I would never have believed that the 160-pound officer could carry Hendrix up that thirty-foot-high wall. I tried to help, but Orgler told me he could handle him. And he did. Luckily, Orgler's quick action and the first aid that followed stopped the hemorrhaging.

In a desperate move to slow the Allied advance, the German army converted all antiaircraft artillery and barrage balloon battalions to infantry. These secondary troops leveled their dual-purpose 20-, 40-, and 88mms at us. The results were mixed, depending on the gunners' level of training and dedication.

We received sporadic rifle fire from community-dug trenches, but received only occasional organized resistance. The *Volkstrum* (Home Guard) proved ineffective, since they had few good weapons and, more importantly, they were reluctant to tangle with the Allied juggernaut. This was proven in the town of Erkenschwick, where the fanatical Nazi Burgermeister (Mayor) and his assistant had ordered their citizens to defend the town to the last man. Both of them were summarily executed by the townspeople.

German forced-labor personnel were of little value in spotting enemy military installations, but many of them volunteered to assist with Allied road and bridge maintenance work. Division engineers took advantage of idle Russian, Polish, French, and Belgian displaced persons and put them to work.

Company D was relegated to motorized patrol duty with orders to make contact with the fading enemy. Four men were assigned to each jeep. Heavy .30-caliber machine guns were mounted on swivels and manned by sergeant section or squad leaders.

Two riflemen rode in back, assigned to watch the rear and flanks. Eight vehicles kept a twenty-five- to thirty-yard interval. I was in the second jeep from the front, and Private First Class McAdoo Potter, from Kentucky, was the driver. Lieutenant Verne Morse, from Pennsylvania, was in charge of the eight-vehicle patrol, and a three-man crew was in the lead jeep.

Our task force had been patrolling for hours on dirt and secondary roads and had seen no sign of the enemy. Traveling the back woods of a mostly uninhabited rural area, we became tired and lethargic after many hours of monotonous miles.

Then, as we topped a rise, all hell broke loose.

A torrent of machine gun tracer bullets sprayed the patrol. Enemy machine guns, rifles, and burp guns sent what seemed like a zillion tracers popping and cracking around our heads. One of them hit and killed Private First Class Emmett Journell, from Salem, Virginia, a D-Day veteran and friend. The rest of us were extremely lucky.

I don't know how they missed hitting us all. Potter, my driver, showed unusual driving skill. He hit the brakes, bringing the jeep to a screeching halt. Then he threw the vehicle into reverse, and we fishtailed back over the slight knoll. We quickly dismantled our machine gun from the swivel to the tripod and went into action. Lieutenant Morse radioed for help. By the time it arrived, the ambush party had dissolved into thin air.

That was our last combat of World War II. My friend Emmett Journell was the last D Company man to die in combat. He had joined the Virginia National Guard from Salem, Virginia, endured all our harsh training, survived the assault on Omaha Beach, and made it through the hedgerows of Normandy. But an ambush by second-rate soldiers stopped him, just two weeks before the end of the war. His English fiancée later gave birth to a child that would never see its father.

As we continued our patrols and other assignments, evidence all around us testified to the end of the war. Sad-looking, unescorted German soldiers, hands over their heads, limped slowly to the rear, and for many of them, to a better situation at a POW stockade. On occasion we heard the sound of distant artillery or small-arms fire. But mostly what we saw was an entire nation in defeat.

White flags made of bed sheets hung from windows, and the main roads were jammed with displaced civilians. Entire army units surrendered en masse, and many individual soldiers simply shed their gray uniforms and changed to civilian garb. The German army boots they wore revealed their true status, but it didn't matter. These ex-soldiers had already given up the war. Like us, they just wanted to go home.

Later, as we marched to the bivouac area, someone lobbed a smoke grenade into the area. A soldier up in the front of the column yelled, "Gas! Gas!" Our gas masks were packed away on company trucks a mile or so away. We didn't care. We were so war-weary we didn't give the nonlethal smoke grenade a second thought.

Hours after the false alarm, a weapons-carrier sped toward us, wildly honking its horn. "The war's over! The war's over! The war's over!" the driver gloriously shouted. Even before this pronouncement, it was clear to us all that the war was ending, but they still were good words to hear.

Although the war was over, there was danger everywhere. Mines, booby-traps, unexploded bombs, artillery shells, and even enemy souvenir weapons were hazardous leftovers. Some of us became careless, and let our guard down.

My turn at carelessness nearly cost me.

One day, a stunning blond fräulein bicycled over to where I was standing, and after our clumsy attempt at conversation, she invited me home for dinner. I was pleased to accept the offer. We were bivouacked about a mile away from where she lived with her mother.

Their house was extraordinarily comfortable, and I could tell the family had been prominent and wealthy. When I asked the young lady about her family, I learned that her father, who was absent, was a prominent physician and had once headed a hospital in occupied France.

I kept wondering why she had chosen me to be invited for dinner, and I also thought it strange that she insisted I bring my rifle along. I soon found out why.

About midmeal as we sat around the dinner table—*mutter, fräulein,* and me—there was a pounding at the front door. *Mutter,* visibly shaken, exclaimed, "Ruskies! Ruskies!"

I grabbed my M1, removed the safety, and casually stepped outside to the front porch. There stood ten or twelve armed Russian soldiers, either escaped or displaced POWs. Camped in the nearby woods, they were living off the land. They had come to the house looking for anything of value, I supposed, but mostly in need of food.

I knew my life was on the line, and I was scared. I ordered them to leave. I held tight to my rifle, ready to shoot the first person who raised his gun. They left without saying a word.

When I went back inside, I was a big hero to the German family. But I felt ashamed. Here I was, dining with prominent Nazis and I had taken their side against ragged, hungry Allied comrades. I should have insisted the Russians be fed.

Early in May, the 29th Division moved up to the spring-swollen Elbe River. Previously, the Pottsdam Big Three—President Roosevelt, Prime Minister Churchill, and Marshal Stalin—had agreed the Allies would halt at the west bank of the Elbe river. The Soviet Union was given sovereignty over the German capital, Berlin, and all territory east of the Elbe. Politically, this treaty was a mistake that would cause a half-century of Cold War tension between the Soviet Bloc and NATO Allies. At the time, I was only happy that the 29th Division didn't have to storm Berlin, and inevitably, be awarded the thousands of Purple Hearts.

About this time, it occurred to me that I had failed to get a substantial souvenir out of the war. The ultimate trophy, in my opinion, was a 9mm German Luger pistol. Among the thousands of prisoners thronging to the rear, surely one of them had a Luger that rightfully belonged to me. Soon, I would find it.

The 116th Infantry was hunkered down along the west bank of the Elbe awaiting the arrival of the Soviets. Thousands of displaced civilians and ragged German military were desperate to surrender to the Americans rather than to the Russians. Many of them died trying to cross the swollen river in homemade rafts and leaky rowboats—and some even tried to swim.

At one point, I was scanning the riverbank near an artillery observation post, using powerful artillery binoculars. I spotted a lone German climbing a steep path partly hidden by tall reeds. I asked one of the 2nd Section to cover me while I intercepted him. I followed the contour of the riverbank and waited for the soldier to come to me.

The soldier looked very tired and disheveled. He was wearing a civilian raincoat but I could see army boots and gray army trousers beneath the coat. "*Kamerad!*" he pleaded, then dropped his satchel and raised his hands. The second thing he said, shaking his head, was "*Fuss kaput!*"—My feet are killing me!

I relieved him of the satchel. Inside was a brand-new Luger, a Belgian .765mm pistol, a roll of explosive material, and a pair of great-looking binoculars. I gave the binoculars and the smaller pistol to members of the section, and kept the Luger.

Early afternoon, volleys of gunfire could be heard from across the river. Ivan announced his arrival by firing small arms tracer bullets skyward. He then began to torch every flammable dwelling on the eastern bank of the Elbe River. I worried the Ruskies would keep coming: shooting, burning, and looting.

At first light the next morning, the first wave of Soviet soldiers began to show up. We had been through hell, but these folks looked worse. Next to the Germans, I have never seen an army so used up. There were female infantry who looked like they could hold their own with any man. All of them were filthy and ragged. Their eyes were hollow, their hair was straggly, and their teeth were bad. This army looked like it operated on one hundred-proof vodka.

They tried to communicate as we exchanged gifts of chocolate, cigarettes, and vodka. A Russian noncom offered a drink of his vodka, and in exchange I gave him a pack of my Chesterfields. The soldier seemed pleased and gave me a wide-grin smile, showing very bad teeth.

As a friendly gesture, I found a bar of pink scented soap that my mother had just sent from home. Ivan smelled the soap and gave another wide grin. I turned the bottle of vodka up to show friendship. When I lowered the bottle, Ivan had taken a big bite out of that sweet-smelling soap. "NO! NO!" I screamed—but it was too late. He spit out the bite, and gave me another big grin.

Soon, hundreds of Russians, those who could find boats, began to arrive on our shore. They were worn out and edgy, and the more they drank their vodka, the more they fired their weapons into the air. They needed to boost their morale in some way. They still had to take Berlin.

But our war was over.

Right away, the army was anxious to rotate surplus soldiers back to the United States. They used a point system to discharge us fairly. It took 85 or more points to be considered for the first rotation. Luckily for me, I had 135 points, one of the highest in D Company. Captain Murphy announced that I would be leaving immediately, and told me to turn in my weapons and all the equipment I didn't need for the journey home. I turned in everything but my watch. I had carried that watch through hell and high water, and I thought I deserved to keep it. I quickly packed and hopped into a waiting jeep.

As the driver was about to leave, Supply Sergeant Eugene "Jack" Martin, from Richmond, ran out of the supply tent.

"Slaughter! Slaughter!" he screamed. "I've got to have that watch!"

I was stunned. The watch was a cheap Elgin GI timepiece with an OD canvas strap and it already had seen its best days. But I still wanted it to keep.

"This is *my* watch!" I said.

But Martin insisted, so I gave him the damned thing.

Looking back on it now, I guess it didn't really matter. Time changed for me at that moment, and my life would never be the same.

I lived through eleven months of pure hell.

I was at that day and time just twenty years old.

I left the company without saying goodbye to anyone.

My war was over!

The 29th were seated nearby.

EPILOGUE

I stood there speechless and awestruck, my throat tight, my heart pounding. Next to me was a Medal of Honor winner, the president of the United States, numerous United States senators and congressmen, the Virginia governor, Virginia state legislators, and other dignitaries of every description and importance. There were the secretary of the army, generals and colonels, D-Day veterans and others who had fought in World War II and later wars. And there were young adults, and school children—all together, over twenty thousand people gathered from near and far.

It was June 6, 2001. The place was Bedford, Virginia, the occasion, the unveiling of the National D-Day Memorial. This was the D-Day celebration I and so many others had dreamed about and worked so long to achieve. Before my eyes, the fruit of our labor rose up: the elegant architectural carpet of multicolored granite; the Overlord Arch representing victory, forty-four and one-half feet high; the twelve colorful flags symbolizing the victorious Allied nations; the bronze plaques for every military unit that contributed to the Allied victory; and the plaques depicting the name of every soldier, sailor, airman, and marine who died on June 6, 1944, a day that changed the course of world history.

I turned my eyes to the figurative, heroic-size bronze statuary representing the men who had valiantly stormed the beaches. Warmed and glowing in the late spring sun, their bodies and faces looked so real, I could almost hear them breathe. The men they represented had waited all too long for public recognition for their sacrifice. I was painfully aware that the overwhelming majority had been cut down in their youth. Twenty had come from my hometown of Roanoke just thirty miles away; nineteen had come from Bedford, which lost more of its sons per capita on D-Day than anywhere else.

Bedford was thus the perfect site for the National D-Day Memorial, a $25 million venture to rival any war memorial anywhere else in the world. Its unveiling was a swirl of excitement—rousing tunes by a military band, liturgies, speeches, smiles, backslaps and handshakes. And yet, as I watched the military flyover from Langley Air Force Base, as the naval chorus from Washington broke into song, a sense of peace came over me. At long last, the armed forces of D-Day, their families, and their friends could take comfort that their fallen sons and comrades were receiving the honor they deserved. The long march had come full circle.

The last leg of the journey, the building of the memorial, had begun as a concept in 1987. It was a pie-in-the-sky dream I could not shake. It was a dumb idea many of my D Company cohorts couldn't or wouldn't embrace. Their stance continued into the 1990s. "Hell, we've had three wars since then," some of them said. "Forget the damned thing! Bury it!"

I couldn't understand their logic. Or perhaps I should say I no longer could accept it. As the philosopher George Santayana wrote, "Those who cannot remember the past are condemned to repeat it."

EPILOGUE

And yet I, too, had long been one of the silent. On July 13, 1945, I was suddenly separated from the service, discharged at Fort Meade, Maryland, with a few dollars in my pocket and the khaki uniform on my back. I was suffering mental as well as physical wounds, but there was no one to counsel me. I was a civilian again, but I was not comfortable socializing with other civilians. I was twenty years old, with an eleventh-grade education and no skills other than soldiering. I was left alone to find my way home to Roanoke, Virginia.

In my mind, I never left the army, but I had to get on with my life. In this, I was luckier than many of my comrades, for I met a wonderful young woman, Margaret Leftwich, who agreed to become my wife. In 1947, we settled down to raise a family in Roanoke, where I worked for the *Roanoke Times & World News.*

Without Margaret's love and understanding, and the stability of family life, I dread to think what I might have become. There was no treatment for "post traumatic stress syndrome." It was simply called "battle fatigue." Those of us who had returned from the war were left to tough out what it meant to have survived.

The years rolled by, our hair grayed and thinned, waistlines grew, and many of our Company D associates developed health problems. Our generation smoked cigarettes and drank hard liquor. Many of our men who had hiked halfway around the world became sedentary. We didn't like to exercise. We traveled to the beach or went to swimming pools, thinking that sunshine was good for the skin. Many were disabled by wounds, drank and smoked too much, and died prematurely. The war still took its toll, long after it was over.

Rarely did anyone talk about the war. The media were silent, our children were uninterested, and we ourselves sought to forget. Some of my buddies did join veterans' associations—the American Legion, Veterans of Foreign Wars, Disabled American Veterans, and the 29th Division Association—but I was not among them, although I was often invited to join. And yet, whenever one of my D Company buddies called on the phone, or came through Roanoke, I was always glad to see him. Reunions were not discussed.

One of these buddies was George Kobe, another survivor of the D-Day landings, and a very special friend, despite the fact that he had been a mortar man and I a machine gunner. During the war, the big blond and I always looked for each other during breaks in the action. It was like looking for your brother to see if he was all right. Both of us were promoted to staff sergeant during the bitter fighting at Saint-Lô. Later, George was seriously wounded on Hill 203 overlooking Vire, which left him with a permanent disability. I had other friends, but in combat situations, George Kobe had always been different.

I have George to thank for my first change of heart toward the idea of reunions. The first, informal D Company gathering took place in 1950, largely to please him. The big Polack missed his old army buddies, so he and his wife took off on a road trip to half a dozen states. Along the way, they spent a couple days in Roanoke with Margaret and me, and while they were here, I assembled the Roanoke D Company bunch for a night on the town.

George was a prolific letter writer, and he kept in touch with most of his beloved mortar men. On rare occasions he called me on the phone, but his multipaged letters came every other day. Over time, he decided to get D Company organized. He was joined in this project by Vic Crimone, a former first sergeant, who had copies of the company roster. The two of them set about to update every soldier's home address, city, and state.

Our first official reunion took place in Roanoke on Memorial Day weekend, 1982. George selected the site because most of D Company had been formed in Roanoke back in National Guard days, and the city was centrally located on the

East Coast. George took the role of West Coast chairman and overall honcho. When he enticed me to be the East Coast chairman, how could I possibly refuse?

Like many other D Company men, I was close to retirement. Our children had left home and I began to think about reestablishing old friendships. I found myself becoming interested in writing my remembrances for my children and grandchildren. Many of my former comrades were ill, and our memories had turned fuzzy. Getting together might help all of us to remember all of those names and places from the 1940s.

And so it was that I got involved. I printed up the first D Company newsletter, advertising the reunion: "Have you considered the possibility that the men you will be united with in Roanoke on Memorial Day weekend are the only people on Earth qualified to share the good and the bad times we experienced more than a quarter-century ago?" I wrote. "Make plans now and I will see you there. *29, Let's Go!*"

Since our coffers were zilch, I booked the Thrifty Inn on Peters Creek Road in Roanoke. Thirty seven former soldiers with fourteen wives came along for the first-ever reunion, hailing from eleven states and the District of Columbia. We were off to a great start. The next year, we were overflowing when fifty former machine gunners and mortar men returned to the Thrifty Inn.

George did a bang-up job that year, moving Company D up into the major leagues. He produced a twelve-page brochure that would have made a journeyman printer proud, and paid all of the costs out of his own pocket. There was one stipulation George always insisted upon: "Nothing is too good for 'the D Company Champs.'" His pension was modest, and he lived frugally all year long so he could spend lavishly on his D Company buddies. We accused him of having a money tree in his back yard.

These company reunions were the first step in the last long leg of the journey of remembrance. Even now, over twenty years later, the exuberance of this beginning, and its positive effects on Company D survivors come through loud and clear in the write-up that followed our 1983 reunion:

> The years melted like hot butter when we mustered for our second D Company Reunion. The talk centered on Fort Meade, Carolina Maneuvers, Jolly Ole England, the moors, Captain Schilling, "Blue Bill," Ivybridge, London and eight-day passes, 25-mile hikes, Spam, Ed Walton, "Slim" Callahan, "Fats" Williams, "Ajax" Bowling, air raids on Plymouth, Stonehenge, Weymouth, Duck Problems, the real McCoy, Jack Simms who ate two dozen bananas in order to weigh enough to join the army, and then paid the supreme sacrifice on D-Day, Lieutenant Verne Morse, Vierville-sur-Mer, Grandcamp-les-Baines, Couvains, Saint-Lô, Vire, Jack Ingram, Brest, "Razz" Jones, Stanley Koryciak, Romeo Bily, James Wright, Lieutenant Merle Cummings, submarine pens, George Johnson, a glimpse of Gay Paree, Belgium, Holland, closing the Aachen Gap, Wurselen, November Offensive, Lieutenant William Gardner, John Dylik, Tony Carusotto, Koslar, Julich, Lieutenant Vincent Labowicz, Munchen-Gladbach, "won't this damn war ever end!" K-rations, burp guns, Lieutenant Wallace Riddick, 88s, Tiger Royals, the rest areas and the quick reunions to see who is still with us, how much longer can the luck hold, the lucky ones who got wounded (not the bad ones) and sent home, on and

on . . . lie . . . lie . . . and more lies, laughs, tears,
vows to return to Roanoke and the third reunion of
Company D, 116th Infantry, 29th Division.

But although we were meeting and talking among ourselves, D-Day was fading from public memory. Those of us who remembered our buddies who had died storming Omaha Beach were not prepared to allow that to happen.

The year of our third reunion, 1984, was the fortieth anniversary of D-Day. This nice, round number presented a significant opportunity to jolt public memory and recall the events of the war, and particularly the sacrifice of so many men from my local area. Company A of the 116th Infantry, originally part of the Virginia National Guard, had been formed in the 1930s at the Bedford Courthouse Armory. On D-Day, the company landed on the Dog Green Sector of Omaha Beach in the first wave: ninety-one men were killed, and most of the others were wounded, many severely. It was reported that when the sun set at the end of that momentous day, only fifteen A Company soldiers were left to fight.

Since I worked for a newspaper, *The Roanoke Times & World News,* I was in a position to remind the editors that the D-Day anniversary was imminent. I asked the executive editor what he planned to do. "Nothing," he said. "There is no demand for that."

"Really?" I thought. Roanoke lost twenty men that day, and Bedford lost nineteen, and many other men from the region were permanently maimed. Company A of the 116th Infantry, which hit Omaha Beach first, sustained some of the highest casualties. And what about their families? Weren't they part of the casualty statistics?

My efforts at the newspaper failed that year, for these imploring arguments fell on deaf ears. Meanwhile, those few 29ers who could afford it made plans to revisit the beaches and cemeteries in Normandy, where President Ronald Reagan would speak in honor of the fortieth anniversary of the invasion. This was the first return to France for the vast majority of veterans on the trip. Many were overwhelmed as they stood on Omaha Beach. Feelings of terror, grief, and horror mingled with amazement at what they had accomplished and their own gratitude at being alive. This occasion, too, was an important step, both in public recognition and private remembrance.

Those of us who could not make the trip were invited to Washington, D.C., to attend the reorganization of the 29th Division into a "light infantry" division. The new 29th contained highly mobile combat and combat support units. These consisted of the 116th Infantry Brigade, based in Staunton, Virginia; and Maryland's 58th Infantry Brigade, based outside of Baltimore. Both were Army National Guard existing commands.

With help from Milton L. Aliff, a retired army lieutenant colonel, former H Company Supply Sergeant Harry Richardson organized a bus convoy to the nation's capital for former 29th Division combat veterans and their wives. Off we went, expenses paid, for a day of ceremony. Virginia state police escorted the two buses into Lafayette Park, where military bands, marching units, color guards, and reviewing stands were reserved for us. Someone said that there were more generals and colonels assembled at the ceremony than at any other time in recent history.

D-Day veterans were recognized by Secretary of Defense Caspar Weinberger, who announced the 29th (Light) reactivation, and shook each veteran's hand. Afterward, we were feted at a northern Virginia restaurant, and we watched a training film depicting the role of the 29th Division on D-Day. The Maryland adjutant general, Brigadier General James F. Fretterd, spoke briefly about D-Day and history. Photographs were taken of everyone before we departed for our respective hometowns.

To my knowledge, this ceremony in 1984 was the first time that an important government official individually honored D-Day veterans. Most of us appreciated the recognition. Our government acknowledged the survivors, and we remembered the dead. But what about the larger American public?

In 1987, I retired from the newspaper, and wondered what I would do with the rest of my life. I was in good health and did not wish to play golf or go fishing every day. It was clear to me that the signal event of my life, the largest air, land, and sea battle in history, had been all but forgotten by everyone except those who participated in it. Schools skimmed over World War II and D-Day. Students were left ignorant of how and why the United States became a world power and the leader of the Free World.

Then a minor miracle occurred: on December 4, 1987, a former Roanoke journalist reawakened the local public to D-Day. A story written by feature writer Brian O'Neill appeared in *The Roanoke Times & World News*. The article suggested that D-Day veterans deserved a permanent acknowledgment of the unique contribution that Virginia made on D-Day. Another newspaper employee, Steve Stinson, added a crucial suggestion: "It would make a fascinating exhibit," he said. "We're talking film clips, live remembrances . . . a statue, too." This article was the germ of an idea that evolved into the $25 million D-Day Memorial in Bedford, inaugurated in 2001 by President George W. Bush.

After the article appeared, I asked my friend Milton Aliff what he thought of a D-Day exhibit at the Roanoke Valley History Museum. Milton had served on the committee for the recently unveiled Roanoke War Memorial. He suggested the head of the committee should be William B. Bagbey, a retired navy commander, who had just completed a stint as chairman of the board of the History Museum, and who knew many old-line Roanokers. Bagbey's former father-in-law, the late C. Francis Cocke, had been appointed in 1942 to head the local World War II Memorial Committee. Its mission, to build a suitable memorial to the men and women who had lost their lives during the war, had unfortunately never been realized.

This modest D-Day exhibit was the next step in public recognition. The museum's executive director, Ms. Mitchell Bowden, said if the exhibit drew enough visitors it might stand for six months. We began the arduous task of raising funds from downtown business friends; in the end, $7,000—almost half of the needed funds—was donated by a philanthropic friend and history buff.

All this while, the idea of a statue had never left my mind. I envisioned it at the time as a modest, life-size soldier with a replica 29th Division patch on his left shoulder, standing guard somewhere downtown. Commander Bagbey and others insisted that D-Day was much too important, and that we should plan a more robust memorial.

Again we went to work, forming a committee to make the memorial become a reality, with Commander Bagbey as chairman of the board. We needed enthusiasm, funding, and some very good people. Anyone willing to serve was considered. A request was presented to Roanoke City Council that Mill Mountain, a scenic mountain owned by and contained within the city, be considered as the memorial site. After a year of wrangling, a special committee appointed by the city rejected the idea. By 1993, we still had no memorial, and figured the idea was DOA—dead on arrival. Then, again, a miracle happened.

June 6, 1994, was the fiftieth anniversary of D-Day. Public acknowledgement still was weak, but with a half-century now gone by, the Department of Defense had decided on a "last" great commemoration for D-Day veterans. Many veterans and officials would be gathering in Normandy for the anniversary. I, for one, wanted to be there. The 29th Division Association assembled 150 veterans and their families—ten busloads—to make the trip to France.

The most important event of the trip for me, and for the future of the D-Day Memorial, turned out to be a forty-five-minute stroll that I took with President Clinton on Omaha Beach. I had received a phone call from the White House, informing me that I had been selected to represent the 29th Division as one of three escorts for the president at Omaha Beach. Also selected were Captain Joe Dawson, who led G Company, 116th Infantry, 1st Division, ashore in the first wave; and Staff Sergeant Walter Ehlers, 18th Infantry, also of the "Big Red One." Ehlers, a Medal of Honor recipient, lost a brother on D-Day, and later received a battlefield commission. Dawson, who introduced President Clinton at the main ceremony, was awarded the Distinguished Service Cross.

How did they choose me? Ken Ringle, feature writer for *The Washington Post*, had written a story that someone at the White House undoubtedly had read. That story included an interview with me, and it caused my phone to start ringing. Calls from old army buddies, long-lost friends, and relatives soon were followed by reporters from newspapers, television stations, and magazines from around the country and even from abroad. Suddenly, everyone seemed to be interested: reporters from the *Los Angeles Times*, *USA Today*, *People*, *U.S. News and World Report*, *Newsweek*, the *Discovery Channel*, ABC, NBC, CBS, CNN, *Ouest France News*, and *Paris Match* magazine, to name a few.

We arrived in Paris on June 1, and were bused to the Ibis Hotel Normandy in Saint-Lô. While I was unpacking my things, some-one paged me. Brent Blakely of the White House staff had left a message for me to call ASAP. Donald M. McKee, the 29th Association national commander, Colonel Alvin Ungerleider, D-Day veteran of the 115th Infantry, and I were to meet at the Colleville Cemetery at 7:30 p.m. for a D-Day ceremony rehearsal. National Commander McKee was selected to greet the president at the helicopter pad, and Colonel Ungerleider was to help the president lay a wreath.

We arrived at the cemetery to find Colonel James R. Chambless in charge of military protocol. He was well organized, with plenty of help. The colonel acted the part of the president; after a few dry runs, we performed a dress rehearsal. It was approaching 11 p.m., and all of us were hungry and tired. All downtown and hotel restaurants were closed. Our dinner that evening was stale, leftover bar peanuts.

At 9 a.m., June 6, the big day, the White House driver met us at the hotel, precisely on time. The preliminary ceremony was not until 2:30 p.m., so why did we need such an early start? We soon found out.

The driver's instructions were to proceed through Bayeux. Our military vehicle immediately ran into gridlock traffic, and encountered many checkpoints. We sat for over half an hour while a vehicle in front of us received a security clearance. McKee had a Michelin road map and ordered the driver to turn around. By traveling the back roads, we arrived at the cemetery with time to spare.

About 2:15 p.m., we vacated the hospitality tent. Our names were printed on the backs of metal chairs in the front row. The preliminary portion of the program began with soothing band music. It was cold, windy, cloudy, and threatening rain. The front-row seats across the aisle were reserved for the official presidential party.

The master of ceremonies was Walter Cronkite, who began by describing to the hushed throng how he flew over the fleet in an American bomber early on D-Day. Following remarks were made by Chairman of the Joint Chiefs of Staff Army General John M. Shalikashveli and Captain Joe Dawson, who then introduced President Clinton.

The president's message was a stirring tribute to all D-Day veterans. "On these beaches the forces of freedom turned the tide of the twentieth century," he said. "Let us not forget when they were young, these men saved the world!"

After the speeches, the president's handlers whisked Dawson, Ehlers, and me to the path leading to the steep steps down to Omaha Beach. Clinton began to exit, shaking hands with the front row veterans and those bold enough to reach over the front row for a touch and a handshake. First Lady Hillary Rodham Clinton was the first to reach the three escorts. She shook hands and thanked each of us for serving our country. She said to me, "Thank you so much for what you did." I replied, "Thank you, Mrs. Clinton, for coming."

Brent Blakely reminded me that I was to walk on the president's right, Dawson on the left, and Ehlers to the left of Dawson. When the path narrowed at the steps, I was to step back and let Ehlers move to the president's right. While walking, we were to talk about our respective roles on D-Day. Brent introduced each of us to the president.

Clinton led the entourage of handlers and Secret Service. Shaking my hand, he looked into my eyes and said, "Thank you for what you did." I replied, "Thank you, Sir." He moved to the others, shaking hands and thanking them as well. Then each of us assumed our assigned positions, walking slowly down the path.

Secret Service and TV cameras were hidden along the pathway. Every blind bend in the path was covered by the Secret Service, and by newspaper and TV cameramen. *CNN* and *The New York Times* were conspicuously present. We were informed that other television cameras were aimed from a small ship in the channel.

After descending the steps, I assumed my original position to the right of Mr. Clinton. He grabbed me by my elbow to steady me along the uneven path to the sand. At the edge of the sand, there were beach shingles laid out to read, "OMAHA BEACH 1994." Major General Matthew A. Zimmerman, chief of army Chaplains, concluded the walk with a prayer.

As we walked across the loose sand to the waiting Humvees, Mr. Clinton held my left shoulder for a moment and removed a shoe, shook sand from it, then did the same with the other. Captain Dawson pointed up the hill, to where he and his rifle company were the first to penetrate the enemy defenses.

Arrangements had been made to transport us back to the cemetery separately. As Brad directed us to our respective vehicles,

President Clinton said he would ride with us. He leaped into the back of the Humvee, and sat on the railing of the vehicle. The president instructed me to ride up front with the driver. The driver, a staff sergeant, said, "Will you be all right, Sir?" The president replied, "Go ahead. I'm okay."

It was a very bumpy ride plowing over the loose sand and rough shingle. We followed the Colleville Exit Draw road, which was the route the "Big Red One" had opened up for traffic fifty years before. Halfway up, a formation of army troops were standing at attention. An officer ordered, "Present Arms!" The president saluted from the back of the truck.

He then jumped over the railing and into the formation of eager, smiling soldiers. He moved easily from one trooper to the other, shaking hands and asking questions: "Where are you from? Do you like the army?" He obviously made a big hit, and seemed to be enjoying himself. We left him talking to his men and women in uniform.

All of us had postceremony media appointments. I am not sure who all spoke with Joe and Walter; Don had an interview with CNN's Larry King; Al with CBS; and I with CNN's Frank Sesno and CBS' Dan Rather. All of the networks were situated in temporary broadcast booths overlooking the 9,387 white crosses and white stars at the American Cemetery. Dan Rather and I had a casual interview as we slowly walked through the immaculate cemetery, between the crosses and stars.

I can only hope that the fiftieth anniversary of D-Day meant half as much to President Bill Clinton as it did to Walter Ehlers, Joe Dawson, all the other D-Day veterans, and me. That unforgettable stroll down the beach with two bona fide World War II heroes and the most powerful leader on earth changed me forever, and will always remain a highlight of my life. The walk brought back chilling memories of 1944 that will never go away. All the attention focused on the anniversary also gave me hope that others might finally be willing to remember as well.

EPILOGUE

Five months later, on a happy November 11, 1994, Veterans' Day, that hope came true. On this date we officially announced that Bedford, Virginia, would be the site of the proposed D-Day Memorial. Although we had feared the project was DOA, we had never given up trying, and the preceding months had been full of activity aimed at funding and securing a site.

During the bleak, uneventful years of struggle, three of our board members had died. Others had quit in frustration. I, too, became very tired and considered quitting. And yet, as time went by, our generation's veterans also began to incite new interest, especially in the public school system. Demand was rising for classroom visits and talks about the causes and the possible prevention of another world war.

I did not quit the board, but carried on with a handful of other dedicated individuals. Finally, we had our breakthrough. We had heard that the Bedford City Council might offer a memorial site with amenities within the city limits. Then a letter from Bedford Mayor Michael Shelton and Bedford County Commissioner Lucille Boggess stated their interest in the project. Mrs. Boggess had two brothers killed on D-Day, and she was especially eager to have the memorial located in Bedford. Mayor Shelton had received permission from the Bedford City Council to persuade the D-Day Memorial Foundation to move its operation to Bedford.

The package of incentives included a quiet twenty-acre hill that overlooked the city and the scenic Blue Ridge Mountains. The view featured the stunningly picturesque Peaks of Otter eleven miles distant. A pot sweetener worth $250,000 was offered, giving free use of city utilities, security, and limited upkeep. Accepting the offer was a no-brainer.

This was not a step, but a giant leap forward toward the construction of a permanent national D-Day memorial. The offer enticed Roanoke City Engineer Richard B. Burrow to accept the important executive director job. Another indispensable professional was a (then) little-known Roanoke architectural firm, Byron R. Dickson & Associates. General William B. Rosson, whose four stars added unbelievable prestige to the venture, was a jewel of a find. Not only did he help tremendously with fundraising, keeping an eye on what was promised and seeing that the promises were kept, it was he and Byron Dickson who suggested the height of the monument be raised to forty-four feet, six inches—6/6/44.

The project took work and a lot of money. We met with many influential people, driving to Richmond to speak to the Virginia General Assembly and to Washington to meet with our legislators. We also spoke to students, church groups, the DAR, Ruritans, Rotary, Lions, and Kiwanis—anyone who would listen, and many folks who would not. At times, I thought we would have to give up, and I did, indeed, come close to doing so. But in the end, the cause prevailed. On June 6, 2001, as the monument was unveiled and my heart swelled with emotion, I knew it had all been worth it, and far more. The symbolism of the monument and all it conveyed struck me anew with gratitude and awe—gratitude to the thousands who gave their lives on D-Day, and awe at their towering achievement.

Nearly three years later, as the sixtieth anniversary of D-Day was approaching, I received an invitation to participate in a documentary to be aired regionally on ABC and over most of Europe on June 6, 2004. I again packed my bags for the trip to the battlefields of France. This trip, however, was a joy ride compared to some other journeys I had made abroad.

The big Boeing 777 eased down on the runway at Charles de Gaulle Airport in Paris, at 11:35 a.m. France Channel 2 Public Television had scheduled for me to be the principle interviewee. Eric Ellena of French Connection Films, the producer, director, and overall manager, had arranged for (government-owned) Channel 2 to underwrite the expenses for my nine-day trip. He and his crew were attempting to capture on

206

film the effects of D-Day and the war on my life. I didn't sleep a wink the entire flight over.

How can I ever possibly describe the excitement and emotion of that whirlwind experience? That night, the elegant Paris Four Seasons Hotel offered free lodging, meals, and full amenities to D-Day veterans; at 6 p.m., Eric escorted me to the hotel conference room, which was arranged for interviews with each of the many journalists from radio, television, and the printed press. The regional director of the Four Seasons opened the event with a champagne toast. Waiters hovered, serving wine, hors d'oeuvres, and more champagne. As far as I know, I was the only American and D-Day veteran. The number of interviewers was unexpected, but I tried to answer all their questions.

And this was just the beginning. The next day, Eric took me to the American Omaha Beach Cemetery at Colleville-sur-Mer, where journalists from *Cityzen TV* and *Ouest France News* fixed a microphone on my jacket and followed as we walked between the white marble crosses and stars, musing about D-Day. Afterward, at Omaha Beach, we met journalists from *La Voix du Nord* and *Midi Libre* newspapers. Later still, we drove to Cherbourg, to be present when the mayor unveiled an art museum. At the reception, German D-Day veteran Franz Gockel and I were interviewed by many reporters. As a nineteen year old, Gockel had been a machine gunner defending Omaha Beach. A Cherbourg hotel provided free accommodations, and I went to bed early for a change.

The following days featured visits to Saint-Lô; La Madeleine Chapel, a medieval stone sanctuary donated to the 29th and 35th Infantry Divisions; and Couvains, where Ray Moon of the 115th Infantry Regiment joined the party and helped retrace the steps made a few days after D-Day. We parked the cars and began a hike down a sunken road that brought back dark memories of 1944.

Doctor Claude Paris, our host in Couvains, was the son of the wartime mayor of the village. He wanted me to find the wagon path that led to the partially demolished church. I believe we found the spot where I gave first aid to the wounded German paratrooper. The sunken road with the opening where the German paratrooper lay, and the church steeple, now restored, were just as I remembered them. A local print photographer and reporter were on hand to record the occasion. Afterward, Claude invited us to his home in Saint-Lô for drinks and more talk.

On June 5, at St. Jean de Savigny, 29th Division veterans and friends gathered at a Wall of Remembrance ceremony; and then came the trek to Ste.-Mère-Eglise and the program sponsored by Channel 2, with Michel Drucker as moderator. The town was swarming with mobs of red bereted airborne veterans, reenactors, and history buffs from all over Europe, Canada, and the United States.

I again was interviewed with Franz Gockel, German veteran of Omaha Beach. Drucker, speaking for the audience, wanted to know if former enemies could now become friends. Both of us said we could. The program was broadcast live for ten hours in France, and shown in 205 countries around the world. Outside the Ste.-Mère-Eglise church, nearly four thousand spectators watched the event on a giant television screen.

The biggest day of all, June 6, began very early for us. Because of the large crowds expected, the tight security, and the congested drive from Saint-Lô to Colleville, we were advised to leave Saint-Lô at 6 a.m. I caught one of the 29th Division buses to Colleville, where I was escorted to the VIP section, in the third row, near the presidential podium. The first two rows were reserved for the presidential and White House dignitaries. Roanokers Hugh Wills of the 30th Division and Allen Levin and Chuck Neighbor of the 29th were seated nearby.

On the backs of the special reserved chairs in front of me, I read many important names: Secretary of State General Colin Powell, Presidential Advisor Condoleezza Rice, Chairman of the Joint Chiefs of Staff General Richard Myers, a four-star marine general, First Lady Laura Bush, Presidential Adviser Karen Hughes and her husband, director Steven Spielberg, and actor Tom Hanks, among others.

These luminaries drew applause as they were escorted to their seats some thirty minutes early. Then two identical helicopters appeared, hovering behind us: a roar of applause preceded President George W. Bush and French President Jacques Chirac, who were escorted by bodyguards to their seats on the stage.

The program was extremely moving. It included the rendering of honors, an invocation, the laying of memorial wreaths, a salute to the fallen, speeches by Presidents Bush and Chirac, a benediction, the national anthem, and a fly-over. There were many weeping eyes, but despite the sadness, we all were proud and glad to be there.

The next ceremony took place at the Vierville Draw on Omaha Beach, where the 116th had been so badly mauled on D-Day. About two hundred members of the 29th Division assembled under the canvas of a large tent, erected as shelter from the intense rays of the afternoon sun. American dignitaries in attendance included Maryland Governor and Mrs. Robert L. Ehrlich Jr.; Lieutenant General H. Steven Blum, head of the National Guard Bureau; and Major General Daniel Long, 29th Division (L) commanding officer. I was one of the speakers, but in my haste to catch the 6 a.m. bus, I had left the paper with my speech at Saint-Lô.

To make matters worse, I had just paused for a quick pit stop at the Omaha Beach Hotel, when someone came running: "Slaughter, they're waiting for you!" I raced the one hundred yards up the exit draw road to the tent, and had to wing it from there. I think I did all right. My words were sincere and truthful, and I hope they honored the mixed emotions that most of us there were feeling.

The rest of the trip continued apace, as lower Normandy, always warm toward American veterans, outdid itself in generous hospitality, copious food and wine, awards, speeches, and lavish entertainment. One of the most touching moments of the entire tour was an *au revoir* awards ceremony in Saint-Lô. Again, in accordance with tradition, a Saint-Lô child led each veteran of the 29th as we walked, holding hands, down the main street. It was a memorable moment, made all the more so by the children whose forebears we may have saved during that terrible time in the past.

The townspeople cheered and clapped as they crowded sidewalks and windows along the way. I walked hand-in-hand with Dr. Paris's grandson, Clement Bossard, right behind the leader of the parade. Someone in the crowd had given me a souvenir cap from Saint-Lô, so Clement was sporting my 29th Division Association cap.

I felt proud and very moved by the ceremony, as surely the Normans did themselves. I think I can speak for all the veterans in attendance, when I say we came home to America fully satisfied. The sacrifices we had made in 1944 and 1945 were remembered and truly appreciated by the people we had come to free.

I began the long march as an adventurous schoolboy, just turned sixteen. I suppose I was looking for some dramatic juvenile excitement. If that was the case, I found plenty of it as a United States Army foot soldier. Fifty-two months later, I returned to my home a bewildered and disillusioned twenty-year-old man. I have often wondered what happened to my laid-back, carefree youth—those irreplaceable teen years that come only once in a person's lifetime.

On my return, I accepted a much less dramatic lifestyle. I got married, raised two sons, and went to work for a midsized newspaper in a midsized community. I found time to acquire a modicum of education, coached Little League baseball, and was grateful to live a normal American life.

Too many of my army buddies failed to reach their 25th birthday, and many of those who did were never the same. After what they had been through, they couldn't adjust to the real world. Many of them fell prey to alcohol, loose women, radical religion, or isolation—anything to help them get through each day, month, and year. Seven of our D Company men committed suicide. Compared to those and thousands more, I have been blessed.

In some ways, writing this book, a process that has taken me almost fifteen years, has been the last leg of the journey. I realize that I speak for many who never had the chance to speak for themselves, and I have done my best to pay them tribute. My hope is that this memoir, in however small a way, will perpetuate their memory and stand as a witness to their sacrifices. It saddens and worries me that so much of the world, including America itself, refuses to learn the hard lessons of the past.

Now that I am in my eighties, I am well aware that the long march that began so many years ago is about to come to a halt. I am proud to say my generation helped save the world from tyranny, prevent the extinction of an entire group of people, and preserve the democratic freedoms of our wonderful American way of life. I wouldn't change a thing, except to wish that my dear army buddies could be here to see and touch the magnificent National D-Day Memorial that was built for us all.

EYEWITNESS ACCOUNTS OF OMAHA BEACH, 29TH INFANTRY DIVISION

PRIVATE HAROLD BAUMGARTEN
COMPANY B, 116TH INFANTRY

Private Harold Baumgarten, from New York City, was a rifleman in B Company, 116th Infantry. After being discharged from the army, he attended medical school and became a physician. Doctor Baumgarten is now retired in Jacksonville Beach, Florida. Following are his edited memoirs of D-Day.

Clarius Riggs (Company B, KIA) was hit in front of me as he exited the boat. As I ran through the water carrying my M1 rifle at port arms, a bullet hit the receiver plate. I was able to fire one shot and the stock broke in half. I threw the thing away. Private Nicholas S. Kafkalis (B Company, KIA) picked it up and handed it back to me.

He thought I was giving up. Bullets ripped through my field jacket and one glanced off my helmet. I left my assault jacket on the

LCA. As we worked our way to the sand, I noticed three amphibious tanks, and two of them were knocked out. Many of the Company A soldiers were hanging on to the tanks, one of which was firing its 75mm gun into the pillbox over to the right of Dog Green sector. The bunker, nevertheless, kept on firing at us.

When I reached the sea wall, blood was gushing from my left cheek. My gums were lying on my tongue. I met Private First Class Dominic Surro (B Company, KIA), who then was unhurt. He was a rather large kid from Georgia. He and I were the same age of nineteen. He tried to help me, but we were under intense fire from the same pillbox, which was over to the right.

Private Robert L. Ditmar (B Company, KIA) was hit in the chest and soon died. Bullets were ricocheting off the ground and there was the scary whining of 88mm artillery shells coming in, and then exploding nearby. Staff Sergeant Clarence E. "Pilgrim" Roberson (B Company, KIA) was over to my left and behind me. He was shot in the forehead and was helmetless. He was also down on his knees as if in prayer.

Twenty yards to the left front, I saw Private Bedford Hoback (Company A, KIA). *(His brother, Technical Sergeant Raymond Hoback, was listed as MIA [missing in action]. It was reported that Raymond was wounded near the water's edge. As the tide rushed in, it washed Raymond's body out to sea. His Bible was all that was ever found. Both Hoback brothers were from Bedford, Virginia's, Company A. J.R.S.)*

As I crawled toward the sea wall, I saw Staff Sergeant Elmore Wright, Private First Class Frank Muzzo, Private Richard C. Brandtonies (all from A Company and all dead). Lieutenant Donaldson (B Company, KIA) was not with us. I didn't see him after the landing.

I picked up another M1 rifle and followed Surro, who was moving left toward the Vierville Draw. We were seeking safety from the deadly pillbox over to the right. I then found my best buddy, Private First Class Robert L. Garbett (B Company, of Newport

News, Virginia, KIA), lying facedown and dead. Men from Company A, Private First Class Harold Webber (KIA, company scout) and some fellows named Gilbert E. Pittenger (WIA)), Herbert Kaufman (WIA), and Private First Class Donald J. Szymczak (WIA) were at the sea wall. We could see two more amphibious tanks that were knocked out.

I got up to cross the road above the wall and the beach, when Pittenger tackled me and probably saved my life. Just as I started to run across the road, a hail of bullets cracked overhead, barely missing me. I helped Sergeant Frazier (A Company, of Orange, Virginia), who was wounded and paralyzed, to get behind the wall. That is the last I saw of him.

A mortar shell exploded; three pieces got me in the left side of the head. My helmet had three holes but it probably saved me from much worse. More mortar shells began to hit around our exposed position, so we jumped behind the wall. One of the medics, Tech 5 Cecil G. Breeden, leaned over me as shells and bullets were flying. He applied a pressure bandage and sprinkled sulfa powder on my face wound. I tried to pull him down to safety but he refused, saying, "You're hurt now. After I get it you can take care of me." That was the last time I saw Cecil until we both took a trip to Normandy in 1988.

LIEUTENANT-COLONEL SIDNEY V. BINGHAM JR.
COMMANDING OFFICER, 2ND BATTALION, 116TH INFANTRY

Colonel Bingham, a West Pointer, was sent to the 29th Division to bolster its leadership for the Normandy invasion. He joined the regiment in September 1943 and assumed command of the 2nd Battalion, 116th. He led them ashore on D-Day and during the campaign was decorated four times for valor. He received the Distinguished Service Cross, Silver Star, and Bronze Star with two Oak Leaf Clusters. The colonel was wounded on August 1 near Vire and rejoined the 116th near Wurselen at the German border. He was later promoted to commanding officer of the 116th.

Colonel Bingham died August 22, 1993, at his home in Aspen, Colorado. Following are excerpts of the colonel's remembrances during the European campaign.

The 2nd Battalion, plus spare parts, loaded at Weymouth, England, aboard the very comfortable SS *Thomas Jefferson*. We were at home aboard this ship, in view of the two previous exercises we had with her. Our vehicles were loaded on seven landing craft. The voyage was rather uneventful as we watched our air force bomb the coast, as they were being fired on by enemy flak batteries. H-hour was 6:30 a.m. The navy herded us into assigned landing craft at 4:30 a.m., some twelve thousand yards off shore.

Maybe I am wrong about the time but it was pitch dark, ice cold, and the sea was rough. Everyone was soaked to the skin and at least ninety percent were desperately seasick. While circling, we waited our turn to go in. We had grandstand seats of the naval bombardment, which was very impressive.

At dawn the beach was partly obscured by smoke and dust, but a few landmarks were still discernible. There were no German planes, but ours were plentiful. There was no evidence of our bombing of the beaches. In fact, though preinvasion bombing by British heavies, American mediums, and fighter-bombers was planned, there was none; and to date, I have heard no good reason why. In my opinion, this lack of bombing was one of the chief reasons why Omaha Beach was such a deadly operation.

This was our mission that day: The 2nd Battalion, 116th, was to land three rifle companies abreast from left to right (E, F and G Companies) on a 2,500-yard front at H plus 3 minutes. E Company was scheduled to land just left of the Les Moulins beach exit and to the right of G Company, which was just left of the Vierville Draw.

Appendix I

The swimming DD tanks were to land at H plus 10 minutes, the same time underwater engineer demolition parties were due. Most of the tanks foundered, but those that did get ashore saved our necks. They had about ninety percent casualties.

H-hour was at low tide (three hundred yards of sand to cross) so the underwater obstacles would be exposed. At H plus 30 minutes came H Company and Battalion Headquarters Company. The battalion's objective was to cross the beach, secure the Les Moulins exit, neutralize the German defenses, move rapidly inland and take up defensive positions. Needless to say, this was not immediately accomplished.

Company E landed too far to the left and was in the 1st Division zone. It was cut down just as the ramps lowered. The company commander, Captain Lawrence Madill, was killed, and chaos reigned. F Company landed on target but fared worse, casualty-wise, than E Company. The company commander was badly hit, three lieutenants were killed and two were wounded. Company G seemed to have landed all over the beach, but didn't fare too badly.

Later, at H plus 30 minutes, parts of H Company and Battalion Headquarters Company came in where G Company was supposed to land and were badly cut up. The H Company commander got hit; the company executive officer was killed, and three other officers were wounded.

My reaction was probably typical. On the way in, the beach was obscured by smoke and dust, and it wasn't until we got about a thousand yards from shore that I could see anything. I noticed some explosions and thought they were the engineers blowing the beach obstacles.

For some reason I thought all was well until after struggling ashore through shoulder-deep water I paused for a breather behind a steel tetrahedron (antiboat obstacle) and noticed sand kicking up nearby. It then occurred to me that I was getting shot at and that these were machine gun bullets. There was no doubt in my mind. I was scared and exhausted. The fancy assault jacket issued for the operation was waterlogged and weighed a ton. I finally crossed the beach, getting to the shingle along the beach road.

I joined a few men from F Company who were seeking shelter. The only officer I could find was a wounded and dazed Lieutenant Lamb. A noncom was running up and down the beach ordering the men to start shooting and move forward. It then became apparent they couldn't shoot—their rifles were clogged with sand. Ludicrous as it sounds, I had them tear down their rifles and clean them.

I then moved east toward a three-story house, found my radio and the navy gun fire support party and tried to establish communication. I couldn't make radio contact. I had no control and might as well have been in the States for all the good I did that day. Everything accomplished was by small groups led by the true heroes—most of whom were killed. Sad to say, very few were decorated because there were no witnesses. Dead bodies were strewn everywhere up and down the beach, in the minefields, behind the beach, and at the hedgerows on the bluffs.

That night was spent with about one hundred men just south of St. Laurent-sur-Mer. The next morning we rounded up some three hundred more. The regimental commanding officer (Colonel Charles D. W. Canham), sent word to go back to the beach and take care of a few still-active snipers. We followed the St. Laurent-Les Moulins road back to the beach and dug out a few diehards. We received a good many casualties from small arms and antipersonnel mines.

About noon we returned to Asnières, about a mile south of Vierville. I was with remnants of E and G. It was pretty rough going with what seemed like Krauts behind every bush. We spent the night there. I sent the remainder of the battalion under direction of my executive officer to Vierville. That night, they took an awful drubbing from artillery. The next day (D plus 2) we got fairly well organized and followed the 3rd Battalion into Grandcamp-les-

Bains. We performed some mopping up without suffering too many casualties. That night was spent just southwest of town.

The next morning (D plus 3), we returned to Grandcamp for more mopping up and a "champagne" breakfast. That afternoon we moved into defensive positions along the La Cambe-Longueville road, just short of the flooded area. We took a breather and picked up about three hundred replacements. We spent nights D plus 3 and D plus 4 here. On D plus 5, we crossed the flooded area and spent the night about half way between Longueville and Marguerite d'Elle. The next day (June 12), we arrived at l'Epinay-Tesson and were told to halt and button up for the night. The 115th Infantry at the time was trying to cross the Elle River—actually a creek—and take St. Clair-sur-Elle.

We had just dug in and bedded down quite comfortably when about 4 p.m., Colonel Canham, regimental commanding officer, called for me to meet him in St. Marguerite. He, the chief of staff, and the assistant division commanding officer (Brigadier General Norman Cota) ordered us to relieve the 115th at 9 p.m., attack across the river, and take St. Clair. There was no time for adequate reconnaissance. I got them started, G Company on the left, E on the right and F in reserve. The .30-caliber machine guns were with E Company.

The attack began about 5:30 p.m. G Company didn't get to first base. E Company did better, and finally crossed the river about dark—approximately 11 p.m. As usual, all communications were out. I was with Company E, where the commander and two platoon leaders were wounded and other casualties were relatively heavy. Confusion was complete, Krauts popping up where they had no business being. We finally secured St. Clair at daylight (June 13) and held it for three days with pressure from three sides. We received mortar and artillery casualties but they were not too heavy.

On June 17, we were relieved; we moved south through Couvains, then west toward the Saint-Lô highway with the village of La Lucerne as our objective. That night we ran into trouble between Couvains and the highway, were held up and had quite a scrap. The Krauts pulled out during the night, but we ran into them the next day about a mile to the west along the Saint-Lô road. Here we had another rough fight all day (June 18) and didn't get near La Lucerne.

The next day, the 115th Infantry relieved us, and we went back through Couvains and into a defensive position just north of St. André de l'Epine. The 2nd Division was on our left, with the famous Hill 192 looking down their throats and ours too. We stayed there until July 11, exchanging patrols with a German parachute division and also trading lots of artillery and mortar fire. We were curtailed for a time as a result of the storm that wrecked the Mulberry harbors—and we took an appreciable number of casualties daily.

This wasn't such a bad situation. Now and then we were able to take a platoon at a time back for a hot bath. They also brought us hot food occasionally, and just in rear was an aid station that provided hot water for shaving, etc. There was plenty of cider, calvados, and fresh beef on the hoof that also furnished milk—regulations notwithstanding.

July 6 through 10 was spent readying for our next move. We distributed aerial photos to squad leaders, rehearsing with division engineers and the 747th Tank Battalion methods of going through hedgerows and sunken roads. Artillery prepared an elaborate fire plan. The attack was set for dawn, July 11. The 116th was to attack in column of battalions—2, 1, 3: the 3rd Battalion was in the line and the 2nd and the 1st were to pass through them. That night (July 10 to 11), the Bosch on our right came close to upsetting our plans by staging an enthusiastic show of their own against the 115th.

We took a terrific amount of artillery fire; all wire went out, but our attack shoved off on schedule. Our plan was to move south astride the road through St. André de l'Epine with Company F on the left, E on the right and G in reserve. About two thousand yards south, we were to make a ninety-degree turn on the high ground and move west along the ridge to the village of Martinville.

F Company did very well, but by noon E Company was in bad shape, so I relieved them with G Company. Casualties were heavy and the Kraut parachute lads were determined. By dark we had made our right turn and were about a thousand yards short of Martinville.

The 115th had not gotten off in the way they had planned, and our right was exposed as was our left and, of course, our front. That day was expensive—the three rifle companies were down to about sixty men apiece, and these were well shaken. Very, very few of the noncoms and officers from England remained. We were depleted. The next day we moved about six hundred yards and were stopped cold. The following day, we made three abortive attacks and may have picked up two hundred yards. On June 14, the 3rd Battalion pulled back to St. André de l'Epine, where we spent the night. While here, we received 250 replacements.

The next day (July 15), at 3 p.m. we were ordered to attack through the 3rd Battalion toward Martinville, bypass Martinville and go to Saint-Lô. Again, we attacked astride a road, F Company on the left, G Company on the right and Company E in reserve. At dark, I got a message to hold what we had and button up for the night. At the time I was with G Company, and actively engaged with the enemy on the outskirts of Martinville.

I got G Company settled and since wire and radio were out, I started to look for F and E Companies on the left to tell them to dig in. (E Company had been committed on the left with a platoon of .30-caliber machine guns from H Company.) I followed their wire and found them about a mile away, astride the Bayeux-Saint-Lô highway near a stud farm and racetrack that was on the outskirts of Saint-Lô. At the time, I'm sure we could have gotten back up the hill to the rest of the battalion, but there were approximately 200 of us in the two and a half companies, and we thought we were completely cut off. I decided to stay put. Fortunately, the radio of the artillery liaison officer was working, and we sent word to regimental headquarters of our predicament.

The situation looked gloomy, but the Germans weren't sure where we were or in what strength. We had them very confused. With us were E and F Companies, four 81mm mortars and four .30-caliber machine guns from H Company. All day (July 16), the Krauts harassed us from the south, east, and west. For some strange reason, those to the north didn't seem to give us much trouble. We surprised by shooting them from the rear.

We were taking casualties and had but one aid man. He did remarkable work. On June 17, we captured an enemy medic (an Austrian) and put him to work. We were low on ammunition and without food, and our only water supply was from a well under enemy observation. That afternoon (July 17), a bazooka man knocked off a couple of German trucks loaded with mortar ammunition. We used it in ours very well.

The enemy was beginning to figure out our position. That night (July 18), regiment sent us a strong patrol with rations and ammunition. Next morning, 3rd Battalion got down to us after a bold night attack in fog with bayonets and hand grenades. This attack is the only one I've heard of actually using bayonets. They caught the Germans asleep in their holes and gave them the business end of their cold steel. My good friend, Tom Howie, the gallant "Major of Saint-Lô," and 3rd Battalion commanding officer, was killed by mortar shrapnel shortly after the rescue.

There were now two battalions cut off, but not for long. About noon (July 19), the Germans hit from the southwest with quite a crew, including tanks. We called for and got the closest air support from P-47s I have ever seen. We also had medical supplies dropped from Piper Cub monoplanes. Except for incoming mortar and artillery, our lives became much easier.

Appendix I

That night a task force (Task Force C) was organized by division and sent into Saint-Lô. The 2nd Battalion was not involved. The next day (July 20), we were relieved by the 115th Infantry and sent back to St. Clair for a week's rest.

Our casualties for June 16–19 weren't too bad in view of the tight situation—twenty-five dead and sixty wounded. However, it was a nerve-wracking experience for all of us. The remainder of the 2nd Battalion at Martinville accounted well while protecting the regiment's right flank. They stacked quite a pile of dead Krauts.

Technical Sergeant Felix P. Branham
Company K, 116th Infantry

Felix P. Branham was born near Charlottesville, Virginia, on July 5, 1921. On November 19, 1939, he joined the Charlottesville National Guard's Company K, 116th Infantry. Branham's decorations included the Silver Star, Purple Heart, Bronze Star, and three Oak Leaf Clusters. Felix Branham died on December 9, 1997, at Holy Cross Hospital in Silver Spring, Maryland.

"This story is not hearsay, it is not something I read about or saw in the movies. It is something I was a part of." This is how Branham began his hour-and-a-half taped oral history with me. Excerpts here include a description of his encounter with General Montgomery, the commander of all Allied ground troops as he inspected the 116th Infantry while on an exercise, the D-Day assault through Vierville, Pointe-du-Hoc, and Grandcamp, under the leadership of Colonel Canham. Also his recollections of one of the most honored and decorated soldiers of World War II—Technical Sergeant Frank Peregory of K Company. Peregory, who was killed in action, won the Soldiers Medal in North Carolina and the Medal of Honor posthumously.

On one of his last inspections, Monty asked that we remove our helmets. He then said in his high-pitched voice, "A fine bunch of

lads you are, a fine bunch. I know you will do an outstanding job."
As he departed he waved his beret and said, "Good luck and happy
hunting!"

General Montgomery had said earlier that we, the 116th, were
to play an important part in the upcoming invasion. He didn't say
where or when the invasion would take place, but he wanted us to
take our training very, very seriously. General Bradley, American
ground forces commander, said the same thing. After that we had
no doubt about our upcoming role.

*Branham next fast-forwarded to trucking to Weymouth and
marching to the ship, the SS* Charles Carroll.

As we marched to the ship, people lined the streets, undoubtedly knowing this would be the great invasion. Military police cor-
doned off well-wishers from talking to the troops. We stoically kept
our eyes straight ahead, ignoring the flowers and kisses that were
thrown by the ladies.

After climbing the gangway, we deposited our gear and found
our sleeping quarters. We had been issued crazy-looking money
that was different from the English currency we were used to. Each
enlisted man received a two-hundred-franc invasion note that was
worth about four dollars, American. We were told that the money
was to be used for bartering. Officers received one-thousand-franc
notes, or about twenty dollars.

On Sunday, June 4, Rome fell. D-Day was scheduled to be the
next day—June 5. Our living quarters aboard ship were canvas
hammocks with metal frames about five feet high and two feet
between each bunk. We had to squeeze in and out of our bunks.
These quarters were below deck.

That afternoon we assembled on deck with our gear. I had
286 rounds of M1 ammo, ten hand grenades, a twenty-pound
satchel charge of TNT, a twenty-pound pole charge of TNT,

and a half-dozen number fourteen blasting caps. All of us were given a quarter-pound block of TNT with a seven-second fuse lighter on it. This was to be used as an aid to dig a quick foxhole or to blow up a German fortification.

We were about to rail-load onto landing craft, which was suspended by davits. We had practiced this operation many times and knew exactly where our location on the LCVP would be, but it was still a tricky maneuver because of the high seas. We were tense after being cooped up in tight living quarters and, of course, the uncertainty of the outcome of our mission.

A storm had been brewing out in the English Channel, and later that night the wind began to howl and rain came down in sheets. The sea became very rough and the invasion was in peril. General Eisenhower had to make a hard decision to go ahead as planned, or postpone and risk detection by the Germans.

A command decision was made to delay the invasion for twenty-four hours. We had to retrieve our equipment from the landing craft and take it back to the *Carroll*. Another case of hurry-up-and-wait: overcrowding, tense nerves, being ready to go and now this damned postponement! We wanted to go! We were past ready to evacuate that rocking boat! We weren't anxious to ride those small landing craft twelve miles in that rough sea, either. Of course we were frightened, but if the delay lasted too long we would surely lose our edge. Also, Jerry might find out what was going on and alert his troops.

To relieve tension we joked with each other. The twenty-first birthday of one of the men, Gino Ferrari, was June 21. We kidded Gino that he wouldn't live long enough to become a man. We told him that sometime on June 6 he was going to be shot and killed. Another of our men carried huge sums of American money in his wallet. He didn't believe English money was worth anything; besides, when the war was over, he didn't want to waste time exchanging foreign currency. Jokingly, we told Smitty,

"When you hit that beach a bullet will hit you in the head and one of us will be in that wallet." In reality, we were ready to die to save any or all of our buddies. I'm sure, and I pray they knew we were kidding.

On June 5, the *Charles Carroll* left Weymouth and joined the huge convoy in the channel. This was *it*, and there was no turning back. About twelve miles from France, we lowered the anchor and prepared to disembark. At 2:20 a.m., we went to our last meal aboard ship. While standing along the railing we could see explosions along the shore. It was raining and a cold wind was blowing that dark, dreary morning.

Just prior to loading, we met with friends, telling them, "Good luck," or, "See you in France," and "Keep a stiff upper lip," etc. I admit I was scared, but we really wanted to get this thing over with. I remember saying, "Fellows, we could stay in these British Isles forever and never get to go home. After landing in France, every step we take is a step closer to the good ol' USA."

At 4:20 a.m., we loaded into our landing craft and were lowered to the extremely rough water by hydraulic winches. The English Channel had swells six or seven feet high, and the cold spray blew in, soaking us to the skin. But we were thankfully on our way! Let's get this thing over with! My wave of six landing craft circled around and around until all had disembarked and formed into other waves. We then straightened the line and headed toward Normandy.

At first light, the navies began firing toward the coast. The battleship *Texas* opened up with its 14-inch guns launching one-ton missiles, and rocket-firing craft began firing in unison at the coastline targets. The sky was overcast but we couldn't see a single enemy aircraft. Our planes, thank goodness, had the skies to themselves.

Shells going over, bombs being dropped, the strafing by medium fighter-bombers, plus the incoming fire from German artillery batteries and heavy mortars caused all of us to shake with fear.

About fifty yards from shore, we hit a sandbar. Back in England we were told that sand barriers might keep us from getting in close, but to buck over them as the water would probably get deep again. Several landing craft let their ramps down too soon, and many men drowned. I had close friends who died that way.

As we approached touchdown, tracer bullets were cutting the air inches above the ground and ricocheting off the beach area. Explosions from mortars and artillery were all around us. Men getting hit by shrapnel and bullets began to scream for help. It was pure hell! There is no other way to describe it. Much of the chaos was due to fear of drowning and the incredibly loud explosions. The rattling of machine gun and rifle fire sent panic and chills up our spines. We were sitting ducks with no way to defend ourselves. My rifle was jammed with sand, but I couldn't see anything to shoot at anyway. There was plenty of smoke but no visible targets.

Our boat team lost four men on the beach and we considered ourselves lucky. One of the first men to get killed was Gino Ferrari, the young man who would not live to celebrate his twenty-first birthday. He was about four or five feet from me when he got hit and his brains splattered on my jacket. The man who carried large sums of money was also hit and killed nearby. I can assure you no one from our company pilfered Smitty's pockets. That was just a cruel, bad joke that backfired. Men were getting hit right and left. The Lord up above undoubtedly saved those of us who survived for a more important mission.

We crossed the beach and moved up the path to the left of the Vierville Draw. The Vierville exit draw was about a quarter-mile from our scheduled landing zone. We were lucky to have gotten within five miles of our targeted area. After topping the hill, we followed the road paralleling the beach. At this point, I still hadn't fired a shot from my rifle.

Colonel Canham, whose regimental command was on the *Charles Carroll*, was screaming for us to get across the beach. He previously had a BAR shot out of his hand. The bullet had gone through his right wrist and he had a makeshift sling. His bodyguard, Private First Class Nami, followed closely behind the colonel, keeping his .45 pistol loaded as he fired clip after clip.

Back in training, we used to call Colonel Canham everything not fit to print. When he took command of the 116th he made life miserable for us. We thought he would be another rear-echelon *prima donna* commander. After seeing him in action, I sure had to eat a mess of crow. He and all of our officers would have made ol' Stonewall Jackson proud!

We headed toward Vierville. Back in the marshalling area, we were briefed to assemble the battalion about two miles off the beach. Several were wounded along the road. We had stragglers from other companies and rangers fighting alongside us. We were leaderless individuals fighting independently.

One thing you will never read in the history books, but it happened. High command instructed us that we were to capture real estate, not prisoners. No prisoners were to be taken the first three days because we simply didn't have facilities or the manpower to secure them.

(We did capture a few prisoners, because I saw one being interrogated on the beach.)

We eventually made our way to the assembly area, where approximately forty men had gathered. My boat team was the first to arrive. We immediately dug foxholes in a perimeter of defense and there we spent the night. We could see Germans moving some two hundred to three hundred yards away, but could not fire at them because we were so outnumbered and outgunned.

The next morning we retraced our steps back to the beach. It was shocking to see how many men were washing in the surf, and many of them were from K Company. Men I grew up with, caddied

228

with, double-dated with, puffed off the same cigarette with, drank out of the same bottle with, all washing in and out with the tide. It went through my mind that we were brothers and always would be. They died so that we could live. I thank them and our Heavenly Father for what they gave us.

The tide was coming in and we stared in disbelief at this wasted scene. Hundreds of dead bodies and wrecked hulks littered the now somewhat tranquil shore. There were wrecked, burned-out tanks, landing craft, and military debris of all kind. By far, the most shocking were the cold and bloody bodies washing in the surf.

We moved through Vierville and Pointe-du-Hoc—the ranger objective on D-Day—and on to Grandcamp, a German strong point. We could see it about two miles off the beach and up on higher ground. Grandcamp became the 3rd Battalion's initial objective. We were working our way into position when I jumped over a rock wall, and on the other side I landed on the back of a 2nd Ranger captain.

He shouted, "Soldier! Where in the hell are you going?" I replied, "Sir, we're going to take Grandcamp!" I told him that Colonel Canham, who was leading us, had vowed that Grandcamp would be ours by 9 p.m. This was D plus 3. The captain told me he had already lost two tanks out there and that we ought to wait until morning. I replied to him that Grandcamp would fall tonight.

The ranger then said there was no reason to dig a foxhole if we were jumping off tonight. He assembled his men and, with Colonel Canham leading, we began to attack. I believe Lieutenant Colonel Eugene Meeks, 3rd Battalion commanding officer, was there as well. As we moved toward the objective, we came under vicious mortar, heavy machine gun and 88mm fire. We couldn't break through, and the attack stalled.

Here, Felix Branham recounts the circumstances of his wound on June 17, and shares memories of Technical Sergeant Frank D. Peregory, who had

won the Soldiers Medal back in 1942 for saving the life of a fellow soldier.
The following account begins with the description of the action at
Grandcamp, for which Peregory was awarded the Medal of Honor.

A former Virginia National Guardsman from near Charlottesville
(Peregory), acting alone, jumped out of his foxhole and charged the
position. He fixed his bayonet and charged the elaborately built
communication trench strong point.

We could hear grenades exploding and then rifle fire for what
seemed like a couple of minutes. Suddenly Frank appeared with
three German prisoners, hands over their heads, marching in front
of him. He handed the prisoners to his 3rd Platoon and immediately returned to the trench. This time it seemed an eternity. We
heard an occasional burst of fire and then a grenade went off. The
German machine gun stopped firing. Lo and behold, here's Frank
with thirty-two additional prisoners. He gave the prisoners to
Colonel Canham, who had witnessed the entire episode. This
action made him the first of two World War II Medal of Honor
winners for the 29th Division.

Thanks to Frank Peregory, we took our objective before the 9
p.m. deadline. Six days later, at Couvains, Frank Peregory was killed
in action. I was with Frank at Grandcamp and within one hundred
yards of him at Couvains. Peregory was killed trying to knock out a
machine gun nest. It was a devastating loss when my friend was killed.
Frank deserved all of the awards he got, but he didn't deserve to die.

I had known Frank and his family intimately for over twelve
years. I soldiered with his cousin, who was my first squad leader in
the National Guard. I hunted and fished with his brothers, his
uncle, and his cousins. They were a very poor family. He lost his
father at a very early age and had to quit school and go to work. He
made next to nothing, but had to help support the rather large family. His mother died when Frank was fifteen or so, and he inherited
the upkeep of his six or seven siblings.

Appendix I

On June 17, I was wounded and evacuated to the rear. The doctor checked the tag hanging on my shirt and he replied, "Son, can you stand a twenty-minute ambulance ride?" I replied, "Sir, after what I have been through I can stand anything." As he was leaving the ambulance he looked back and said, "Son, you are going home." I straightened and said to him, "Sir, you're nuts!" He saluted and left. After treatment, I made my way back to France. I returned to K Company on July 12.

Tech 5 Cecil G. Breeden
104th Medical Attachment, 116th Infantry

Tech 5 Breeden, from Deer Trail, Colorado, landed in the first wave on the Dog Green Sector of Omaha Beach as a medical aid man with rifle Company A, 116th Infantry.

This particular landing area was fraught with antilanding obstacles. The rough sea and tricky tides made the ride to shore miserable. Omaha Beach was sewn with thousands of mines, and miles of barbed wire added to the danger. Concrete bunkers and trenches protected the well-concealed and dedicated enemy. When the ramps of the landing craft dropped, the slaughter began. A total of ninety-one men of A Company died very early that morning. Wounded soldiers lay everywhere. These were the conditions Tech 5 Breeden faced on D-Day.

Every man was a hero that day; I never saw a coward. When I found Baumgarten, he had his cheek about over his ear. I patched him up and went on my way. I glanced now and then at the boys trying to take that damn pillbox. As I remember, it took six or more to do it. As far as I know none of them survived. I couldn't tell you who any of them were. I was just too busy tending to the wounded to know what was going on around me.

I remember patching up Butch, the A Company mail clerk, and Lieutenant E. Ray Nance (of Bedford, Virginia, WIA). Then "Big"

Bill Pressley (First Sergeant, B Company), came by and I asked him what he was doing. He said, pointing up on the hill, that he had some men up there. *(I was one of them. J.R.S.)*

Then he told me to get down or I would get hit. I said, "What the hell are you talking about? You are a damn sight bigger target than me." He just grinned and went on up the beach. Soon he came back with a rifle, just waved, and went on. That was the last time I saw him. I thought for sure that he had gotten it until I saw you (Bob Slaughter) and Curtis Moore in France in 1988.

That house down on the beach from the pillbox sheltered many of our wounded. Tech 5 Bernard Layne, a medical corpsman with B Company, was in that bunch, and was hit through the face and gave me hell for not recognizing him. He and I were kin. His granddad and mine were brothers. They were from eastern Iowa. I still don't know who gave them first aid. I didn't see anyone.

I worked my way around the base of the hill following the road and into the draw. When I got to about where the 29th Memorial now stands, General Gerhardt, Colonel Canham, Lieutenant Colonel Metcalfe, and some other officers had set up a command post. Canham was shot through the right hand. I fixed it up. While I was there, a man came through looking for a noncom, saying there was a sniper up there in the cliff. Metcalfe said that he wasn't a noncom but would he do. They both left going up the hill, bearing to the left. *(Lieutenant Colonel Metcalfe was later killed in action.)*

TECH 5 VICTOR J. CRIMONE
COMPANY D, 116TH INFANTRY

Instrument Corporal Victor Crimone was drafted from Pittsburgh and on D-Day was in Headquarters Platoon of Company D, 116th. He was a demolition expert, making pole charges and TNT packs for blowing up fortified bunkers and gun emplacements. He was later promoted to the company's first sergeant. Following are excerpts from his memoirs.

As we approached Omaha Beach, a landing craft that had already deposited its human cargo and was on its way back, gave us the thumbs-up sign, giving us confidence that all was well. In minutes all hell broke loose. The ramp blew in from an 88mm, killing Captain Schilling (Roanoke), first Sergeant Obenshain (Roanoke), Private First Class John C. Dylik, our bugler, and others.

As the boat started to sink, I became terrified because I couldn't swim. Nevertheless, I jumped into the English Channel, inflated my Mae West, and prayed to God for help.

My friend George Kobe came by and I grabbed his assault jacket. He was a rather large fellow and was trying to help other weak swimmers from going under. I was pulling him under, so I let go. I gave up struggling and put my fate into the Lord's hands.

I floated with the tide, in and out, each time drifting farther to the west and away from our sector. When I finally worked my way to the shore, I was five hundred yards too far to the right. I was frightened, exhausted, and shivering cold. I took cover behind a crossed I-beam beach obstacle, which was no cover.

There were soldiers pinned down in front of me, which I finally decided were 2nd Battalion Rangers. After what seemed an eternity, Lieutenant Verne Morse (Pennsylvania) and Staff Sergeant Edward Fatula (Gray, Pennsylvania), who was my closest friend, came by and rescued me to safety.

We worked our way up the hill and, near the top, I encountered an enemy soldier who was hiding in a foxhole. Hands over head, he surrendered, and in broken English said that he was Polish and was forced to fight. I covered him with a carbine that was fouled with sand and salt water. I turned him over to the military police.

That evening, we found 249 survivors of the 1st Battalion, 116th RCT.

CAPTAIN ROBERT E. GARCIA
COMPANY E, 116TH INFANTRY

Captain Bob Garcia of San Jose, California, joined Company E, 116th, September 1942 at Camp Blanding, Florida. On D-Day, he was company executive officer and had been battalion transport quartermaster. He and the 2nd Battalion embarked on the SS Thomas Jefferson, formerly of the United States President Line. He and Company E landed in the first wave on Omaha Beach. The commander of E Company, Captain Lawrence Madill, was killed, and 1st Lieutenant Garcia inherited the job of company commander. Following are edited excerpts of Captain Garcia's memories of that eventful D-Day.

Early on D-Day, we dressed for a good breakfast. Afterward we got our stuff together and went out on deck to our assigned stations. We loaded from the rail instead of climbing cargo nets. One of the men refused to board the LCVP and a noncom brought him to me. I didn't know what to do with him, so I turned him over to the navy. The boarding was smooth due to the ship's competent crew. Aboard the LCVP were eight or ten men from E Company, plus some special engineers and a few air force and artillery liaison personnel.

As we departed the *Thomas Jefferson*, our wave began to circle while waiting for orders to align abreast and proceed toward France. The circling maneuver was tough on all of us because of the high seas. One minute we were on the crest of a swell, enabling us to see the entire show. The next minute, we were swallowed by mountainous waves allowing us to see only walls of water. Many of the men were getting very seasick and all of us were wet and cold.

One thing that stands out vividly was the deafening muzzle blasts of the battleship *Texas'* 14-inch guns. Believe it or not, one could actually see the projectiles spiraling through the air. What their targets were or what good they did, I do not know. Observing this bombardment was mind-boggling.

During our run to the beach, I tried to see what was going on, but smoke and dust from the bombing and shelling obscured my view. As we got closer, I soon recognized we were too far to the left of our sector, Easy Green beach. It was too late to change course. The coxswain was anxious to lower the ramp and cast us off and get out of there. Who could blame him? That is what happened, except we prematurely hit a sandbar and had to wade quite a ways to shore.

Loaded down with sixty pounds of gear, we found the long run across the flat sand was too much in one run. We tried to ignore the screaming of artillery shells, explosions of mortar rounds, and spurts of sand kicking up from small arms while we were lying exposed on Omaha Beach trying to catch our breath. There were eight or nine men of the company still following; the rest had stayed behind or departed. After a short rest, I signaled the men to follow me to the rocky shelf and cover. We were approximately a thousand yards to the left of Easy Green.

I tried to inform the remainders that we were going to look for Company E. It was impossible to yell above the ear-splitting noise. I began to move laterally down the beach, hugging the rocky shelf. The beach narrowed considerably as the tide rushed in. To my surprise and disappointment I found that Private First Class Edward R. Bollinger (of Chase City, Virginia) was my only follower.

Bollinger and I were being subjected to small arms and artillery fire, so we continued to stay close to the rocky shelf. We saw dozens of men struggling through the surf and many were already wounded or dead, tossing in the incoming tide. All of them were exposed to the heavy gunfire.

Our mission was to get to Easy Green as fast as possible. We were trained not to stop to help the wounded. That was what the medics were supposed to do. I saw no medics helping these poor wounded, so Bollinger and I pulled one man out of the water and up on the beach, then another, and another. We didn't like being exposed, but these men needed help and now. At first we tried to take cover whenever the shelling became heavy, but soon we ignored it and did whatever had to be done.

How long this went on I do not know. We were soaked to the skin and very tired from carrying and dragging men up onto the beach. We eventually worked our way down to Easy Green. This beach had fewer men than the one we had just left. Ed and I were tired and very frustrated because it had taken us so long to find our sector. We failed, however, to find a single man from Company E.

We saw an orderly column of men coming up the beach, which, we found out, was Company M. M Company, the 3rd Battalion heavy weapons company, was led by Captain Charley Kidd (of Roanoke), who led them up the bluff and inland.

M Company and the 3rd Battalion were in reserve and came in behind us and were still in pretty good shape. As the tail end of his column passed, we fell in behind them. We slowly trudged up the well-worn path and up the hill, still determined to find the company. *Achtung Minen* signs were on both sides of the path. Either the mines had been cleared or they were decoys. I didn't see anyone hurt by a mine.

Bollinger and I became separated, but I joined with Private First Class Armand O. Berthiaume and Tech 4 Edward R. Wilmoth of Company E. We three were looking for St.-Laurent, a village 1,500 yards from the beach. We spotted in plain view a battery of *nebelwerfers* ("screaming meemies") firing at the beach.

They were about 800 yards from us. There was a light machine gun section set up to fire across the Les Moulins Draw and they were also observing the meemies. I asked the noncom in charge why they weren't firing. He replied, "We don't want to give away our position."

I ordered him to get those guns firing. We watched enemy gunners trying to move the guns but not soon enough. There was a terrific explosion as the ammo or propellant ignited. When the smoke cleared we could see that the guns were destroyed.

About 7 p.m., we arrived at St.-Laurent. As the company grew, one of the men informed me of our captain's death (Captain Madill). It fell to me as company executive officer to take charge of the company.

I assembled the thirteen men of the company and established the CP under a lean-to against a church. I kept Private First Class Robert O. Berthiaume (*the Berthiaumes, probably related, were from Massachusetts*) with me at the CP and stationed the others into a perimeter of defense. Shortly, Lieutenant Leon Harvey's H Company, which had a section of heavy machine guns (two), was deployed to cover the road.

I slept fitfully, trading with Berthiaume for time to sleep. Thus ended the first of many harrowing days for me and Company E. Besides Captain Madill, E Company suffered the loss of approximately thirty-one other men killed on D-Day.

Private First Class Randolph A. Ginman
Company D, 116th Infantry

Private First Class Randolph Ginman, from Old Bridge, New Jersey, was twenty-seven years old on D-Day. He was the mortar gunner in Staff Sergeant Joseph Trona's mortar squad.

Staff Sergeant Philip H. Hale (of Roanoke) was the de facto leader on our boat. The English coxswain tried to drop the ramp a couple of hundred feet from shore when the sergeant ordered, "Take us all the way in!" Just then machine guns opened up and bullets tore through the wooden sides of the landing craft, wounding four or five men. Men began screaming, "Open those damn doors!" Just as the ramp went down, there was a pause in the incoming fire.

We exited fast, diving into the water and holding on. Sergeant Trona was lying next to me and he was shot through the wrist. I crawled over to him and gave him first aid. We just let the tide wash over the lower portion of our bodies, using our fingernails to pull forward, inch by inch, to keep from drowning. I looked back at our assault craft and both English sailors were dead. They were heroes and paid the price for getting us in. They risked their safety to get us closer to shore.

Private Thomas McArtor (of Hazard County, Kentucky) was the first fatality in our sector. His cries to me for help still haunt me. Weighted down and possibly wounded, he frantically struggled in the water as he cried my name, but I couldn't get to him.

It was drilled into us that we must push forward to the objective and to let the medics take care of the wounded. We were subjected to grazing fire from criss-crossing fire from machine guns. I believed at the time that it would be better for me to push forward, since Tom was quite far away. These machine guns kept firing until we got to the sea wall. Tom was my friend and I should have tried to save him.

Our boat was the first to touch bottom in our wave. We were slightly to the left of the Vierville Draw and exactly where we were supposed to be. To the west of us there was a large fortified bunker, which had an 88mm capable of covering the entire beach. That one pillbox and its screaming gun did more damage to our sector than any other. Later, we watched an amphibious tank knock it out. This, and the prodding of General Cota (29th Division executive officer) were the catalysts that got us across the beach.

Brigadier General Cota and Colonel Canham were great leaders that day and deserve all of the credit they received afterward. It took individual riflemen using grenades, satchel charges, and bayonets to neutralize the almost impregnable concrete bunkers. I didn't see any rangers until later. In my opinion, the air force and navy made it possible for us to hang on until reinforcements and more equipment arrived. They also kept the Germans from mounting an armored counter attack. But, you know, it boils down to the bloody foot soldier and his rifle to hold on to the real estate.

STAFF SERGEANT WILLIAM R. HURD
COMPANY D, 116TH INFANTRY

William R. "Bill" Hurd, of Roanoke, was D Company's transportation sergeant. He and Medron R. Patterson, also of Roanoke, manned a halftrack loaded with ammunition and armed with a .50-caliber machine gun. Their vehicle was parked on the open deck of an LCVP. Their job was to resupply heavy weapons ammo for D Company.

My halftrack was the first one off the ramp. The others followed my tracks to keep from rolling over a hidden mine. We tried to cross the beach, but incoming artillery shells forced us out of the vehicle and under it for protection. During a lull, we moved up the draw to find the company. Some riflemen from the 116th told us that D had been wiped out. We later found a few who also were weaponless, lost, and disorganized.

After unloading the ammo, we went to the 1st Division supply depot, begging for food. They didn't want to part with theirs, but finally gave in. We were ordered to go back to the beach and retrieve scattered weapons and ammunition.

PRIVATE FIRST CLASS GEORGE A. KOBE
COMPANY D, 116TH INFANTRY

Private First Class George Kobe was on the same boat with Captain Schilling and Technical Sergeant John Stinnett (mortar platoon sergeant, of Roanoke, WIA, lost an eye). Kobe was a giant of a man who grew up in Chicago, and later moved to Southern California. He was severely wounded in the battle for Vire. After a stay in an English hos-

pital, he returned to the United States for lengthy rehabilitation and a medical discharge. He was instrumental in organizing the postwar Company D, 116th, reunions.

Six hundred yards from shore, the English coxswain lost his nerve and slowed the engine. This improved the Germans' opportunity to hit our boat. Captain Schilling was looking through the vision slit, looked back at the sailor and said, "You're not going to drop that ramp here!" Technical Sergeant Stinnett was standing next to the captain.

Suddenly, an 88mm hit the ramp directly, blowing Captain Schilling backward, killing him instantly. Part of the ramp caught Stinnett's left eye, knocking it out. Stinnett, although seriously wounded, somehow made it to the sea wall. There was no panic. *(Others on the craft believed they hit a submerged beach obstacle that was mined.)*

At this point, I put my mortar base plate with a Mae West tied to it gently into the water. It went straight to the bottom of the channel. With John Stefko (of Lakeland, Florida, WIA June 29), Vic Crimone (of Pittsburgh, WIA August 7), and Eugene Adrian (WIA June 7), we finally made it to the sea wall. How, I'll never know! It was the worst fire I was ever subjected to in all of my combat. *(Kobe was a good swimmer and saved many of his comrades from drowning.)*

PRIVATE FIRST CLASS BERNARD "ROCKY" LATAKAS COMPANY D, 116TH INFANTRY

Bernard Latakas was born in Kennan, Wisconsin, and joined D Company on June 9, 1943. He was twenty-three years old on D-Day. Latakas was Captain Schilling's radio operator and landed in the same boat. Others he recalled who were also aboard were: Technical Sergeant John Stinnett (WIA), Private First Class George Kobe, Sergeant

APPENDIX I

Edward Walton (of Roanoke, KIA July 15), Lieutenant Blair Dixon (KIA July 1), and Private First Class John C. Dylik (KIA), to name a few. As he vividly remembers: "The night of June 5, I crawled into my bunk and wrote on the canvas of the bunk above me: 'D-Day is June 6, 1944. Today is June 5, 1944.'" The following excerpt from his memoirs begins as his assault craft approaches Omaha Beach.

As we neared the wood obstacles, Captain Schilling stood up to see where we were going. He ordered, "Stop the boat!" The sailor cut back on the throttle. About that time a shell hit the front of the assault craft, blowing the ramp back into the landing craft. The British sailor stationed in the starboard compartment went down.

Captain Schilling, mortally wounded, also went down. Lieutenant Dixon went down as well, and I thought at the time he was also killed. The British sailor on the port side had his helmet blown off and was bleeding badly from head wounds. He began screaming "Get off the boat!" I squeezed my Mae West, which exploded with oxygenated air. I jumped over Lieutenant Dixon's prostate body and into the water.

I bobbed and swam through ten-foot waves until my feet hit the sandy bottom. I couldn't swim and wade with my sixty-plus pounds of baggage, so I dumped the assault jacket. I also lost my walkie-talkie radio and all my grenades. All I had left was a carbine and cartridge belt, canteen, and first aid packet. There were 88s firing over to my right, hitting many of our men. There were men trying to help the wounded, some of whom were crying for help. I thought for sure I was going to be killed.

Machine guns were cross-firing the beach. I got behind one of the log obstacles as an 88 fired for the second time. I aimed and fired my rifle into the pillbox port where the 88mm was firing from. My carbine didn't eject the empty shell and I couldn't fire again. I tried to use my foot to eject the shell but it was frozen hard. The 88mm, after a while, stopped firing.

I ran back to the breakwater and dived under a three-legged steel obstacle for protection. Sergeant Ed Walton joined me under it. Machine gun bullets began ricocheting off the metal, causing sparks and a weird pinging noise. I yelled, "Walton! We can't stay here!" He then ran for the breakwater and I followed him. I looked back and three mortar shells hit where we had just left.

The tide was bringing dead bodies in with their life preservers inflated. A ranger had been hit in the forehead and fell back on his helmet. Another ranger's boat team had tried to land at the cliffs but he said it was too rough over there and they decided to land here at the beach. I swapped my carbine for an M1 rifle from a soldier who was dying.

I joined with Lieutenant Dixon, who had revived enough to get ashore and was the only D Company officer in our sector. (He was later killed on July 1.) A few riflemen cleaned out some German positions in the cliffs and took about a dozen prisoners. I saw one tank that made it to the beach. Lieutenant Dixon tried to organize what was left of D Company.

We finally joined with Lieutenant Morse and D Company on D plus 3. It was good to see them and become organized again. I opened a can of chicken soup, which was the first food since D-Day. Lieutenant Morse and I went back to the beach to collect some heavy weapons. Weapons and ammunition of all description were plentiful.

There were some guys playing softball on the beach with little concern for the hell of a price that had been paid for the privilege. Bulldozers and explosives were being used for digging temporary graves to bury our dead buddies.

STAFF SERGEANT WILLIAM H. LEWIS
1ST BATTALION HEADQUARTERS COMPANY

J. E. Kaufmann, San Antonio, Texas, a writer and teacher, advertised in the Twenty-Niner newsletter for eyewitness accounts of D-

Day. I answered the ad and we began corresponding. He asked if I knew a Twenty-Niner from San Antonio named Bill Lewis, whom he had already interviewed. I did know him. Mr. Kaufmann kindly shared his taped interview with Bill Lewis.

William H. Lewis, ASN 20806717, was born in 1922 in Wichita Falls, Texas. Staff Sergeant Lewis was a squad leader in the Antitank Platoon, 1st Battalion Headquarters Company, 116th Infantry, 29th Division. Following are excerpts of the interview.

After Carolina maneuvers I was sent to Fort Richie and the 36th Division and was assigned to the intelligence section after receiving basic training for linguists. Our job was to demonstrate German equipment and tactics. One night my friend Ernest Lee and I pulled into a drive-in hamburger joint. We were wearing full-dress German uniforms. Lee was operating a German military motorcycle and I was riding in the sidecar. It was unbelievable, no one asked us, "What in the hell are you Germans doing here?" We could have stayed at Fort Richie for the duration, but being rather dumb and wanting to fight for our country, we asked to be transferred. That was a huge mistake!

Soon we were in a one hundred-ship convoy going overseas. *(The years 1942 and 1943 were particularly dangerous, because the German wolfpacks were ravaging the British shipping lanes, and traveling in the winter added to our discomfort.)*

Chronic sea sickness, plus the unheated sleeping quarters with backbreaking hammocks to sleep on, made the trip anything but pleasant. It was wintertime and we took the northern route by way of Newfoundland, Greenland, and Iceland. Confusion, especially after dark, caused the convoy to drift apart as we plied ice all night and then re-formed the next morning. Eerie whistles blowing and foghorns bellowing to prevent us from ramming each other added to the uneasiness. A few small Canadian corvettes were all the protection we had against the German navy.

At daybreak, a convoy was spotted on the horizon and at first we didn't know who they were. As we closed with them, we could see two American navy cruisers were escorting it. They passed peacefully, moving on to their destination. We were on an old British merchant marine ship, the HMS *Esperance Bay* and the flagship of the convoy. It had just returned from a trip to Tobruk in the Mediterranean, where her sister ship, the HMS *Empress Bay*, had been sunk. The ship had one heated mess deck. It was miserable trying to sleep in hammocks in the unheated, crowded quarters. Breakfast consisted of fish and tea with some old milk. Ugh! We bellyached to the poor cooks, "This is *breakfast*? What *is* this stuff?"

When the convoy came into range of the Luftwaffe, we broke off from the others and started running alone. We zigged and we zagged, avoiding those dreaded unseen U-boat torpedoes. It was dark when the ships from a convoy up ahead could be seen under attack from German submarines. The night sky was ablaze with what looked like a giant sunset reflecting off the dark clouds of the North Atlantic. We stood guard behind six-inch guns that we didn't know the first thing about.

We had to chip ice off the firing mechanism even though we didn't know how to use the guns. Ice-chipping all night long plus trying to stay alert for submarines was a duty that we knew had to be performed. If one stared into the darkness long enough, sure as hell phantom submarines began to appear.

After sailing for what seemed like a month, we finally docked at Liverpool. We then traveled on to Tidworth, on the Salisbury Plain, where I joined the 1st Battalion Headquarters Company. The battalion soon left Tidworth for good, hiking all of the way south to Devonshire and the village of Ivybridge.

We marched in from Tidworth, rested for a day or so, and then we got paid. It had been a while, so we went into town to blow off a little steam. Tidworth didn't offer much in the way of good pubs.

There wasn't much to drink there either. There might be one bottle of Scotch or gin, maybe some wine or that old warm, bitter beer that always gave me heartburn.

That night the bars were full with the additional Yankee customers. Soon we had drunk our share of double Scotches and water and then we began to fight all the Englishmen. After we whipped the limeys we beat up each other. The people thought we were a bunch of maniacs.

At the time I was delivering mail, which I picked up in Plymouth each day. I traveled the twelve miles, picked up the mail, brought it back to the local post office, and checked it in. I will never forget that first morning after we had that night on the town. The people pulled back the drapes, and you could just see half of their faces and hear them muttering, "Goddamn, there is one of those bloody Yanks!"

We trained in the moors, living and hiking over those windy, spongy hillsides for nearly a year, and then we began the assault amphibious training. We used amphibious trucks (DUKWs) a couple of times in practice but they didn't have near the load we had on D-Day. We practiced on all kinds of landing craft that were used during the invasion. We made lots of dry runs and many wet ones.

We left Ivybridge and the townspeople, who had at first despised us, were out in droves lining the streets, and some of them were waving out of their windows to us. We had marched out many times before, but this time they knew this was it. The men were looking very sad and the women were crying. They really did learn to like us and we liked them as well. The economy boomed while we were there and many of us became their friends. We knew and they knew that we had to leave eventually and go to war.

We trucked down to the coast near Blandford and set up tents. We were surrounded by a ten-foot barbed-wire enclosure and MPs guarded from the outside. The briefing officers told us what we already knew, that this time it wasn't a dry run. I had heard of Normandy in school but didn't know exactly where it was.

A year earlier, we often asked, "If we were going to invade the damn country, why don't we do it today and get it over with?" We didn't realize the logistics problems involved: five thousand ships and 250,000 men, supplies, airplanes, and other things that go into making war that we hadn't thought about. They kept telling us, "When you hit the beach be sure to do so-and-so." We thought, "Goddamn, if we're going to hit the beach, let's go hit it!" We knew that Joe Stalin was fighting a desperate war and the 36th Division (Texas National Guard) was slogging it out in Italy, but this mission was the Mother Goose of them all.

We loaded on an LCT the night of June 4 because the invasion was scheduled for the 5th. The worst channel storm in many years forced us to postpone for twenty-four hours. Some of the ships went to sea and were forced back, but I don't believe we left port. The night of June 5, we raised anchor and were on our way. Early the next morning we lowered the ramp and drove the DUKW down it into the ocean.

We left the LCT before daylight so we could rendezvous. We had to circle round and round, waiting for time to go. We lost half of the DUKWs in the rough seas while awaiting the signal. They just shipped water, turned over sideways and sank. The DUKWs, not very seaworthy, would ride up a swell and instead of coming back down, they would go into it and go under. The coxswains had never experienced a storm like this. We didn't have any problems in practice as long as the water was calm.

As dawn began to break, we received the signal and headed to shore. I remember the battleship USS *Texas* firing broadsides into shore while we were close by. It was godawful, with terrible explosions—muzzle blast in our ears—when they fired. The smoke ring passed by us and it looked like a funnel of a tornado, growing larger and larger as it finally dissipated.

They then fired another one. I don't believe we should have been that close, because we actually felt the muzzle blast. All kinds of ships were firing. A French cruiser, painted in camouflage, did a good job of getting close to shore, inviting the Germans to do battle. She shelled the hell out of the beach.

All of the ships did a good job except the LCT(R) rocket ships, which didn't get close enough to hit their targets. Destroyers came within a thousand yards of the shore and let go their five- and six-inch guns. It must have been terrible on the other end of that artillery. The flash of the big guns was blinding and the explosions from the muzzles were deafening.

The DUKW was piled high with equipment like an overloaded barge. The coxswain had to use great skill guiding us through the water. The guy stayed busy maneuvering us into the waves so we didn't turn over and sink. If we headed into a trough he knew we were going to turn over so he kept the bow into the waves, letting them push us along. It was an ugly situation.

When we got to the metal obstacles we saw a man hanging on to one of them. He yelled to us for help. We kept going on past him because we were out of control. Platoon Leader Lieutenant Leo Van de Voort yelled, "We are out here to kill people, not save them! If you want on this damn thing you had better jump on!" The soldier grabbed hold and climbed aboard.

We sheared a pin in the motor and lost power. We were between the obstacles and their teller mines and helplessly adrift. We were drifting sideways into the mines, which could be seen sticking out of the water. We brushed one of them more than once but it failed to explode. I suppose salt water had deteriorated the firing mechanism. Mines were strapped onto the slanted log obstacles.

We were 110 minutes or so after the first wave. They began to machine-gun the DUKW, so we jumped out of the thing into deep water. We had lost the gun and control of the DUKW. I jumped into the water, and by standing on my toes, I kept my head barely above the surface, except when a wave crashed over me. The natural assumption was the closer one went to shore, the more solid the footing was going to get.

That wasn't true though, because sand had built up around the obstacles and I stepped off into a hole. I was a good swimmer and wasn't afraid of water, but the equipment was pulling me under. We carried over sixty pounds of gear on our person. Every time a wave crashed over I felt for the bottom again. I wasn't about to go back the other way, I'll guarantee you that. We kept going in and I don't know how we did it. The water was dancing to the tune of that damned machine gun that was firing all around us.

Private First Class Louis Lorditch climbed back onto the landing craft. I'm guessing that he hitched a ride in order to help him to get in with his heavy load. The Germans began shelling the DUKW. A shell exploded close by, hitting the craft.

Lorditch got off as it beached sideways and it began to burn. He was near me when they shelled and he came over to where I was. We both ran over to the sea wall, cold and scared. Corporal Larry Vogt piled in on top of both of us. He asked, "Is that you shaking, Sarge?" I said, "Damn right!" He said, "My God! I thought it was me!" I could see that he was shaking all right! Both of us were.

We were huddled there just trying to stay alive. There was nothing we could do except keep our butts down. There was no place to go, and the automatic fire became heavier.

As others landed, they, like us, took cover behind the wall. Then old Van de Voort, a tough old cookie, said, "Let's go, god-damn, there ain't no use staying here, we're all going to get killed!" The first thing he did was to run up to a gun emplacement, and he threw a grenade in the embrasure. He soon returned with about five or six prisoners. So then we thought, "Hell, if he can do that, why can't we?" That's how we got off the beach.

Lieutenant Van de Voort was shot in the groin later at

Couvains. I was with him when he got it. He received the DSC for bravery and damned well deserved it. He wrote us later saying that he had joined the paratroopers where he could see some "real" action. He was a tough old Dutchman. The lieutenant's radio operator, Jeffreys, and a fellow named Belinski talked to me about him on the radio. Jeffreys said, "He kept me scared to death all the time, because he took me to places I didn't want to go!"

The first time I saw Lieutenant Van de Voort was when he rode the DUKW in with us as our platoon leader. After we got in on the beach he picked up a couple of "volunteers" to scout up the beach. He turned to me and said, "Sergeant Lewis, you get some rest." I don't know why he said that to me, but I damn sure took advantage of it. I stayed hidden behind the wall with some others who were taking cover. The lieutenant soon came back with the prisoners. After he got wounded at Couvains I didn't see him anymore.

There were dead guys washing back and forth in the surf. I remember a tractor or a bulldozer hitting a land mine and it blew into nothing. Two pieces of track were all that was left where that baby hit. Even the camouflage nets were blown to pieces.

There was a 1st Division sergeant who had seen combat in North Africa (who) said, "I see what that bunker next to the exit is doing. Get some fire on that baby!"

A fire control sailor got on the radio and tried to direct fire on the pillbox, but the shells were ineffective. The sergeant with the Big Red One on his jacket ordered, "Everyone, start firing on that embrasure! Keep them away from that hole! Keep them from running back in there!" He sure knew what he was doing.

We got up there and started firing on that embrasure. The sarge took some men with a bangalore torpedo and placed it under that baby. He stopped that thing from murdering us with its 88s. The bunker was in the face of the cliff and they were using it as a command post. It was a killer, and the man with the Big Red One on his shoulder helped to blow it up.

There were quite a few 1st Division men in our area and they helped a lot. That sergeant taught us how to fire at the Germans. I didn't fire my rifle, but some of the others did. The 1st Division sergeant got things going with four or five of our men. The Germans ran down the trench away from the embrasure, and then he put the bangalore up to the hole. They might have had a BAR, but I just don't know.

We were disorganized because everyone was in the wrong place and three out of four of the company commanders were killed: Captain Taylor N. Fellers, Company A; Captain Ettore V. Zappacosta, Company B; and Captain Walter O. Schilling. Many officers and noncoms were casualties, so we became disorganized and didn't move off the beach as soon as we would have liked. They went in where they could find a hole in the obstacles; if they couldn't, they worked on down the beach until they did. It took a week to find our units and get organized.

We went up the Vierville Draw before the beach defenses were cleared. After getting to the top of the bluff, we turned toward Pointe-du-Hoc with a ragtag bunch of rangers, some sailors, and some 1st Division boys. We joined with Major Tom Dallas, 1st Battalion executive officer, and skirted Vierville and headed for the Pointe. Taking Pointe-du-Hoc wasn't any fun. It was a tough little thing.

I was lucky to miss stepping on one of those mines. There were signs all over the place saying, *Achtung Minen!*—Beware of mines! That first day, the weather was cold as hell with the wind blowing, and it was cloudy and, at times, raining. It was nasty weather. I don't remember seeing the sun shining at all that day. I don't remember where we slept that first night. I faintly remember sleeping in a yard of a chateau or something. We were trying to get organized.

I had liberated a big jug of wine and we all had a drink. This was not far from Vierville and we were heading out to Pointe-du-Hoc. It seems we were there most of the day. We were caught between a tank that had gotten ashore and some fortified houses that Germans were shooting at us from. There was a huge naval dud from one of the battleships lying next to me. I was afraid the thing would explode.

From the top of the hill, the view of the fleet out in the channel was awesome. As I looked down, the slaughter of the men and the destruction of equipment was hard to fathom. I never heard anyone say, "Hell, this is not what it was supposed to be like! Let's go back!" There was so much going on that all you could think about was to keep your ass alive. I don't remember eating until that night.

Major Dallas was with a fellow named Vincent. They started across a field and Vincent was killed. We followed a hedgerow and had about one hundred yards to run when one of the men froze and wouldn't move up. Major Dallas kicked him in the butt and screamed, "Get going, soldier!"

On D plus 3 or D plus 4, I saw Dallas jump on the hood of a jeep and scream, "Shoot me, you GD sons of bitches!" He didn't have any fear of the Germans at all. I heard him say to the chaplain, "You better get your little ass to the rear before you get it shot off, Chaplain!"

LIEUTENANT COLONEL LAWRENCE EUGENE MEEKS
COMMANDING OFFICER 3RD BATTALION, 116TH INFANTRY

Lieutenant Colonel Lawrence E. "Gene" Meeks, wartime commander of the 3rd Battalion, 116th Infantry, 29th Division, was executive officer of Company D, 116th, when I joined the Virginia National Guard in 1940. Colonel Meeks distinguished himself as combat commander of four different battalions of the 29th and led the 3rd Battalion, 116th, ashore on D-Day. He earned four medals for bravery and merit. Colonel Meeks died in November 1995, in a Richmond hospital after a lengthy illness.

The following by Colonel Meeks is partially based on an account given to his son Larry Meeks, whom I taped in an interview concerning his father's wartime memories. As the colonel recalled preparing and leading the 3rd Battalion on June 6, 1944, he confided that the 3rd Battalion was originally scheduled to hit the Dog Green sector of Omaha Beach at 6:30 a.m. instead of the 1st Battalion. Just days before the invasion, Regimental Commander Colonel Charles D. W. Canham changed his mind and sent the 1st Battalion to assault the Vierville Draw sector.

Following is Meeks' version, as told to his son, of why Canham changed the 116th Regimental assault plan for D-Day. The words are those of Larry Meeks in his interview with the author.

Colonel Canham briefed the regimental staff and command officers on their respective missions on D-Day. They were shown a wall map oriented from the sea toward land. The various beaches and code-named sectors were marked on the map, and it revealed where the different units of the 116th were scheduled to land and at what time. The map showed the 1st Battalion was scheduled to hit Easy Green; the 2nd, Dog White; and the 3rd, Dog Green. Colonel Canham turned to (then) Lieutenant Colonel Meeks, and he asked, "Colonel Meeks, are you and your men ready to die?" Lieutenant Colonel Meeks reportedly looked the colonel squarely in the eye and responded, "Hell, no! But we ARE prepared to do our jobs, Sir!"

Canham reportedly didn't like that answer, and immediately changed the plan of battle: 1st Battalion would assault the Vierville Draw's Dog Green sector; 2nd Battalion would hit Dog White; and 3rd would follow the 2nd in reserve.

(If true, the decision changed history. The 1st Battalion had the highest casualty rate of any unit that day. Its Company A alone lost ninety-one men killed, and most of the rest were maimed. Companies B and D were also hard hit. Meeks' 3rd Battalion received moderately high casualties.)

The source of the following is a taped interview in which Colonel Meeks personally recounted to the author his recollections. It begins

252

with events on June 4, while the USS Charles Carroll *is still anchored at Weymouth Harbor.*

I was given special permission to visit other ships of the regiment. I chose to visit my former unit of the 1st Battalion, Company D, which was on the *Empire Javelin*. I found former Roanoker and old Viscose buddy, Captain Walt Schilling. (Both men had previously worked in a rayon mill together as civilians.) I had known Walt since we were ten years old, and we both joined the National Guard together. He was in a mood I had never seen before.

When we were alone, he said, "Do you think you will live through this and return home?" Knowing him as I did, this caught me by surprise. I said, "Sure, with our training and fine equipment, we've got it made." His reply was, "Gene, I don't believe I'm going to make it."

I assured him he would return home. (I was wrong—his landing craft was hit by an 88mm before it touched down. Schilling was standing behind the ramp that took a direct hit.) I visited and shook hands with many men of Company D and the 1st Battalion. Too many of them didn't survive the landings.

When I returned to my ship, I noticed the men were unusually quiet and a few were playing cards. There wasn't any of the usual horseplay. I remember eating a good evening meal. I checked my clothing and equipment and turned in about 10:30 p.m. I was not the least bit nervous and tried to look at tomorrow as just another training exercise. I began wondering what we would be doing this time the next day.

We were awakened at 2 a.m. the next morning. I got out of bed, checked my gear, and ate a good breakfast. I assembled the battalion officers, reminded them that this was the real thing and to keep in mind what we had learned in training, and I then wished them all good luck!

We heard Colonel Canham's and General Eisenhower's messages over the ship's intercom. Everyone knew where their stations were and how to get there. We loaded into our landing craft by davits; others used cargo nets. By now, the water had some fair sized swells, and one had to be careful. We were in total darkness. We had about thirty men in our landing craft. A 4.2-inch chemical mortar detachment and its captain (Gaffney) were assigned to us for support.

It became apparent that some of our men were getting nervous about the mission they were soon to perform, and understandably so. We didn't know what to expect on the beach or even if we would make it to the beach. Then the battleship USS *Texas*, less than a mile to the right, began firing its 14-inch guns against the French coast. All turrets pointing shoreward were belching pure hell toward the area where we were heading. This tended to uplift all of our spirits, at least temporarily.

As we got closer in, we soon realized there was resistance and that we were in for a fight. Machine guns began firing across the ramp and into the side of the landing craft. This injured no one. I was, at the time, talking to the other officer, Captain Gaffney, when enemy artillery shells landed close by. The coast guard coxswain became very nervous and tried to steer our craft behind and close to another boat in our wave.

This, of course, created a good target for the shore batteries. I had already cautioned the sailor to keep a good distance, but to no avail. I then drew my .45 Colt pistol and ordered him to disperse. He finally steered away from the others. After trying to calm the sailor's nerves, I returned to the front of the boat.

I had just gotten settled, and had my hand on Captain Gaffney's shoulder, when an incredibly loud explosion blew the ramp off the landing craft. Captain Gaffney and some of his men were killed. The captain's head landed on my shoulder, and I could see blood oozing from his nose and mouth. It was apparent that he was dead. This was the first battle casualty, and the first person that I saw killed.

Water flooded into the landing craft, sinking it in shoulder-deep water. We shed our equipment (about fifty or sixty pounds) and kept low in the water, wading to shore. It is probably fate that saved us, because if we hadn't sunk we would have landed in front of a machine gun emplacement and probably would have been killed. We picked our way through the obstacles.

There were two guns firing at us and a few of our men were returning the fire, which neutralized them. Those that survived the boat sinking made it across the beach and to the wall unscathed. We stayed at the wall until the afternoon, when conditions improved. We moved down the beach, where I tried to organize the company commanders. We hadn't heard the terrible news concerning the 1st Battalion's high casualties.

We could see the road up ahead that led to the Les Moulins Draw. We thought it might be under fire, so we avoided it by going over the bluff. On top of the hill a well-hidden coastal gun fired, frightening us because it was only a few feet away. One of our men was killed near the gun.

Battalion S-2 Lieutenant Smith and I encountered a ravine that was a German defensive position. We met strong resistance throughout the night at a rather large church in the center of town. The next morning, Colonel Canham appeared and ordered the battalion to pull back and move up the road that parallels the beach at Vierville.

On D plus 2, we were ordered to help a contingent of beleaguered rangers at Pointe-du-Hoc. We opened fire on what we thought were Germans. After seeing they were American rangers, I ordered a ceasefire. After relieving the rangers at the point, we resumed our march to Grandcamp. As we followed the road, we began to lose sight of the channel.

PRIVATE FIRST CLASS ROBERT L. SALES
COMPANY B, 116TH INFANTRY

Bob Sales, of Madison Heights, Virginia (near Lynchburg), joined the Virginia National Guard's Company B, 116th, at age fifteen. He was the lone survivor of his thirty-man landing craft. Sales fought with B Company as a staff sergeant and went on to Saint-Lô, Vire, down to Brest, and up through Belgium, Holland, and Germany. He received the Silver Star for valor at Setterich, Germany. During the November Offensive, while fighting near the German border, Sergeant Sales was severely wounded in both eyes. He recuperated for two years in army hospitals and regained partial sight in one eye. He returned to Normandy for the 50th Anniversary of D-Day Commemorations. Following are edited excerpts of his written and oral memoirs.

I was Company B Commanding Officer Captain Ettore Zappacosta's radioman and bodyguard on D-Day. Captain Zapp asked me to become his personal bodyguard after I returned from ranger training. He told me that I would ride with him on the company headquarters landing craft. I was the only survivor to get off that boat alive.

I do not remember sleeping aboard the HMS *Empire Javelin*, or what was served for breakfast the morning of June 6, 1944. I made a point to see each of the Lynchburg men and to shake hands with them before embarking into the landing craft. At this time, I didn't notice anyone showing fear of what was to take place. The sea was rough, and the landing craft seemed to be jumping as high as ten feet.

The captain was in charge of our boat. We rail-loaded and were let down to the ocean by davits. We circled the control ship until all of our wave had disembarked and formed up for the ride to shore. The ocean spray blew into our boat and we became soaking wet. Some of the men became sick and began to vomit into their puke bags. I was lucky not to get sick.

Appendix I

We could see and hear the large guns firing at targets on shore from navy ships. There were also rockets firing from LCT(R)s and airplanes flying over to protect the fleet and to soften the beach. All of this noise and action tended to cause assurances that our mission would succeed.

About one hundred yards from shore, the English coxswain said he couldn't get us in any closer. As the ramp lowered, enemy machine guns opened up, firing directly into our boat. Like all great leaders, Captain Zapp was first off the boat and the first one to get hit.

Staff Sergeant Dick Wright (of Lynchburg, Virginia, communication sergeant), was second and also hit, falling into the water. A medic was third, and I didn't see what happened to him. I was fourth. I caught my heel in the ramp and fell sideways out of the path of that MG42, undoubtedly saving my life. All of the men that followed were either killed by Germans or drowned. As far as I know, no one from my craft was ever found alive.

The captain screamed, "I'm hit!" I tried to get to him but he was lost in the surf. It became obvious that we were in mortal danger. Men were all around me in the water bleeding from wounds and screaming for help. I knew the boat was the target so I got away from it as fast as I could.

One of the first things I did was to shed my SCR-300 radio and my assault jacket. That radio was heavy, and I suppose it is still at the bottom of the channel. Mortar and artillery shells were landing all around, and one hit so close that it knocked me groggy. Luckily, a log floated by with an unexploded teller mine still attached. I grabbed hold of it until my head cleared a bit. I remained behind that log, pushing it in front of me, using it as a shield until I reached dry land.

The first person I saw on the beach that I recognized was Dick Wright. He hollered over to me that he was badly hit. I watched him trying to raise on his arms, but a sniper spotted him and shot

257

him through the head. His face fell to the sand, never to move again. I didn't try to go to him because I knew he was dead.

While pinned down on the beach, I watched incoming landing craft being shot at. One of them carried the battalion surgeon, Captain Robert B. Ware, a man I knew from my hometown of Madison Heights, Virginia. The doctor had flaming red hair. I watched him as he disembarked the landing craft and that machine gun opened up, cutting him down. What I will never forget was seeing his helmet fly off his head and showing all that red hair.

I crawled on my belly using the dead and wounded as a shield. Some time later, I saw Mack Smith from Shepherdtown, West Virginia, and some other B Company men taking shelter behind a sea wall. Some of them were badly wounded.

I bandaged Smith's eye that was lying out on his face. I kept crawling back to the water's edge, dragging men out if they were still living. I didn't bother if they were dead. I pulled quite a few to safety. One of the medics helped me to give first aid and comfort to the wounded.

The first enemy soldier I saw was a prisoner. Interrogators had him on his knees and his hands were locked behind his head. He didn't look so tough to me, but those guys up in those cliffs were plenty tough. You can't imagine how helpless it was to be lying on that beach, and those machine guns and snipers shooting anything that moved.

At this point, we were not sure the invasion would succeed. Our company was shot up so badly that there was no organization or communication from other sectors to tell us how they were doing. If all of the landing zones were as helpless as we were, the invasion was in jeopardy. We felt helpless and alone.

We had many acts of heroism from our B Company men with many of them unreported. Lieutenant William B. Williams single-handedly, with hand grenades and rifle, charged and subdued a pillbox. Sergeants William Pearce and Odell "Toad" Padgett survived the landing better than we did, and were able to take a few men up into those rocks and cliffs and fight it out with the Germans. It was touch-and-go for quite some time in our Dog Green sector.

Not until Saint-Lô fell in July did we know for sure that the invasion was a success.

D-Day was, indeed, the "longest day," but there were many, many long days after that. Day after bloody day, it was jumping over those hedgerows and getting men killed. We lost some very good men every single day. Saint-Lô was about twenty-five miles from the beach and it was liberated on July 18. When Saint-Lô fell, we felt confident that we were in France to stay. Surviving the war was another story.

PRIVATE DAVID E. SILVA
COMPANY D, 116TH INFANTRY

On D-Day, Private David Silva, a machine gunner with Company D, 116th Infantry, was nineteen years old. After the war, Silva was ordained as a Roman Catholic priest. Father Silva is now retired and lives with his sister in Seven Hills, Ohio. Following are excerpts of his remembrances of D-Day.

On D-Day, I was an ammo bearer in Sergeant Jack Ingram's squad (Russell W. Ingram, of Roanoke, KIA). As we approached the shore, we came under heavy machine gun fire. Already there were many dead and wounded on the beach.

As the ramp dropped, I was wounded while exiting the boat. I was struck in the calf of my right leg, tearing up my legging. The bullet first hit my entrenching shovel, then a C-ration can, and creased my water canteen before entering my leg. I was lucky, as this was a minor flesh wound. There were many dead and wounded from Companies A and B lying on the beach and in the water.

I didn't recognize any D Company men there on the beach.

Most of our boat team died in the water. We huddled in the water for about ten or fifteen minutes before attempting to cross the beach. All of our weapons were fouled by sand and salt water, and I had lost one box of ammunition in the water. About twelve of us reached the sea wall about 7:15 a.m. and stayed there until about noon. Tanks flushed out a machine gun and some snipers holed up in a pillbox.

Early afternoon, tanks neutralized the deadly pillbox and allowed us to regroup and count our casualties. As the tide receded, we retrieved weapons and ammunition that were lost earlier while under fire. We cleaned our weapons and reconnoitered the beach. It was then we learned that our casualties were very heavy. Everyone lost their appetites. Our leaders were wiped out, we were in the wrong sector, and we were exhausted. At dusk, we walked up the draw, which overlooked the beach, and slept like babies—on top of the ground!

At D plus 1, I ate my first meal, and upon inspection, I saw that my pack equipment deflected bullets and probably saved my life. At this time I had not fired my weapon.

MAJOR JOHN W. SOURS
116TH REGIMENTAL S-4

When I began gathering material for D-Day history, I received a letter from Mrs. Grace Sours (Mrs. Bentley H.) Strickland, sister of Major John Sours, Regimental S-4 and ranking Roanoker killed on D-Day. Following are excerpts of this letter, describing the last time she saw her brother, along with the major portion of a letter she received from the regimental surgeon, Doctor Robert Buckley, which graphically detailed Major Sours' death. Doctor Buckley initially sent the letter to Colonel Harold A. Cassell (Roanoke), regimental executive officer, who forwarded it to Major Sours' sister.

To John Slaughter,

Reading your interest in D-Day activities and seeing my brother, John W. Sours' name listed, I wish to oblige your request . . . Thanks for caring enough to exhibit this interest in commemorating the bravery of these Americans of June 6, 1944.

. . . Since this was my brother's last leave before leaving for England, the family needed a get-together . . . My brother, John, and two other brothers and I were alone for these intimate moments . . .

John explained that, since the 29th Division was to be the first overseas, they would be the first to spearhead the invasion, and that there would be no way but that the Germans would "mow" them down . . . He wanted us to remember that his Christian faith would "see them through" and that if he "fell," he didn't want his body returned to Roanoke—that he would be "raised up there as well as here" . . . He asked that we not grieve if he did not return . . . He chose to go because "liberty is in jeopardy and those trained should defend it." He said that liberty was worth the sacrifice. As we kissed, I held back the tears, and we both smiled.

The following letter, addressed to Colonel Cassell, was written by Doctor Robert Buckley from Germany, January 27, 1945.

. . . You were asking what I knew concerning Major Sours' death on D-Day, since he and I came in that day in the same landing craft. I remember pretty clearly, and this is the way it was:

Early on the morning of D-Day, after breakfast, "Big John" and I—he had the bunk next to mine in the same stateroom—got our things together, and he finished sticking some more camouflage material in the netting of his helmet.

We also helped each other make some final adjustments in our web equipment, so that all the stuff he was hanging on us would be as comfortable as we could make it. Then we went down to the colonel's stateroom where we were to wait until time to go over into the small landing craft.

When the time came we climbed over the side of the ship and down the net, which was not any too easy that morning due to the roughness of the sea and the load on our backs.

Looking down from the deck of the ship, that little LCVP seemed a long way down (and it was, too) and with everybody standing on the same side of the little boat it was leaning 'way over to one side, the lower end of the net hanging into the high side when the boat bounced just right and dangling over nothing between times.

The sea was slamming the little boat around like a stick of wood and kept throwing it up against the side of the USS *Charles Carroll*. However, all twenty-six of us made it all right, and then we moved away from the big ship, circling around a little, and headed for the shore, which we could see only as a hazy, thin line in the distance.

By the time we were about a third of the way in, we were all soaking wet clear through from water splashing in great quantities over the bow and sides of the boat. No one I saw became seasick but later I heard several of them say—and I felt the same way myself—that their throats became very dry, so much so they could hardly swallow.

This was due partly to the drying effect of the seasickness prevention capsules we'd taken several hours prior to debarkation, but more, I think, to the excitement of the situation than to anything else. I don't think that fear had anything to do with it, because at that early hour none of us had time to become afraid. We were doing the very thing that we, as a chosen group, had trained so long to do, and we were fascinated and eagerly excited about it— although, of course, we realized that any number of things might happen to us, and knew too that some things we'd never dreamed of might very well be waiting for us on the beach.

Major Sours was standing in the boat just to my right rear, and I was on the left side of the boat, second from the ramp at the front end. When we got almost in, where we thought it would be well to duck down from possible machine gun fire, we all squatted down in the boat's bottom. In a tossing small craft with a wet, slippery floor, it's no mean accomplishment to do this and keep one's balance— and many of us did fall over more than once.

I remember Major Sours, two privates, (Rosen [Private Abraham, Security Platoon] and Namey [Private George B., Security Platoon]) and myself trying to disentangle ourselves from a sprawled knot on the floor during the excitement of a couple of minutes—which seemed like almost a half-hour instead— when the boat became stuck against the side of a beach obstacle in the form of a large pole (the size of a telegraph pole) sticking up from the ocean's floor and carrying a teller mine fastened loosely on its top.

Here we were, with about eighty feet of water between us and the beach sand, bouncing up and down, scraping against the side of a pole so that, as the boat went up with each incoming wave, it slid up the side of the pole toward the mine, and then—after approaching to within six or eight inches of it—went down again.

If a little bigger wave had come in—a perfectly good possibility—we'd have hit the mine, and the reasonable expectation is that would have been the end of the whole business for our LCVP. Because of the high spot on the bottom of the sea the navy crew couldn't get the boat off the pole, so several of the men began yelling for the ramp to be let down right there.

All this time we were under fire from the beach and the high ground overlooking it (artillery, mortar and small arms fire), so finally the boat crew decided to lower the ramp where we were. The moment it dropped the whole boatload of men surged out into the water at once, just at H-60 minutes, exactly as scheduled.

As many times as I'd done this landing business in practice, I still lost my balance in running off the side of the ramp and fell forward in about two feet of water on my hands and knees. But I got up immediately and went on toward the shore. The further I went, the deeper the water got, till finally my feet left the bottom.

In addition to our inflated life belts, we all wore on our backs gas masks in rubber carriers, which acted as auxiliary life preservers, so there was no trouble at all keeping afloat. Across the deep stretch—about forty feet, I'd guess—I paddled along with a small piece of board I picked up from the floating debris.

While doing this paddling—which worked pretty well—I looked over to my right and saw "Big John" coming right along, too. When I got up onto the sand, where there were a lot of spiderlike obstacles made of about eight-foot lengths of railroad rails, crossed on each other at their centers, I flattened out on the sand behind one of them to catch my breath a little and saw Major Sours behind another off to my right a short distance.

He saw me looking, and grinned back as he called over, "How're you doing, Doc?" I replied that I was doing all right, and asked how he was making out, to which he answered that he was doing all right, too.

We could see where machine gun bullets were peppering the water all around us but particularly ahead, all the time we were coming in, and after we'd rested on the sand for not more than a minute or two, there was an extraheavy spattering of them in the water, in a runnel, just in front of us.

This runnel was a narrow strip of water between the sandbar we were on and the beach proper and was probably twenty feet wide where we were and it proved to be little less than two feet deep when we ran through it.

Just as this burst of machine gun fire seemed to die down I jumped up and ran across the sand through the runnel and up the rocky beach to a little ledge about three feet (or less) high, where a roadway running right along the beach was built up.

I think Major Sours was almost immediately behind me—I'm not sure—as he started getting up at the same time I did. Everybody ran in individually and got there the best way he could, so when I reached the little ledge I spoke of, it was hard to tell whether everybody was in or not, as we were pretty well separated.

As it happened, I ran up to where Major Jackson (Asbury H., regimental S-2) was, and just as he was asking if I'd seen Tom Howie ("The Major of Saint-Lô," regimental S-3, KIA), up he (Major Howie) ran, all hunched over, and sat down to do as we were doing, loosening our web equipment and other gear so we could get around better.

While the three of us were catching our breath, there we saw two men who seemed to need help getting out of the water, so with an enlisted man who was sitting next to me, I ran back out to them. The enlisted man (whom I didn't know) began helping one of them—a soldier with a wounded leg—and I went over to the other one, who was lying face down in the water about the middle of the runnel. I could tell from his uniform he was one of our officers and when I lifted him partly up, I saw it was Major Sours. He was already dead when I found him. Although the heavy fire on the beach made it no place for any unduly extended examination, I did make absolutely sure that he wasn't either drowned or partially drowned and there was nothing at all that could be done for him. As best I could tell, he'd been killed by a machine gun bullet wound to the head, although at the time I didn't actually see the wound.

I feel sure, however, that was what happened and this is the reason: a few minutes later, I was helping the enlisted man I've already mentioned with the wounded man he was trying to get into a better place on the beach. I picked up what I took to be the wounded man's helmet. It was floating upside down in the water and I put it on his head. Then we saw that it had two bullet holes in it, one where the bullet had entered on one side and the other where it had made its exit on the other side.

We took the helmet off again, looked at the same man's head and found that he had no head wound. Then, on reexamining the helmet, we saw it belonged to Major Sours and had floated down from where we were working on this man. At that very moment, fire on that stretch of the beach became suddenly very intense—so much so that it was impossible to investigate further as to what happened, but there is no doubt in my mind as to what caused Major Sours' death.

In a very short while his body had been taken up onto a place higher on the beach and while I, myself, didn't do this, I did make it a point to check and see that it had been done before I left the beach for good. His body was carried later on the same day up off the beach proper onto higher ground. This was beside the roadway and was covered, along with many others, with heavy sheeting material brought along for that purpose, by the personnel whose duty it was to care for those of us who were killed.

I believe you said something about a diary of "Big John's" that Mrs. Sours had asked about. I have never seen it and don't know where it could be. Since joining the regiment back in April 1943, I'd gotten to know Major Sours pretty well but I've never heard him speak of a diary.

Since I know you're going to turn this narrative over to Mrs. Strickland, I'd like to add something else here, if I may, and it is this: I just wanted her to know that I share the opinion of all the others in the regiment who knew Major Sours, that he was a fine man—a very fine man, who both deserved and received the respect and admiration of us all.

(Signed) Robert Buckley
Major Robert Buckley,
Medical Corp
Surgeon, 116th Infantry

CAPTAIN ROBERT W. STEWART
121ST ENGINEER BATTALION, 29TH DIVISION

Mrs. Ruth Stewart shared with me the personal memoir her husband had written for the family scrapbook. A captain in the 121st Engineers, 29th Division, he was assigned on D-Day to clear the

beach of obstacles such as mines and barbed wire. He was awarded the
Silver Star for valor. He and his wife made their home in Tahlequah,
Oklahoma.

"We were on our way to the greatest adventure man had ever
experienced," Captain Stewart wrote. "We raised anchor at about
6:30 p.m. for Normandy, France, aboard the USS Charles Carroll."
He thought about his wife Ruth and the kids, and wondered if he
would be fortunate enough to ever see them again. He said that he
must have made peace with himself because he slept very well the night
of June 5, 1944. He slept fully clothed and was awakened by clanging
bells for breakfast. The following excerpt picks up his story from this
point. I have slightly changed some of the wording, but hopefully not
the meaning.

We lowered anchor about twelve miles from shore. The sea was
running high and the air was chilly. This was bad for the men who
were prone to getting seasick. We were fed a dream breakfast and
were able to order almost *anything* and get it.

Our assault wave was due to hit the shore at about 7 a.m. The
Royal Air Force flew over and began their assault on the beach targets. The explosions could be felt from where we were, and I could
see in the semidarkness the wreckage from the planes' bombs being
thrown in the air.

We were ordered over the side, and our landing craft assembled
at a rendezvous point around the control ship. I shook hands with
Al and some of the men who were to go in from other craft. Our
U.S. Navy coxswain and his ensign were veterans of the Salerno
invasion. We also carried three ordinary seamen.

We rendezvoused at about 6:35 a.m., and the control ship
waved us toward Omaha Beach. *This was it!* The battleships
Arkansas, Nevada, and *Texas* were firing broadsides into the beach
defenses. The cruiser USS *Augusta,* a British monitor, and several
new American destroyers were also giving us support. The artillery

fire was deafening. The beach from about four miles out looked like an inferno. Orders were given to stay low in the craft. The assault wave straightened out and headed for the beach at full speed. The sea was rough and, despite taking pills, some of the men got terribly seasick.

The navy began shelling the beach as we approached. One craft took a direct hit and disappeared. Over thirty of our men were surely killed. We were soon passing over dead bodies that had washed back out to sea. The beach became clearly outlined with black objects as far as the eye could see. They were our soldiers. Why didn't they move on across the beach and out of the direct fire? I could see dead men washing in the incoming tide. The interlocking crossfire from machine guns was devastating.

There was great confusion and pandemonium on the beach. Our boat was almost ashore when its bottom scraped a sandbar and came to a halt. Unable to buck over it, the seaman lowered the ramp, and off we went in water about five feet deep. The ensign and some of our men began exiting when small arms fire began hitting the open ramp.

Only twenty-one of our men escaped. What a price to pay! The pounding of the surf muffled the screams of the wounded and only the dead were at peace. Outstretched bodies were so thick one had to crawl over them every five or six feet.

There were disabled tanks, two landing craft, infantry-large (LCI-L)s and one burning LCT. A pillbox firing down the beach from the right was finally silenced after bitter hand-to-hand fighting. We worked our way to the beach exit (Vierville Draw) and into the village of Vierville-sur-Mer, our objective.

Captain Humphrey lost most of his men and all of his noncoms. The beach exit finally opened at 3:30 p.m. and we entered Vierville on schedule. A concrete wall across the draw was blown with three thousand pounds of TNT. The wall was fourteen feet thick at the base, twelve feet high and six feet thick at the top. We then filled an antitank ditch and removed some mines. We bivouacked south of Vierville at 4:30 p.m. Sniper fire kept us under cover till dark. I went after the sniper but couldn't find him. This was very irritating.

We buttoned up at 9:30 p.m. after posting guard. The next morning at 6:30, the Germans struck. We lost a lot of men. Sergeant Pacelli was killed but took fourteen Krauts with him. He was a good man. Some of our casualties included Holmstrup, Humphrey, Martin, Lebegue and McNicholas. The loss of most of our top non-coms was irreplaceable. After being driven back five hundred yards, we got help from a handful of rangers and a Sherman tank. After organizing, we went back on the offensive.

Colonel Ploger and I captured thirteen prisoners who were hiding in a cave at the exit off Omaha Beach. Some of them were wounded and all were foreign nationals led by German noncoms and officers. They were more scared than we. I had to search each man thoroughly.

In the short space of twenty-eight hours we had become a battle weary bunch. It seemed that we had experienced a lifetime of danger in these few hours. So passed D-Day, in which the untried American of the 29th tried to prove his worth as a fighting man.

Our losses continued to mount and the workload of each man doubled. We went forty-eight hours with very little sleep. Everyone became bone-weary tired. We cleared the roads of mines and laid wire for communication. We still hadn't gotten replacements and everyone was doing three jobs. We went through Grandcamp-les-Bains on the way to Isigny. Almost all of the houses, barns, and chateaux were destroyed and all of the cattle were dead.

We reached the inundated area on June 8 and found the bridges still usable. I wondered why Jerry hadn't blown them. Thank goodness, we didn't lose anyone crossing the bridges. The enemy fought stubbornly for St.-Claire-sur-Elle. Our infantry was dishing it out and they were taking it as well.

We proceeded slowly through the hedgerow country. It was Murder, Inc. There is no other way to describe it. We encountered various types of antitank and antipersonnel mines that had to be dispatched. Our losses continued to be heavy and some of our replacements didn't last long enough to become soldiers. We bivouacked near Les Foulons, about twelve kilometers from Saint-Lô.

On June 12, our unit went into the line as infantry. We jumped off the next morning at 7 a.m. Our artillery fell short and killed some of my men. Enemy mortars opened up, and the man walking ahead of me got his face partially blown off. We advanced about 500 yards and were thrown back as Jerry counterattacked, and we suffered heavy losses. Two tank destroyers that were supporting us fled, deserting us. The counterbattery fire was heavy and we took more casualties.

After about a week on the line, we were relieved by a battalion of the 115th Infantry. Behind the lines we made up hedgerow busters (prongs mounted on the front of our tanks) for the final drive into Saint-Lô.

I went into Saint-Lô with "Task Force Cota." This was a contingent of 29th Recon troops and mounted infantry led by Brigadier General Norman Cota. Whew! We had very heavy fighting and there were casualties on both sides. We entered Saint-Lô with four bulldozers, and we lost two of them. Saint-Lô fell on the afternoon of July 18. You can't imagine the destruction of this medieval city and the casualties suffered on both sides.

The Division had earned a badly needed rest. On July 19, we were relieved and for the first time since D-Day we were sent to the rear for rest, clean clothes, sleep, and hot food. We were shelled while retreating through Couvains.

Back in the rest area we received our first air raid. JU-88s bombed and strafed us, killing nine and eleven were wounded. Twenty-seven trucks were disabled and one field kitchen demolished. By now, we had received many new faces and not many of the older men were left.

TRICKY TIDES AT OMAHA BEACH

British Flotilla Commander at Dog Green Sector, Sub-Lieutenant Jimmy Green, and his son-in-law, Dr. Kevin Elsby, who is writing a book on Sub-Lieutenant Green, kindly furnished this Omaha Beach tide and obstacle information.

Here is an apt description of the tricky tides at Omaha Beach and its formidable beach obstacles:

Omaha Beach extended along six miles of the Normandy coast from the Vierville-sur-Mer Draw at the western extremity to Port-en-Besin in the east. Some 555 yards of firm sand separated the high, high water and low, low water marks at Vierville-sur-Mer. The last twenty-five yards of beach was covered with shingle, rising to a sea wall that graduated from five feet to twelve feet at Vierville-sur-Mer. A twelve- to fourteen-foot vertical wall had been constructed across the Vierville exit at the high, high water mark.

Behind the sea wall, steep bluffs rose to one hundred feet. To the west of Vierville toward Pointe-du-Hoc, one hundred-foot cliffs faced straight out to sea. There were five exit draws from Omaha Beach. The Vierville exit at Dog Green was the best, with a paved road. It was also the most heavily defended. The four other exits were a combination of dirt paths and dirt roads.

The average gradient of the beach at Vierville was less than one degree to the horizontal. The beach rose and fell in five distinct steps. To the approaching landing craft, the beach presented a series of firm tidal ridges running laterally across the shallow beach. Behind each ridge was an area of deeper water, two to three feet lower than the ridges.

Two large sandbars ran parallel to the beach at Vierville at a distance of 100 yards from the low, low water mark and 600 yards from the sea wall. Each sandbar was 800 yards long and 100 to 150 yards wide. The sandbars were exposed at low, low water, and were covered by about five feet of water as the first wave landed at 6:30 a.m. The tide was then two to three feet above the low tide mark, and about 400 yards from the sea wall.

The tide rose eighteen feet between low tide at 5:30 a.m. and high tide at 11 a.m. on D-Day, crossing 490 yards of beach at Vierville and leaving a 20-yard gap of shingle beach to the sea wall at high tide. The flat shingled sand stones were a barrier for vehicular traffic.

Low tide was at a level four feet above and forty-five yards up the beach from the low, low water mark. High tide was at a level three feet below and twenty yards down the beach from the high, high water mark and the sea wall.

The assessment of the currents prepared for D-Day Bigot maps reads as follows:

"The currents in this region are complex and their detailed behavior little known. In general, they flow eastward along the shore as the tide rises, reach a maximum about half tide, become slack during high water stand and then reverse, flowing westward as the tide falls, again reaching a maximum at about half tide and becoming slack near the time of low water. Maximum currents are experienced during spring tides and minimum currents during neap tides.

"Maximum currents attain velocities of about 2.7 knots at a distance of five miles offshore and decrease as they approach the shore, becoming about 2.2 knots at a distance of one mile offshore. The currents slack and reverse directions somewhat sooner near the shore than to the seaward. Closer inshore than one mile, the current directions become more confused as the depths decrease, but in general, the velocities also decrease, and it is reasonable to assume that they become insignificant at the proposed grounding points."

A table of contents was prepared for the period from May 25 to June 21, based on measurements taken along the coast.

Tidal velocities were about two knots, flowing eastward as landing craft approached the beach. The larger landing craft such as the LCTs traveled at about four knots, whereas the smaller landing craft such as the LCAs and LCVPs made ten knots.

Beach obstacles had been placed parallel to the beach, starting with a line of posts with mines strapped to the top lying in wait of the approaching landing craft. The first line of posts had been placed about three hundred yards from the sea wall and two hundred yards above the D-Day low tide mark. Lines of log ramps, metal tetrahedra and hedgehogs filled the beach behind the first row of posts. Each was laden with teller mines.

First light on D-Day was at 5:16 a.m. followed by sunlight at 5:58 a.m. At first light the sun was six degrees below the horizon. June 6 was a full moon. D-Day had been chosen to coincide with a full moon to assist the airborne assault.

The first wave of LCAs and LCVPs landed at 6:30 a.m., one hour after low tide, thirty yards from the water's edge and one hundred yards below the first line of posts. The beach obstacles had been placed to defend against an assault close to high tide.

The first wave landed when the tide was very low. Five LCAs from 551 Flotilla made it to the beach in the first wave, and all five returned from the beach. The incoming tide advanced rapidly, providing a different scene for the second and third waves. The sandbars and beach obstacles were submerged as the second and third waves approached the beach. The second and third waves landed among some of the beach obstacles, losing five out of the twelve LCAs.

Regimental Headquarters Company and the 3rd Battalion were to load onto the USS *Charles Carroll*, an amphibious assault troop transport that had a troop capacity of about a thousand men or a reinforced battalion.

FATALITIES, 1944–1945: D COMPANY, 116TH INFANTRY REGIMENT

Pasquale Ardolino
Alton Ashley
Richard Ayers
Herman Bania
Romeo Bily
Aaron Bowling
Albert Bronkhorst
John Brown
Sam Callahan
Tony Carusotto
Rufus B. Carr
Charles Carroll
Roland Coates
John Cox
Merle Cummings
Joseph Davis
Blair Dixon
John Dylik

William Gardner
William Garvin
Thurman Green
Benjamin Hoch
Russell Ingram
George Johnson
Roswell Johnson
Emmett Journell
Stanley Koryciak
John Kozak
Vincent Labowicz
Prudencio Lavin
Charles Leach
Raymond Le Beau
George Longlow
Ralph Lynn
Lawrence Martin
Thomas McArtor

Lundy McClanahan
Roy McKay
Charles Milliron
Thomas Monaghan
Louis Monk
Clyde Moore
James Obenshain
James Ohler
James Paulick
Clarence Peck
Anthony Pisano
David Powers
Charles Quinlin
Frenchman Ratliff
Marshall Ray
Wallace Riddick
Perry Rose
Everett Satzko

Donald Sawyer	Alvin Smith	Edward Walton
Walter Schilling	William Solomon	Irvin West
Henry Schmetzer	George Stearns	Francis Wheeler
Francis Schuster	Robert Stover	Winfred Wiescamp
Harold Short	Elmer Swift	George Williams
Jack Simms	Elmer Tokach	James Williams
John Singleton	Daniel Torowski	Walfred Williams
Sherman Skeens	Nevin Walk	James Wright

ADDITIONAL DOCUMENTS

Prior to D-Day, 116th Regimental Commander, Col. Charles D. W. Canham, issued this letter to be read to all members of the 116th Regiment.

29 May 1944
MEMORANDUM:

TO: To the Members of CT 116, reinforced (to be read by commanders to <u>all</u> personnel prior to embarkation).

    1. The long awaited day is near and prior to embarkation I want to wish each one of you the best of luck in your forthcoming adventure. There is one certain way to get the enemy out of action and that is to kill him. War is not child's play and requires hatred for the enemy. At this time we don't have it. I hope you get it when you see your friends wounded and killed.

    2. Learn to take care of yourself from the start. Remember the Hun is a crafty, intelligent fighter and wi;; not have mercy on you. Don't have it on him. He will try to outwit you. Be on the Alert.

    3. Fighting a war is the same as any athletic event, only war is for keeps. It is you or the enemy. Teamwork is the essence of success. We have the tools, the best in the world, and it is up to you to see that they are used properly.

4. Remember when you run into the enemy, contain him with the minimum to stop him, then move around him and strike him in the flank or the rear. In all your contacts with him be ruthless, always drive hard. The Hun doesn't like Yankee drive and guts. Show him that you have plenty. If you close with him, use your bayonet, show him you can take it and dish it out. Don't be caught napping. Don't let your Yankee curiosity get you blown up by a booby trap or mine.

5. Take care of your arms and equipment. Conserve your ammunition, make every shot count. Keep your weapons cleaned and oiled. Their proper functioning at the right time may mean your life. Every soldier must realize the importance of supply discipline and see that he himself does his part in conserving supplies. More than one battle has been lost because munitions and other supplies were not available.

6. Do not eat your "K" and "D" rations prior to D, D+1 Day. you won't get any more until D+2.

7. The Navy and Air will give us plenty of support. Gen. Montgomery was very optimistic in his talk to the officers yesterday. At this time no one knows how much resistence we will meet on D-Day. We may be able to walk in without trouble, we may have to fight for your life, to meet the worst and make up your minds now that you are going forward regardless and it is a one way ticket. <u>We are not giving ground at any time</u> and not leaving until the job is done.

8. I have the utmost confidence in your ability to take it and dish it out. There is one final word of warning, the Hun will try to lower your morale by firing artillery or mortars in your areas during the time our artillery is firing in an effort to make you believe our artillery is firing on us.

To each one of you Happy Landings and come off those craft fighting like hell!

CANHAM

APPENDIX IV

On the morning of the invasion, General Eisenhower read this
message to all the assault troops, who also received a printed copy.

SUPREME HEADQUARTERS
ALLIED EXPEDITIONARY FORCE

Soldiers, Sailors and Airmen of the Allied Expeditionary force! You are about to embark upon the Great Crusade, towards which we have striven these many months. The eyes of the world are upon you. The hopes and prayers of liberty-loving people everywhere march with you. In company with our brave Allies and brothers-in-arms on other fronts, you will bring about the destruction of the German war machine, the elimination of Nazi tyranny over the oppressed peoples of Europe, and security for ourselves in a free world.

Your task will not be an easy one. your enemy is well trained, well equipped and battle-hardened. He will fight savagely.

But this is the year 1944! Much has happened since the Nazi triumphs of the years, 1940–41. The United Nations have inflicted upon the Germans great defeats in open battle, man-to-man. Our air offensive has seriously reduced their strength in the air and their capacity to wage war on the ground. Our Home Fronts have given us an over-whelming superiority in weapons and munitions of war, and placed at our disposal great reserves of trained fighting men. The tide has turned! The free men of the world are marching together to Victory!

I have full confidence in your courage, devotion to duty and skill in battle. We will accept nothing less than full Victory!

Good Luck! And let us all beseech the blessing of Almighty God upon this great and noble undertaking.

[Signed] Dwight Eisenhower

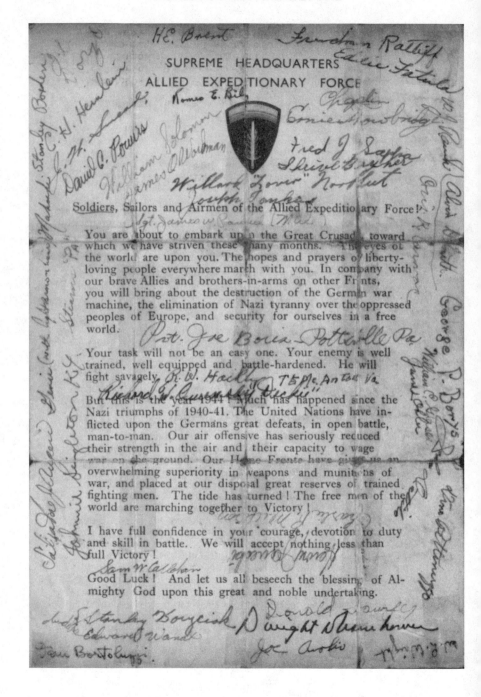

SUPREME HEADQUARTERS
ALLIED EXPEDITIONARY FORCE

Soldiers, Sailors and Airmen of the Allied Expeditionary Force!

You are about to embark upon the Great Crusade, toward
which we have striven these many months. The eyes of
the world are upon you. The hopes and prayers of liberty-
loving people everywhere march with you. In company with
our brave Allies and brothers-in-arms on other Fronts,
you will bring about the destruction of the German war
machine, the elimination of Nazi tyranny over the oppressed
peoples of Europe, and security for ourselves in a free
world.

Your task will not be an easy one. Your enemy is well
trained, well equipped and battle-hardened. He will
fight savagely.

But this is the year 1944! Much has happened since the
Nazi triumphs of 1940-41. The United Nations have inflicted upon the Germans great defeats, in open battle,
man-to-man. Our air offensive has seriously reduced
their strength in the air and their capacity to wage
war on the ground. Our Home Fronts have given us an
overwhelming superiority in weapons and munitions of
war, and placed at our disposal great reserves of trained
fighting men. The tide has turned! The free men of the
world are marching together to Victory!

I have full confidence in your courage, devotion to duty
and skill in battle. We will accept nothing less than
full Victory!

Good Luck! And let us all beseech the blessing of Almighty God upon this great and noble undertaking.

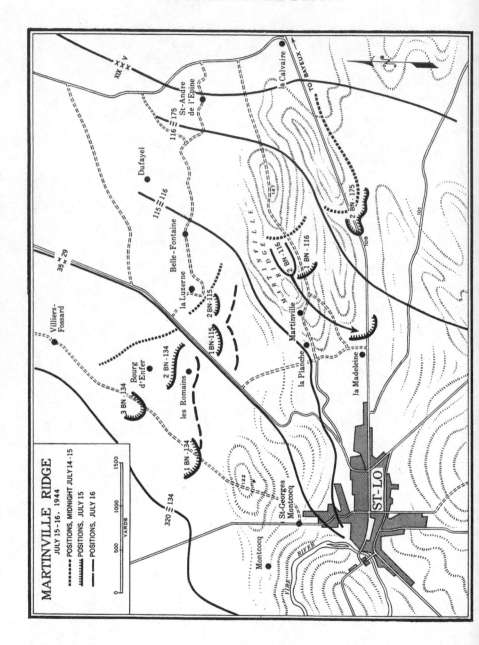

MARTINVILLE RIDGE
JULY 15-16, 1944

POSITIONS, MIDNIGHT JULY 14-15
POSITIONS, JULY 15
POSITIONS, JULY 16

YARDS
0   500   1000   1500

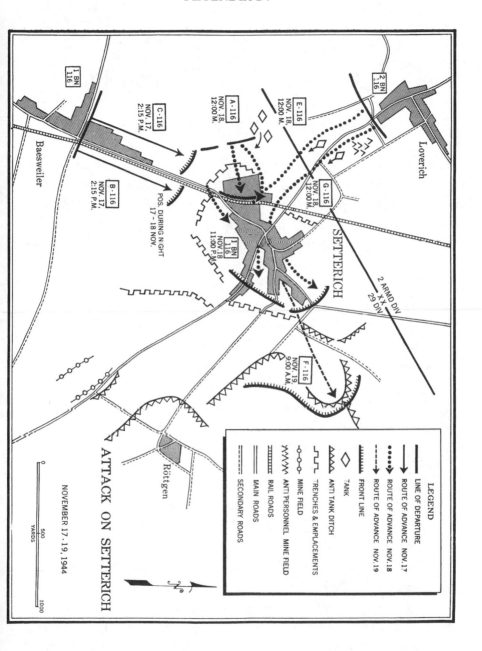

ACKNOWLEDGMENTS

I could not have written about preparing for the D-Day amphibious invasion, the landing plan, execution, and its aftermath without the assistance of many noteworthy people. I would like to thank all who answered my request for written and oral histories.

Extra special thanks go to navy Captain Robert A. Rowe (deceased) who, while writing a book on first-wave assault units, died of cancer. I likewise thank Captain James D. Sink, commanding officer of Headquarters Company, 116th Infantry (deceased), who kept a daily journal of the 116th's Headquarters Company throughout the war. I used excerpts from his unpublished writing that appear in this book.

Army Captain Charles W. Cawthon (deceased), gave permission to use passages of his excellent book Other Clay (University of Colorado Press); Colonel Sidney V. Bingham, Jr. (deceased) shared his memories and kindly wrote a foreword. Texas writer J. E. Kaufmann shared an oral history of his fellow Texan Bill Lewis.

Grace Sours Strickland (deceased), sister of Major John Sours, permitted use of a letter written in 1945 by 116th Infantry surgeon Doctor Robert Buckley, who detailed Major Sours' death on D-Day. My thanks also go to a friend, Harold Howard, for helping to wrap up the final chapters. I am also indebted to Joseph H. Ewing (deceased), Company G, 175th, and author of 29 Let's Go! Ewing allowed me to use excerpts from his very important 29th Division book. Architect Byron R. Dickson, head of the creative design team of the National D-Day Memorial, allowed use of photographs of the imposing Overlord Arch.

ACKNOWLEDGMENTS

Many thanks to all who furnished written or oral accounts, or read this memoir and offered suggestions, such as writer Karen Sulkin, who helped organize and re-write some of these accounts. Thanks to my wife, Margaret Slaughter, who offered suggestions, to special writer Peter Stoudt, proof reader/editors Marty Horne, Bob Teitlebaum, and Roland Lazenby. I am also grateful for suggestions from friends Joe Lindner, M.D., and Richard Dehmel, Ph.D.

Thanks to my French friends Jean Michel Simoni, Richard Catherine, Doctor Claude Paris, Philippe Ygouf, Eric Ellena, and Ms. Junko Forster.

Thanks to British Royal Navy Sub-Lieutenant Jimmie Green and his son-in-law, Kevin Elsby, Ph.D., for allowing me to use information about the tricky tides at Omaha Beach. Thanks to Art Dickens for keeping my computer operating smoothly.

Many, many thanks to the following 29th Infantry Division veterans who contributed their personal memories to the appendix for this book: Dr. Harold Baumgarten, Company B, 116th Infantry Regiment; Cecil G. Breeden, 104th Medical Battalion, deceased; Vittorio J. Crimone, Company D, 116th Infantry Regiment, deceased; David C. Davidson, Headquarters Company, 116th Infantry Regiment, deceased; Randolph A. Ginman, Company D, 116th Infantry Regiment; Bernard Latakas, Company D, 116th Infantry Regiment; William R. Hurd, Company D, 116th Infantry Regiment, deceased; George A. Kobe, Company D, 116th Infantry Regiment, deceased; William H. Lewis, Company B, 116th Infantry Regiment; Gordon B. McDonald, Headquarters Company, 116th Infantry Regiment, deceased; Curtis C. Moore, Company D, 116th Infantry Regiment; Robert L. Sales, Company B, 116th Infantry Regiment; David Silva, Company D, 116th Infantry Regiment; Robert A. Stewart, 121st Engineer Combat Battalion, deceased; John B. Sink, Company D, 116th Infantry Regiment, deceased;

Raymond Moon, Company B, 116th Infantry Regiment, and all of my many friends mentioned in the book, dead or alive.

I must also thank my friend the late Stephen Ambrose for his encouragement and suggestions with this, my first (and probably only) book. He was working on a foreword to *Omaha Beach and Beyond* when he became too ill to finish. Thanks to Steve's son, Hugh Ambrose, who wrote an endorsement for the back cover of this book. And thanks to the prolific Bedford Boys author, Alex Kershaw, who penned a foreword and an endorsement.

I am deeply indebted to Lieutenant Walter Ehlers (Medal of Honor), Ranger Lieutenant Len Lomell (Distinguished Service Cross), "Band of Brothers" participant and paratrooper Major Dick Winters (Distinguished Service Cross), Thanks to Dave "Mudcat" Saunders, Senator Jim Webb, Writer Joe Balkoski, author and paratrooper Spencer Wurst, and author Phil Nordyke.

Special thanks to a Roanoke newspaper colleague and friend, Edward L. McCallum, who by divine accident, found my brilliant literary agent, Gayle Wurst, Ph.D., of Princeton International Agency for the Arts. Gayle and Zenith Press publisher Richard Kane did so much to improve the readability of my work and inspired me to complete this memoir.